NEW FACES IN THE FRAME

A GUIDE TO MARRIAGE AND PARENTING
IN THE BLENDED FAMILY

DICK DUNN

LifeWay Press
Nashville, Tennessee

This book is the text for course CG-0418 in the subject area Home/Family Diploma Plan or LS-0035
in the Leadership and Skills Development Diploma Plan of the Christian Growth Study Plan

Unless otherwise noted, Scripture quotations are from the Holy Bible,
New International Version,
Copyright © 1973, 1978, 1984 by International Bible Society.

Scripture quotations marked KJV are from the *King James Version*.

Printed in the United States of America

Cover Design: Edward Crawford
Cover Illustration: Stephano Vitale

LifeWay Press
127 Ninth Avenue, North
Nashville, Tennessee 37234

ABOUT THE AUTHOR

DICK DUNN lives in a blended family in Roswell, Georgia, where he is Minister of Singles and Stepfamilies at the Roswell United Methodist Church. The singles and stepfamily ministry at the church is one of the largest such ministries in the United States, serving over 3,000 people each year. More than 22 different groups meet on a regular basis.

Dick became aware of the needs of single adults following his own divorce in 1977. When he married again in 1982, he was astonished at how different a second marriage is from a first one. As a result of his own experience in blending a family, Dick authored the books: *Willing to Try Again: Steps Toward Blending a Family, Preparing to Marry Again,* and *Developing a Successful Stepfamily Ministry.*

Dick is a graduate of Baldwin-Wallace College in Berea, Ohio, and Boston University School of Theology in Boston, Massachusetts. In 1993 he received the Pace-setters Award of the Network of Single Adult Leaders, and is an active member of The Stepfamily Association of America. Dick travels extensively throughout the United States speaking to single adults and stepfamilies.

CONTENTS

Introduction 4

Week 1: Progress Through the Stages 5

Week 2: Give Your Marriage Priority 22

Week 3: Build Communication Skills 39

Week 4: Learn to Live Together 56

Week 5: Minimize Interferences 73

Week 6: Rely on God 90

Week 7: Understand the Children 107

Week 8: Avoid Typecasting 124

Week 9: Reduce Refereeing 141

Week 10: Set Guidelines for Behavior 158

Week 11: Develop Problem-Solving Skills 175

Week 12: See God at Work 192

Leader Guide 209

Welcome to *New Faces in the Frame: A Guide to Marriage and Parenting in the Blended Family.* This study is designed for persons who are part of a blended family. Look at the course map, "The Blended Family Tree," on the front inside cover of your book. The tree illustrates the 12 key actions that will help families experience a sense of blendedness. Note that the tree has two branches: marriage and parenting.

The first six units explore issues related to the blended couple. As you read and talk with your spouse and group, you will learn ways to enhance your couple relationship. Topics include how you communicate as a couple, how to incorporate traditions from both sides of the marriage to start new traditions of your own, what role outside influences play in your relationship, and – most importantly – how to rely on God in your new family. During the second six units you will explore parenting issues in the blending family. These topics will range from understanding the concerns facing the children to problem-solving techniques.

New Faces in the Frame is an interactive study. Read *New Faces* as though I am sitting right beside you. When you come to a learning activity—set in **boldface type** and preceded by a 🐛 —respond in writing. When you see a learning activity preceded by a 💙, mentally respond. Often I will follow the activity with feedback to let you know how I may have answered. Many activities will be personal to you and will not have a right or wrong answer. Be honest and open as you respond. Allow yourself the opportunity to express your thoughts and feelings freely in your own book. Your spouse should have a separate workbook. You will share only what you choose with your spouse at the end of the week during CoupleTalk and in your group session.

Set aside a certain time and place five times a week to study each day's lesson. Some days may take as little as 20 minutes while others may take a little longer to process the information. In order to reap the most benefit from this interactive study, spread the lessons out over the week, completing only one a day.

New Faces in the Frame is intended to be discussed in a weekly group meeting, which will offer you invaluable support. To know that you are not alone in the process of blending a family is comforting beyond words. The group meetings provide a safe environment to discuss the information studied the previous week and to share your own experiences. If you are not part of a weekly group, talk to your pastor or church leader. They will probably know of others who would benefit from this study. You may be able to start your own group from your circle of friends. I encourage you to become a part of a weekly group session.

New Faces in the Frame is written with the assumption that you have already received Jesus Christ as your Savior and Lord of your life. If you have not made this crucial decision, I invite you to turn to page 92 for guidance. Your journey through *New Faces in the Frame*—and most importantly through the rest of your life—will be greatly enhanced if you allow the Holy Spirit to guide you.

My interest in this topic grew out of my own divorce and remarriage. Betty and I found the challenges of blending our three children more difficult than we had ever imagined. We look back on those experiences with gratitude for God's help. Be encouraged that I am praying for you. As you begin your study, read Philippians 4:6-7 in the margin.

Do not be anxious about anything, but in everything, by prayer and petition, with thanksgiving, present your requests to God. And the peace of God, which transcends all understanding, will guard your hearts and your minds in Christ Jesus.
—Philippians 4:6-7

PROGRESS THROUGH THE STAGES

Susan and Michael had been married seven months. Susan's daughters, Jennifer and Melissa, had been very excited about Michael and their mother marrying. They loved being involved in the wedding. However, once Michael moved into the house, their relationship started to fall apart. Melissa and Jennifer had somehow never imagined that once Michael lived with them he would start telling them how they should behave. "He's not our father," Jennifer told Melissa. "We already have a father."

For his part, Michael felt he was very restrained in disciplining the girls. Realizing that his presence was a major adjustment for them, Michael ignored many of the irritating things that happened. He intentionally did not say anything about their messy rooms. He knew Jennifer and Melissa needed a father in the home, and they certainly needed more discipline than Susan offered. What else could he do?

Susan felt caught in the middle. While she loved each family member, she watched helplessly as the initial warm feelings between Michael and the girls grew icy. Was Michael expecting too much too soon? It was hard to know. Now, even her former husband was beginning to say: "The girls are so unhappy with you. Maybe they would be better off living with me." What was she to do?

Our culture calls families with children who pre-date the marriage a blended family. A more appropriate term would be blending family, for the state of becoming a blended family involves a process. Michael and Susan probably believe their situation is unique. They would benefit from knowing their blended family will go through some predictable stages before arriving at a sense of blendedness. They would profit from the experience of others who have faced stepparent issues.

Perhaps you identify with Susan and/or Michael. This week you will begin exploring what a blending family can expect in its journey toward blendedness.

What You'll Study
DAY 1
• The Nature of Blended Families
DAY 2
• A Timetable for Blending
DAY 3
• The Early Stages
DAY 4
• The Later Stages
DAY 5
• Keep at It

This Week You Will:
• identify the characteristics of blended families;
• think about a timetable for blending your family;
• determine what stage your blended family is in;
• decide what is involved in moving to the next stage;
• set goals for yourself and your family in the blending process.

This Week's Scripture Memory Verse
"I can do everything through him who gives me strength" (Philippians 4:13).

THE NATURE OF BLENDED FAMILIES

Stepfamilies differ from nuclear families in several ways. They are not just different for a period of time, with the differences ultimately blending into a nuclear family. Stepfamilies differ from nuclear families for a lifetime. Even when we talk of blending two families, keep in mind that the blended family may never completely blend and certainly will never become a nuclear family. Stepfamilies are always stepfamilies. This fact does not make them better or worse; it simply describes what they are.

Those of us who live in blended families must learn to accept these differences as both positive and negative. Stepfamilies have unique advantages.

🌱 **Check any of the items below that you feel are advantages to being a blended family:**
- ❑ more flexibility
- ❑ ability to adjust to new situations
- ❑ a larger extended family
- ❑ experience how other families live
- ❑ other? _____

Where else would you have as many opportunities to learn patience, flexibility, sharing, unselfishness, consideration, and sacrificial love?

Blended family life provides a laboratory to grow—and grow up!—in ways unique to two merging families. Where else would you have as many opportunities to learn patience, flexibility, sharing, unselfishness, consideration, and sacrificial love? Children in stepfamilies often take on responsibilities at an earlier age, learn to function independently, and thus mature faster than their peers.

🌹 **Make it a point today to thank one member of your blended family for how he or she has enhanced your life. Be specific and don't expect a return compliment!**

The joys of blended families are numerous, and we could all share happy memories of good family times together. However, you are probably reading this workbook because you have questions about how to blend two separate family units. Perhaps you have encountered significant obstacles along the way. You may even be thinking you were crazy to attempt such a seemingly unworkable scheme.

Take heart! Many of us have felt those same feelings. Whether you are new to the blended family experience or have been at it for some time, everyone can benefit from studying the nature of blended families. You need to know that blended families have traveled through a predictable course. You will follow that course to some degree as well. Knowing what the course looks like from experienced travelers will give you direction and encouragement along the way.

Throughout the study I will refer to your family as a *blended family*. Keep in mind that blending is a process. When referring to the process, I will use the term *blending family*. Both terms refer to stepfamilies. Unfortunately, in our culture the word *stepparents* has a negative connotation. Most stepfamilies do not use that term to describe themselves. I will use it only when I feel it is the most descriptive or appropriate way to convey my thought.

Did you know that blended families are as old as the Book of Genesis? In the polygamist culture of the ancient Hebrews, multiple wives and stepchildren were sources of family friction. Remarriages due to death and divorce were common. Throughout this study we will learn from biblical examples.

🌿 **Of these patriarchs in the Book of Genesis–Abraham, Isaac, Jacob –**

1. Who remarried after the death of his wife? (Genesis 25:1) _____

2. Who had only one wife? (Genesis 24:67) _____

3. Who had multiple wives? (Genesis 29:26-28) _____

God has been in the business of caring for families since Adam and Eve. During this study we will look at God's design for the family and observe what the Bible has to say that will help us have the best family life possible. In the activity above I answered Abraham, Isaac, and Jacob.

Effect of Parental Bonding

One of the major differences between blended families and nuclear families is the issue of parental bonding. At least one spouse has a parental bond with a child or children that the other spouse does not have and cannot share. The bonding between biological parents and their children is one of the strongest emotional bonds known to human beings. An adoptive parent, when adoption occurred before the blended marriage, experiences the same type of bond. A stepparent will always be an outsider to this preexisting bond.

Children as well as parents feel this emotional bonding. Keep in mind that they feel it for both biological parents. When parents divorce or a parent dies, children are psychologically torn in half. When a parent then remarries, children feel like they are being asked to replace that torn away half with a substitute that looks, talks, thinks, and acts differently. A stepparent seems like an outsider who has come to take the absent parent's place. Even adult children may resent this intrusion.

> **When parents divorce or a parent dies, children are psychologically torn in half.**

🌿 **Place a check mark by each of the following that you have experienced in your blended family.**
- ❏ at least one of the children resenting the stepparent
- ❏ the stepparent feeling left out
- ❏ the biological or adoptive parent feeling caught in the middle
- ❏ children saying, "You're not my father/mother."
- ❏ feelings of jealousy for the closeness of the parental bond
- ❏ children resenting their stepbrothers or stepsisters

Feeling like an outsider hurts. In the early days and months of a marriage, many stepparents try repeatedly to enter this closed circle. Often, they become angry or sullen when they cannot. Michael, whom you met in the week's introduction, felt isolated from the closed circle formed by Susan and her children.

Stepparents inevitably enter the new family with optimism. They will love these children so much that the children will undoubtedly respond in kind. However, simply loving them, treating them kindly, and doing things for the children will never equal the emotional bond that exists between the children and the biological or adoptive parent. That bond is based not on actions but on a history established since birth. A stepparent simply cannot hope to establish anything similar in a matter of days, months, or even years.

The struggle of the stepparent to become a "real" part of the family is not an impossible dream. Stepparents can create a wonderful relationship with children over a period of time—when the children are ready. Emotional bonding may never equal that between biological parent and child, but bonding does occur with every new experience. Stepparents who are persistent and loving can develop a very satisfying relationship with their spouses' children.

Children with Divided Loyalties

Children view themselves as being one half of two persons—their mother and father. When the blended family has been created by a death, children worry that loving a stepparent nullifies their love for the parent who has died. Loyalty to the deceased parent may block feelings of attachment to a stepparent. In addition, children—even adult children—quickly perceive that a parent's remarriage is going to drastically alter their relationship with their remaining parent.

In cases of divorce, the number one fantasy of most children is that Mom and Dad will get back together again. This dream of Mom and Dad living together again can last a lifetime, even if one or both has remarried and has additional children. The stepparents then become the chief obstacles keeping Mom and Dad apart in the eyes of the children. Even when children want to love the stepparents, they often find it difficult, wondering, "If I love my stepparents, what will that be saying about my love for my 'real' parents?"

Frequently the other biological parent (especially if he or she has not remarried) also views the stepparent as a threat. Worrying about being replaced by the stepparent, the biological parent sometimes says things to the children like: "I don't want you to ever call her (or him) Mom (or Dad). I'm your Mom (or Dad)." And if the biological parent is really insecure, he or she may undermine the stepparent whenever possible. All of this scenario happens more often than not.

The children are caught in the middle. They simply do not know how to respond. They may display undesirable behavior. Even if they do not act out in negative ways, children in a blended family must sort out where they fit in.

Of course, not all children desire for their parents to reunite. Some children have watched home life with their parents deteriorate to a point that even they do not want it back. Some are ready for Mom or Dad to marry again. However, these reactions are more the exception than the rule.

Your stepchildren are reacting to a situation you did not create and cannot solve. Knowing not to take their reactions personally can help you give the relationship time.

Loyalty blocks feelings of attachment to a stepparent.

How sensitive are you now to your children or stepchildren's divided loyalties? Place an *X* on the following scale.

very sensitive   somewhat sensitive   not sensitive

Knowledge Enables You to Act

Perhaps today's study has opened or re-opened some wounds. You may feel burdened by the challenges that lie ahead. Finding out that other blended families confront similar issues may have been an encouragement to you. My purpose has been to take a realistic look at what blended families face.

Just being familiar with the nature of a blended family gives you a real edge on making your family work. Ignorance is anything but bliss. Ignorance is usually chaos. Knowledge and the grace of our Lord Jesus will enable you to move ahead in the blending process. If you don't know Jesus as your Lord and Savior, turn to page 92 and read the section titled "The New Covenant." This is the most important decision you will ever make—for yourself and your family.

In the weeks that follow, we will look more intentionally at what specific steps you can take to function more effectively in a blended family. You are already doing many helpful things that you can share with your group.

 God has been teaching you what works and what does not work in a blended family. In the margin write some things that seem to help and some things that seem to hinder the blending process.

Begin to memorize this week's Scripture memory verse. Think of one particular area of your life that you will ask Christ to strengthen today.

HELPS _____

_____

_____

HINDERS _____

_____

_____

DAY 2

A TIMETABLE FOR BLENDING

*A*s we observed in day 1, the blending process is rarely totally complete. The emotional bonding between biological parent and child will never be equaled in the child/stepparent relationship. Trying to make the blended family into something it cannot become will only be frustrating. Therefore, it is important to relax and accept the blending process for what it is.

All major life adjustments take time. When you moved out of your parents' home for the first time, it took some getting used to. You had to shop for food and other household necessities. You had to clean the house or apartment, cook, and do laundry. If you moved in with other people, you had to learn to live with others who did things differently. Each adjustment took time and effort.

Grief in a Blended Family

Every major life adjustment involves a grieving process. Even positive changes, such as a promotion at work, require leaving behind familiar faces and comfortable ruts. Losses may seem minor in light of the gains, but they are a part of change. Grief always precedes a remarriage and blended family.

The grief of losing a mate to death or divorce is one of life's biggest adjustments. People often expect to recover from the loss of a mate within a year or two. However, grief is an individual process that cannot be rushed. Those who grieve never forget the past, but they do learn how to live with it. One widow said: "It is not the past we need to let go of. It is the future. The past is who we are and it can never be put aside. We must let go of the future that can never be."

David pleaded with God for the child. He fasted and went into his house and spent the nights lying on the ground. The elders of his household stood beside him to get him up from the ground, but he refused, and he would not eat any food with them.
—2 Samuel 12:16-17

King David mourned for his son every day.
—2 Samuel 13:37

The king was shaken. He went up to the room over the gateway and wept. As he went, he said: "O my son Absalom! My son, my son Absalom! If only I had died instead of you—O Absalom, my son, my son!"
—2 Samuel 18:33

King David mourned the loss of his three sons. Read the passages in the margin and underline the ways David grieved.

Grieving takes many forms. Consider David as a role model. He openly grieved his losses. Loss of a mate takes time to heal and process grief. If you have been divorced or experienced the death of your spouse, how long did the adjustment process take for you? In the following question, record your answers in terms of months. Accept your timetable as appropriate for you.

How long did it take before you no longer thought about the divorced or deceased person with an emotional reaction?

_____ months

How long did it take before you felt good about life in general and your own life specifically? Check your answer.
❑ less than a year
❑ more than a year

Members of a blended family are in varying stages of grief over the past. As a couple, you and your mate have chosen to move beyond your grief and establish a new relationship. Your children may feel rushed and unprepared to give up their grief. Try to understand their resistance.

In the manual "Stepfamilies Stepping Ahead" published by the Stepfamily Association of America, Patricia Papernow discusses the timetable for moving through the stages of blending a family. She says, " 'Fast' families make it through the entire cycle within about four years. 'Average' families take about seven years."[1]

Major life adjustments simply take more time than most of us are willing to admit. Adjustment is not merely a matter of feeling down for a period of time and then finally one day feeling positive about the circumstances you've been handed. It is a gradual process, with twists and turns along the way. In a similar way, blended family adjustment is so gradual that it can usually only be measured by looking back at where one has been and noting the progress.

Adjustments in a Blending Family

Many of the initial adjustments of a blended family are similar to those of a nuclear family. Like all couples, the blended family couple must learn to adjust to each other. They must accommodate different ideas about keeping a house, paying bills, what food to eat and where to eat it, how to celebrate birthdays and holidays—things that are seldom talked about before the wedding.

Unlike nuclear families, blended families begin life with an instant family. Children make a big difference. The blended family couple must adjust to the interaction of a new spouse with their biological children and/or their own interaction with their mate's biological children. The children must adjust to sharing the biological parent. They usually experience strange, uncomfortable feelings about this new stepparent who represents drastic change to their lives.

Which of the following adjustments have been the most difficult for you? Rank the top 10 in terms of difficulty with 1 being a piece of cake and 10 being like swallowing an elephant.

___ watching how your mate interacts with his/her children

___ your own interaction with your mate's children

___ interaction with your mate's former spouse

___ interaction with other relatives or friends

___ developing an agreed on set of rules for the new family

___ knowing when to say something and when to keep quiet

___ finding alone time with your spouse

___ finding time alone for yourself

___ listening to complaints about your children from your spouse

___ listening to complaints about your spouse from your children

Good Things Take Time

So many tasks in your blending family shout for your attention all at once. Like any tasks, the tasks of blended family adjustment can be learned. Good things take time. One day, almost on a whim, I decided I wanted to learn Spanish. I bought two cassette tapes that promised to help me. Every time I listened to a new lesson, I felt certain I would never learn those strange words. However, after playing the tapes over and over, repeating the words endlessly, and practicing on my friends, the words gradually became familiar. Those early lessons now seem easy, although I must say the new ones that expect me to put together whole sentences seem totally impossible. I keep at it only because I know that one day I will look back at the current lessons and find them easy as well.

The timetable for blending your new family is probably going to be slower than you expected. Slow growth sometimes produces the best crop. A father once asked the president of a college if it was possible for his son to graduate in three years rather than the usual four. The college president replied: "I suppose it is possible. It just depends on what you want to grow. When God grows a squash, He only takes two months. When God grows an oak tree, He takes twenty years."

Good blended families do not just happen. They are created with God's help, along with plenty of time and much effort on the part of everyone involved.

When God grows a squash, He only takes two months. When God grows an oak tree, He takes twenty years.

On the following continuum, chart your family's blending process. Use initials to represent each person's progress.

...in terms of how the children are accepting the stepparent and new rules.

Not at all	Some	Completely

...in terms of how the stepparent feels accepted in the family.

Not at all	Some	Completely

Now, looking over the progress you have made in specific areas, rate your blended family's overall progress.

Not blending	Blending	A Sense of Blendedness

DAY 3

THE EARLY STAGES

Bill, Martha, and their children were a blended family similar to yours. When Bill and Martha began dating, both hesitated about getting married. They did not want another unhappy experience. They especially did not want to experience another divorce. They worried about causing the children more pain. Putting aside their lingering fears, Martha and Bill married. In some ways, their marriage far exceeded their expectations. They had made good choices in their selection of mates. They were deeply in love and really appreciated most of each other's qualities. If it were just the two of them, their marriage would be perfect.

But it wasn't just the two of them. This family did not seem to blend. Neither Bill nor Martha understood why. Never having studied much about the blending process, both of them were perplexed. Each began to wonder if the other really cared. They worried that they had made a mistake. They watched as the children expressed their displeasure in no uncertain terms. What had gone wrong?

Nothing had gone wrong. As with predictable stages of childhood development, they were experiencing a predictable stage in the development of blended families. While not all blended families have identical experiences because of the makeup of the family and the ages of the children, most blended families do proceed in a very systematic way through the stages. As you read about these stages of blended family development, try to be aware of your own progress, noting where you have been, where you are now, and where you are going.

The Infatuation Stage

When two people fall in love, their bodies are altered by naturally produced chemicals which cause a state of euphoria. Falling in love is one of life's most pleasant experiences. Few people would consider marrying without it. However, the old saying that "love is blind" contains a lot of truth. When people fall in love, they really do not see or comprehend things that seem so obvious to others. I remember one couple who could not understand my reluctance to perform their wedding, even though they had known each other only two months and were trying to blend a family of five children. They were in love; therefore, all the glaring difficulties I saw were perceived as minor irritations to them.

My wife Betty and I wonder how we ever believed that our marriage was only going to be about us. It really never occurred to us that having children from a previous marriage would matter. Talk about being naive!

🍂 In the margin list some of the things you were blind to in the early months of your relationship with your present spouse.

One blind spot many couples have in the infatuation stage of a relationship relates to their children's feelings. While some children are very vocal about their feelings toward this stranger Mom or Dad has brought home, most are not. Feelings are not always easy for children to identify, especially negative feelings. When asked how they feel about an upcoming marriage, children often respond, "Fine." Children may get caught up in the wedding plans and seem excited about the marriage. All of these positive affirmations sound positive to Dad or Mom who want to believe them.

Even when children have dismissed any notion that Mom and Dad will reunite and really do look forward to a new family, they are rarely prepared for life in a blended family. Some children remember happier times when they lived in a home with their biological mother and father. These children can easily imagine that when Mom or Dad marries again, home life will be idyllic. Since their former home life was never as good as they remember, reality cannot match their expectations. The illusion dissolves quickly.

🍂 Looking back, what was the attitude of each of the children prior to your marriage? What is it today? Write the children's names in the margin. Beside each name, label the child's present attitude as negative, neutral, or positive.

The Questioning Stage

While falling in love is certainly a wonderful feeling, infatuation does not last. Illusion and fantasy ultimately give way to reality. Even the chemical changes the body experiences during the stage of infatuation disappear. The body adjusts and no longer produces feelings of euphoria. Couples move out of the wonderment phase into the next stage. Although it may happen gradually, many blended family couples suddenly look around at their situations and ask, "What have I done?"

A new marriage requires time for the couple relationship to grow. If couples have children living with them, this instant family makes it very difficult for them to have any alone time. Even if the children are present only part of the time, the interaction between biological parent, children, and stepparent is often so stressful that raw nerves are quickly exposed.

Understandably, many couples in blended families are overwhelmed when infatuation gives way to conflict. They may move rapidly into the Questioning Stage while others take as long as six months to a year.

🌿 **At what point in your marriage did you ask, "What have I done?"**

1 month	6 months	1 year	longer?

Since it may have occurred gradually, what factors led up to the question? Record them in the margin.

The Questioning Stage of a marriage is not very pleasant, for at this point people begin to doubt the sensibleness of their decision to marry. More specifically, they begin to question their decision to marry this particular person, whom they may not know as well as they thought. These feelings are scary, especially for anyone who has already experienced divorce. Many think to themselves, *I can't believe I've done it again.*

🌿 **Check the feelings you had (or are having) during the Questioning Stage.**
❑ My mate loves her/his children more than me.
❑ If he/she really loved me, he/she would understand me better.
❑ I can't stand how the children treat their mother/father.
❑ His/her children give me no respect.
❑ My wife/husband is not supportive of my authority with the children.
❑ My wife/husband worries more about losing the children's love than about what is best for them.
❑ I can't stand being ignored by the children.
❑ I knew it would be difficult, but not this difficult.

You are perfectly normal if you have had or presently have these feelings. These feelings do not mean the marriage was a mistake or you do not love this person any longer. Stage 2 is part of the normal progression of growth, and while it may be somewhat unpleasant, this stage has its function. At this point, people in blended families either move ahead or break.

Learning to love people as they really are – and not how they make us feel – is a difficult aspect of the spiritual pilgrimage God has placed before us. And, I assure you, our marriages are indeed part of our spiritual journey. God instituted marriage for our growth as well as our enjoyment. We demonstrate our commitment to Christ's lordship as we "grow up" in Him.

🌿 Read Ephesians 4:16 in the margin. Beneath the verse, list some ways you need to grow.

From him the whole body, joined and held together by every supporting ligament, grows and builds itself up in love, as each part does its work.
–Ephesians 4:16

The Crisis Stage

The most important stage of all is what I call the Crisis Stage. The Crisis Stage in one family may be a small bump in the road compared to another family's experience. Think of crisis as a turning point. A turning point is a place or time when you can choose to go in a different direction. The scary part about a turning point is that one of those directions is the choice to give up. To come to the point of saying, "Things are going to have to change," troubles us because we can never be completely sure how our mates will react. Some may react by refusing to work on problems.

Unfortunately, many couples use a crisis as opportunity to call it quits. That's why the divorce rate for second marriages hovers at around 60 percent. However, also at this stage many blended families seek help and their family situation often begins to improve. In my own experience, couples that risk moving into the Crisis Stage early (within the first three years) have a better chance of succeeding than those who retreat and repress their anger. Keeping angry feelings bottled up inside may appear to work for a short term. But the only way to move forward in blending is to express and resolve pent-up anger.

I still remember the night Betty told me she was leaving. She announced she would not be there when I got home. She even called to make a plane reservation. Talk about getting my attention! I was stunned. I managed to reach the senior pastor of the church where I was serving as an associate, and he persuaded her to wait at least until we could talk. At that time he gave us two excellent pieces of advice. First, since our schedules prevented us from talking together with him for three days, he instructed us not to discuss our problems until that meeting. We could talk about anything else, but not the issues troubling us. That directive allowed a nice cooling-down period.

Secondly, he suggested we attend a stepfamily seminar being held at a local university. Just being with other couples in similar situations made us realize quickly that we were not unique. We both felt tremendous relief. If others could make it through these difficulties, we could, too.

Crisis can be one of God's gifts because it pushes us to do something about our situation. God allows difficult situations to bring about growth. God does not intend that we feel miserable forever. The pain of crisis is meant to prompt us to action. Often, the only way we are motivated to change is if we feel badly enough. Many who inquire about the stepfamily program at our church do so while they are in the Crisis Stage of their blended family development.

🌀 Read Genesis 21:8-21. What was the crisis experience in this blended family? Think about how God demonstrated His commitment to each family member. God cares for each person in your blended family. Thank Him for His commitment to each of you.

In my book, *Willing to Try Again: Steps Toward Blending a Family*, I related the story of Mack and Ginger who lived through the Crisis Stage experience. They had been married two years when Mack finally exploded. Mack felt Ginger and her children had their own little group, and he was on the outside. Things finally came to a head over a seemingly trivial incident.

As was her custom, Ginger asked the children what they wanted for dinner before consulting Mack. The children decided on pizza. Ginger then asked Mack, "Is that OK with you?"

Although the incident seemed minor, Mack's resentment over feeling like a second-class citizen in his own home reached the boiling point. "I don't care what we have, but we're not having pizza!" Mack shouted. "And either this group starts including me in its plans, or we're not going to BE a family."

With that, Mack stormed off to the bedroom.[2] While that particular evening was very turbulent and uncomfortable for everyone, it did force the family to talk about what they were feeling and begin making changes that would bring them together. This incident was a major factor in their blending process.

Rather than labeling crisis as a negative stage, consider it a stage of opportunity to confront and deal with issues as they arise.

🌿 Recall a crisis experience you have encountered in your blended family. What were some positive results? Record them in the margin.

🌿 How does this week's Scripture memory verse apply to crisis experiences? Thank God for His strength that sustains you.

DAY 4

THE LATER STAGES

*N*ot every blended family experiences the early stages as dramatically as others do. You may not have questioned your decision to marry, or lived through what others might consider a crisis. Perhaps you moved into one of the later stages of blended-family living without much trauma. These stages usually occur sometime between the second and fifth year in a family that is blending.

The Possibility Stage
When you finally hear various family members begin to say, "I think we are going to make it," you have entered the Possibility Stage. Some stepfamilies may have never doubted it, but for others this stage comes as genuine relief. After years of struggle, guided only by hope, they see the light at the end of the tunnel and know that it is not a train coming toward them.

The struggles that led up to the Crisis Stage and beyond will not be over at this point, but you will begin to see possibilities emerging. This new optimism may result from the blended family reaching out to others for help. Just as Jesus instructed us to seek in order to find, many discover that this truth extends to help with family life also. Read Matthew 7:7-8 in the margin.

"Ask and it will be given to you; seek and you will find; knock and the door will be opened to you. For everyone who asks receives; he who seeks finds; and to him who knocks, the door will be opened."
—Matthew 7:7-8

Ginger and Mack in the story from day 3 found help through a blended family group at their church. One idea from the group that they implemented was regular family meetings where everyone could share what he or she was experiencing. At family meetings they strategized ways to solve various problems. Although Mack's feelings of being left out of the relationship between Ginger and her children did not change immediately, the family meetings helped him feel included. He began to observe some change as a result of their discussions.

🍃 **If you have experienced the Possibility Stage in your blended family, what new ideas or approaches have worked for you? List them in the margin.**

🍃 **If you have not entered the Possibility Stage, check which of the following seem to be pointing you in that direction:**
❑ I am reading this workbook and completing learning activities.
❑ I am attending weekly group meetings.
❑ I am open to new insights about myself and my family.
❑ I am willing to change to encourage the blending process.
❑ I feel optimistic about my family's future.
❑ other? _____

The Growth Stage

Moving from the Possibility Stage, blended families enter the Growth Stage. Growth has been taking place from the very beginning of the relationship; however, it probably has not felt like growth until now. In the early stages, growth usually feels like one step forward and two steps backward. Of course, even the mistakes teach us, and learning is taking place amidst the struggle and pain.

As a family enters the Growth Stage, those backward steps become fewer and strides forward occur more often. Take heart. Backward steps are not necessarily regression. Sometimes we must step back to regroup or complete some process that was interrupted. Stepping back can provide perspective, such as an artist stepping back to survey the landscape. God's concern is that we continue the journey, not how rapidly we arrive at our destination.

🍃 **To see if you have already entered this stage, check the phrases below that apply to your family:**
❑ The biological parent does not feel like he/she is walking on eggs all the time trying to keep peace.
❑ The stepparent feels accepted into the family some of the time.
❑ The children actually talk with the stepparent, even when the biological parent is around.
❑ The tension within the blended family has begun to relax.
❑ The relationship with former spouses is not so antagonistic.
❑ The couple can go out for an evening without talking only about the children's behavior.
❑ The children's overall behavior has greatly improved.
❑ When problems surface, usually they are resolved quickly.
❑ Everyone feels certain that this marriage is going to last.

If you checked at least six statements in the previous list, you have probably entered the Growth Stage. If you checked less than six, you are probably still in one of the earlier stages. But take comfort; you are headed for the Growth Stage! It is seldom entered in less than four years. Those early years are not all struggle. Many good times occur during the beginning years in a blended family. However, good times are often overshadowed by the difficulties.

Growth is much easier to see in retrospect. Today I can look back and recognize the growth spurts in my life. At the time, I was aware only of the struggle and pain. In the early years of our blended family, neither Betty nor I were at all sure that we would survive. It was difficult to hang on. We loved each other, but there were many times when the problems seemed overwhelming. As we moved past the Crisis Stage, through the Possibility Stage, and into the Growth Stage, that sense of being overwhelmed diminished greatly. We gained confidence that we would make it. We experienced more good times than bad. Looking back, after 14 years of marriage, the struggle and pain are hazy and faraway. However, they were necessary to the growth that occurred.

The Reward Stage

When you enter the Reward Stage of blended family development, characteristics of the Growth Stage are more common than not. At this final stage, the stepparent, biological parent, and children have learned to live with one another in positive ways. The gears finally mesh without always grinding.

Sadly, many blended families give up before reaching this stage. In Luke 9:62 Jesus says, "No one who puts his hand to the plow and looks back is fit for service in the kingdom of God." Those who fail to complete the blended family journey through the difficult stages will never experience the tremendous rewards a stepfamily has to offer. I keep a picture of a plow on my desk just to remind me of this passage.

Blended families require constant work. By the time you reach the Reward Stage, you will have succeeded at an extemely difficult task. One reward is the sense of accomplishment you feel for having kept your family together. Another reward is the love family members feel for one another. They are able to rejoice and express sorrow with genuine caring. Random acts of kindness occur without prompting. Family gatherings spark anticipation, and old resentments seem as faded memories. There's an exciting today and tomorrow to celebrate!

In the margin list some of the rewards you have already experienced as a part of a blended family. Then list some rewards you look forward to in your family's future.

Say this week's Scripture memory verse to a family member. Share with that person one way God has strengthened you this week.

KEEP AT IT

Frequently I hear from blended families, "I knew it would be difficult. I just didn't know it would be this difficult." Knowing the stages of blended family development and recognizing the signs as you move from one stage to another enables you to keep your perspective and focus on your goals.

Look at the course map, "The Blended Family Tree," on the inside cover of this book. The marriage and parenting branches of the tree each contain six goals that will move you forward in the blending process. Read each goal (lesson title). Put a star by the ones you feel would be most helpful to your family.

For now, let's look at some of the tasks to be accomplished in the weeks ahead:

1. *The purpose of this workbook is to assist you in your journey as a family.* Do the daily reading and complete the learning activities. Set aside time five days a week to read and write in this workbook. Daily work is important. Learning occurs when information is studied and retained over a period of time. Each day's content will receive more of your attention and focus if you spread it out over five days.

2. *Use the CoupleTalk section to discuss with your spouse what you have read.* If possible, find a time to talk before the group session. Remember to speak the truth in love (Ephesians 4:15). Your goal is to understand each other better, not to convince each other of the rightness of your position.

3. *Attend and participate in the weekly support-group meetings.* You will find acceptance and encouragement for whatever difficulties you may be experiencing as you share with others and hear their stories. Attend the meetings each week, even (or especially) when you do not feel like it. Attend even if you are not on friendly terms with your spouse that day. Receive the support you need. If your mate is out of town or unavailable, attend anyway. Attend!

4. *Pray.* While prayer may not fall within the category of tasks, it is essential to growth. Pray each day. The prayers need not be long, but they should include thoughts such as these: "Lord, I will try to be open to Your Spirit as my spouse and I work on blending our family. If there is something more I can do, show me." Pray for your spouse, your children, and your spouse's children.

5. *Relax and trust God.* Learning to let go and let God is not something any of us do easily. We want to be in control, even when our way is not working. Read Matthew 6:27,33-34 which appears in the margin.

How do you feel about the above task list? Check those thoughts that apply.
- ❑ How will I ever find the time?
- ❑ I have trouble putting my thoughts into words.
- ❑ The idea of sharing in a group scares me.
- ❑ What if I fall behind or have to miss a session?
- ❑ What if my spouse disagrees with me?
- ❑ I feel vulnerable.

Knowing the stages of blended family development and recognizing the signs as you move from one stage to another will enable you to keep your perspective and focus on your goals.

"Who of you by worrying can add a single hour to his life?
But seek first his kingdom and his righteousness and all these things will be given to you as well. Therefore do not worry about tomorrow, for tomorrow will worry about itself. Each day has enough trouble of its own."
—Matthew 6:27,33-34

The process we are suggesting for this study has a successful track record. Trust the process. You will become more comfortable as time passes. Feel free to discuss any reservations with your group or group facilitator.

Using the CoupleTalk Activity Each Week

The CoupleTalk activity at the end of each unit will help you structure a conversation with your spouse about the unit content. Find time for you and your mate to process this material before the weekly group session. Then, what you say in the group will not come as a surprise to each other. If you are not able to talk before group time, then by all means do so afterwards. The main objective is for the two of you to discuss the most significant ideas from each unit. Occasionally, you will be asked to do some goal-setting as a couple.

Using the CoupleTalk page will enable you to keep your written activities in the unit as private as you wish. Your workbook is like a personal diary. It is your property and should not be read by anyone unless you give specific permission. You are asked to reveal to your spouse only what is written on the CoupleTalk page. Make an agreement with your spouse that you will not ask each other to divulge any answers that either of you feel uncomfortable sharing. Then you can be open and honest as you respond to the written activities.

Allow Yourself to Dream

The very nature of blended families moves us through definite stages. This movement is not linear. It is more of a spiral. As you move upward toward the next stage, you may find yourself circling through some previous stages. This back-and-forth motion characterizes relationships. Expect to repeat stages.

While most of us would like to avoid pain and struggle, real growth requires us to work through these stages rather than avoid them. Even couples who begin the blending process well prepared usually discover they still have much to learn. While you can learn a lot about swimming from reading a book or listening to an instructor, getting into the water is still the only way to learn to swim.

What are your hopes and dreams for the weeks ahead? When you finish this workbook, what would you like to have accomplished? Write your goals in the margin.

You must do more than wish if you are to achieve your goals. In fact, the difference between a dream and a wish is activity. A wish is something you make and simply wait for. A dream is something you are willing to give your life to. Wishes, although often as noble as dreams, come from human desire alone. Dreams come from God. God wants good things for your blended family.

Write Philippians 4:13 from memory in the space below.

_____

A dream is something you are willing to give your life to.

1. Patricia Papernow, *Stepfamilies Stepping Ahead* (Lincoln, NE: Stepfamilies Press, 1989), 31.
2. Dick Dunn, *Willing To Try Again: Steps Toward Blending a Family* (Valley Forge, PA: Judson Press, 1993), 20.

COUPLETALK

For you to complete

1. List below the six stages of a blended family. Look back at the material in days 3 and 4 if you need assistance.

   (1) _____

   (2) _____

   (3) _____

   (4) _____

   (5) _____

   (6) _____

2. Circle the number of the stage you believe your blended family is in right now.

3. Recall and write at least one idea learned from this week's study that you believe will help move your family to the next stage.

   _____

   _____

For you to share with your spouse

1. Sit down facing each other and take turns sharing how each of you completed the above section.
2. Complete this sentence together: One way we can ask God to strengthen our marriage is …

   _____

3. Tell one thing you love about each other.
4. Say together the Scripture memory verse.
5. Pray for each other, either silently or aloud.

GIVE YOUR MARRIAGE PRIORITY

*T*he church was full. Both Cynthia and Peter had large families and many friends. As the organist played the "Wedding March," Peter and his four children looked expectantly toward the center aisle waiting for Cynthia and her two daughters to enter. Peter and Cynthia were ecstatic! After experiencing very difficult divorces, they had found each other! Life was good again.

Peter and Cynthia were too caught up in the moment to notice that not all of their children were smiling. In fact, Peter's 15-year-old daughter appeared to be frowning. With the attitude of "love will conquer all," Peter and Cynthia were oblivious to any problems.

You can be sure Peter's daughter will let her feelings be known! How disruptive will she be to the new couple relationship? What about Peter and Cynthia's painful divorces? What emotional scars are they carrying into this marriage? Neither has seriously processed their grief. Both have significant trust issues.

Many who marry again are every bit as naive as Cynthia and Peter. Being older and wiser about marriage, they believe this time they have made a better choice in a mate. The past seems far away in time, out of reach of this new relationship. What good would it do to rehash old memories?

Often, grief and guilt held over from the past rob the present marriage of its focus. In order to truly begin anew, couples need to be free to focus on today and the future. Looking honestly at factors that keep us lodged in the past will enable us to move ahead in the blending process.

A good marriage is the foundation of a successful blended family. No matter how formidable the obstacles, our Lord has committed Himself to our present marriages. We need to see God as not just a matchmaker but also a match-keeper! As you give Him priority in your life, He will enable you to give your marriage the priority it deserves.

What You'll Study
DAY 1
- **Healing from Grief**
DAY 2
- **Healing from Guilt**
DAY 3
- **Letting Go of the Past**
DAY 4
- **Trusting Again**
DAY 5
- **Focusing on the Present and Future**

This Week You Will:
- apply the lessons of grief to a blended family;
- deal with unresolved guilt from previous relationships;
- identify past ways of feeling and behaving that interfere with the present;
- determine how to build trust in your marriage;
- set marriage goals for the present and future.

This Week's Scripture Memory Verse
"Two are better than one, because they have a good return for their work" (Ecclesiastes 4:9).

HEALING FROM GRIEF

*S*ome blended family spouses have never been married before. Perhaps you are one! You may not have experienced the feelings and events of a marriage that ended in divorce or a spouse that died. If this is your situation, you may think you do not need to read today's material. However, for two reasons I urge you to read on and complete the learning activities.

First, a better understanding of your mate's experience will contribute to a better relationship. Second, you also have experienced loss sometime in your life. Even if you have never faced the death of a spouse or the pain of divorce, you surely have dealt with the loss of a relationship. The mourning experience is common to us all.

As you complete the learning activities, identify a particular loss and what it taught you. As you study the material consider this question: How does the way you and your mate process grief affect your marriage and your parenting?

What Grief Teaches Us

When a person loses a meaningful relationship, a void occurs in that person's life. Such an emptiness is usually quite painful. Sometimes we call this emptiness loneliness. Loneliness, however, is not the same as being alone. Loneliness is not cured simply by filling up the space with another person. Indeed, if a person initiates a new relationship with the one-dimensional purpose of filling a void, that new relationship basically will be unfulfilling in most other ways. Rushing to fill a void presumes that the void has no purpose or value.

Following the loss of a relationship, time is needed to process the loss. We identify this time as grief. Grief is God-given transition time that allows us to end a relationship emotionally, mentally, and spiritually when it has already ended physically. The intensity of the grief has a lot to do with the intensity of the relationship. Even when divorcing persons feel very angry with each other, they still may experience intense grief when the marriage is officially over.

Grief is a God-given transition time that allows us to end a relationship emotionally, mentally, and spiritually when it has already ended physically.

🍃 Briefly describe a major loss you have suffered.

_____

How did you know you were grieving? Check the responses that apply.
❑ obsessive thoughts about the loss
❑ disrupted pattern of eating, sleeping
❑ tears, visible emotion
❑ withdrawal from social relationships
❑ feelings of anger, bitterness, disillusionment

While grief feels extremely painful, it teaches many valuable lessons that benefit us throughout our lives. The following three lessons of grief have significance for blending families.

1. Grief teaches us that all relationships are temporary.

We think of a 50-year marriage as amazingly long when in fact 50 years is a brief period of time. While the transitory nature of our lives is quite obvious, many of us live in denial about this truth. We must face the fact that earthly relationships do not last forever. We have no guarantees on a future together. All relationships end eventually, and the best anyone can hope for is "until death do us part." Grief teaches us this truth in no uncertain terms.

> **How can you benefit by remembering that relationships are temporary?**
> ❏ I can learn not to take relationships for granted.
> ❏ I can evaluate my priorities to give more time for what is really important.
> ❏ I can appreciate the small details of life.
> ❏ Other _____

Facing the reality of mortality frees us to appreciate the time we do have with one another. Have you noticed that when a person is diagnosed with a terminal illness, suddenly everything about living becomes important—colors, smells, nature, relationships, sunrises and sunsets, birds, children, and breath itself? That person takes nothing for granted. In a similar way, grief following the loss of a relationship teaches us to maximize our time together in new relationships. We learn to nurture rather than neglect those who are most important to us.

2. Grief teaches us to rely on God.

When we finally realize that we cannot survive grief on our own, God is there, reaching out with a power greater than our grief. Although He frequently does not give us all the answers we want, in His presence we can rest and receive comfort. Jesus said, "Blessed are those who mourn, for they will be comforted" (Matthew 5:4).

God is not surprised or dismayed when we express our grief to Him. In the Old Testament Book of Job, the main character is anything but patient or quiet about his grief. Job complains loudly and says, "Let the Almighty answer me" (Job 31:35). Finally, God does indeed talk with Job. God does not give him answers as to why innocent people suffer. Yet after God's speech, Job is satisfied. "My ears had heard of you but now my eyes have seen you" (Job 42:5).

The truth of grief is that it provides the opportunity to experience the reality of God's love and care. We fellowship with His suffering (Philippians 3:10). We rely on His power. When we do that, we too are satisfied.

> **In the first activity today you identified a major loss you suffered. Did that experience affect your relationship with God?** ❏ Yes ❏ No
>
> **How could you apply lessons from that experience to strengthen your relationship with God? Write your ideas in the margin.**

The best relationships are founded on God's love and sustained through His lordship. When we ignore God (a result of our bent to sin) and act as if we are in control, relationships flounder. When God is in control, we can trust the direction and decisions of our lives.

3. Grief teaches us to take responsibility for ourselves.

Relying on God and taking responsibility for ourselves are two sides of a coin. Only God can provide the unconditional love, acceptance, and forgiveness that we need to recover from grief. His comfort sustains us through the hard times. However, God intends that we accept responsibility for our grief-recovery process. He wants us to have a healthy interdependence on others, not an unhealthy dependence. Read the verses from Galatians in the margin. Although these verses sound contradictory, they point out the balance between our responsibility for others and our responsibility for ourselves.

After your previous marriage ended, perhaps you realized that because you and your former spouse had divided tasks there were many things you simply did not know how to do. Maybe you paid the bills and serviced the car, or you did the laundry and expected him to repair appliances. Or, you mowed the lawn and she did all the cooking. Perhaps you were dependent emotionally, hesitating to make decisions or initiate actions. Maybe you waited for someone else to take charge.

Widowed or divorced persons must learn to care for themselves rather than rely on someone else. While learning to do new tasks may have been a challenge, pride came from discovering that we are not as helpless as we thought. Grief has a powerful way of teaching us that God created us stronger than we realize.

In the margin list one task you have learned to take responsibility for as a result of loss.

Some people approach relationships like simple addition. Feeling like only half a person, they go through life seeking another half to make them whole. While we may feel torn in half after a divorce, God did not make any half-people. Relationships are like multiplication, not addition. Consider this: If you multiply 1/2 times 1/2, you get 1/4—a sum less than either of the two original numbers. Similarly, if you take a person who has not yet learned to be whole and couple that person with another, you get a relationship that is much less than what God intends or desires for you. He intends each of us to be whole and complete. The grief experience helps us become more than we ever believed possible.

Reflect on the three lessons—that all relationships are temporary, that God is still here with us, and that we can do more than we ever believed. Write a brief statement about how these lessons can help your blended family.

_____

You have already come a long way. At the time of your divorce or the death of your mate, I doubt you believed you would ever recover or marry again. At that point, you simply hurt. You did move forward. If you are struggling again, remember the lessons grief taught you. Make the most of today because there is no

Carry each other's burdens and in this way you will fulfill the law of Christ.
—Galatians 6:2

Each one should carry his own load.
—Galatians 6:5

promise of tomorrow. God is still with us. Value His presence and comfort more than any answers you seek. Adapt and learn positive ways to handle life in a blended family. Think about the new situations you faced as a single adult. Now you can learn to blend a family. You are capable!

🐟 **Read this week's Scripture memory verse in the margin. This verse encourages us to move beyond grief to enter again into new relationships. Beneath the verse, list some ways "two are better than one."**

Two are better than one, because they have a good return for their work.
—Ecclesiastes 4:9

HEALING FROM GUILT

*O*ne day a woman sat in my office crying. She was breaking up with a divorced man who simply could not end his relationship with his former wife. Every time the former spouse needed something, she called and he responded—immediately! It was not that he still loved her; he felt guilty because his obsession with his job had contributed to the breakup of their marriage. The woman in my office believed, legitimately I think, that she could not experience a healthy relationship with this man until he dealt with his guilt.

Everyone experiences guilt, for "all have sinned and fall short of the glory of God" (Romans 3:23). Widowed persons sometimes experience guilt after losing a mate. They may believe they did not do everything possible to prevent the death. They may remember less than ideal times in the marriage. They may have been unavailable to the other person physically or emotionally. Divorced persons also feel guilt because their marriage did not last "until death do us part." Unresolved guilt from the past creates a strain within the new marriage. Issues that led to the end of a relationship must be dealt with if a subsequent marriage is to succeed.

When we feel guilty, we may do things for others that we would not do otherwise. For example, guilt frequently motivates people to be permissive with children or lenient with former spouses when firmness is crucial. Consider George. George had an affair and his wife left him. George felt guilty for very appropriate reasons. He had sinned. George's children quickly figured out how to manipulate him. George was unable to say no to them, even when he should have. Because of guilt, George's parental and relational skills were damaged.

How do we identify guilt that needs to be resolved before we can truly reinvest in healthy relationships? Fortunately, we have a Helper! Speaking of the Holy Spirit, Jesus said, "When he comes, he will convict the world of guilt in regard to sin and righteousness and judgment" (John 16:8). We need only ask with a heart open to hearing the truth and a willingness to obey.

Experiencing Forgiveness

When we commit a wrong that hurts other people, intentionally or unintentionally, we need forgiveness—from God, from ourselves, and if possible, from those we hurt. Even if a person you wronged does not forgive you, you can still feel forgiven by God and by yourself. That is all that is within your power.

The first step involved in receiving forgiveness is to acknowledge the guilt and accept the fact that a wrong has been committed. Unfortunately, humans can live in denial for a long time. Denial may keep us from asking for forgiveness.

Guilt is a gift from God to help us restore our right relationship with Him and others. Through guilt, God pursues us until we are ready to acknowledge our wrongdoing. This process—repentance—means turning from sin toward God.

Step 1: Acknowledge the guilt and accept that a wrong has been committed.

Sin(s):

🌿 **Are there sins in your life for which you need forgiveness? If so, write them in the margin. Until sin is acknowledged, it cannot be forgiven. Writing the sin down will move you past denial.**

The second step in receiving forgiveness leads us to confess the sin to God. Confess simply means to agree with God's assessment. He wants to restore a right relationship with each of us. For that to happen, we must act on the conviction of sin and confess our sins to Him.

🌿 **Look again at the sin(s) you listed. Confess the sin(s) to God. Tell Him you agree with His judgment.**

Step 2: Confess the sin to God.

If we confess our sins, he is faithful and just and will forgive us our sins and purify us from all unrighteousness.
—1 John 1:9

The third step in receiving forgiveness is faith. Faith means believing God. Read Hebrews 10:23 in the margin. God keeps His promises. We can forgive ourselves, knowing God has forgiven us. Jeremiah 31:34 says, "For I will forgive their wickedness and will remember their sins no more."

🌿 **Thank God for His forgiveness. Live today as a forgiven person!**

Step 3: Have faith in God's forgiveness.

Let us hold unswervingly to the hope we profess, for he who promised is faithful.
—Hebrews 10:23

After admitting wrongdoing to ourselves, God, and the person(s) we have wronged, and believing God's promise of forgiveness, the fourth step in receiving forgiveness is to attempt restitution. For instance, if you have stolen money, repay it. Read Matthew 5:23-24 in the margin.

In George's case, restitution may involve "tough love," learning to set boundaries for his own behavior and holding his children accountable. He should ask forgiveness from his former wife and his children. They may or may not be ready to forgive him. However, asking forgiveness is crucial to his spiritual growth.

🌿 **Look back at your list of acknowledged sin(s). Is an attempt at restitution possible? If so, ask God to show you which ideas would be the most appropriate to implement.**

Step 4: Attempt restitution.

"Therefore, if you are offering your gift at the altar and there remember that your brother has something against you, leave your gift there in front of the altar. First go and be reconciled to your brother, then come and offer your gift."
—Matthew 5:23-24

Regret

Many of the feelings we call *guilt* are misnamed. I would call them feelings of *regret*. Regret results from our human condition. We simply cannot always do everything right. We may second guess actions that seemed appropriate at the time. We may wonder if we did enough to prevent a death, or kick ourselves over something we said or did, or worry about what others thought of us. Regret demands we torture ourselves over every imperfection.

When we label regret as guilt, we experience false guilt. Here's a way to identify true and false guilt. True guilt is specific. I feel appropriately guilty when I have done something wrong or when I have neglected to take some specific action. "I said I'd be there for my daughter's ball game and I didn't show up" is very specific guilt. False guilt is nebulous and generalized. "I have been a terrible father" is a general description for a broad situation complicated by many issues. "I regret not spending more time with my children when they were young" may be an appropriate expression of how we would change the past if that were possible. But we cannot go through life looking through the rear view mirror. Regret is inevitable, but it is not synonymous with guilt.

🍂 **Distinguish between true and false guilt by putting a T (True guilt) or an F (False guilt) beside each statement:**

___ I should have known the end was near.

___ I often lied to my spouse about my whereabouts.

___ I didn't keep the checkbook balanced and sometimes overspent.

___ I didn't try hard enough to communicate with my teenager.

While false guilt (feeling guilty without having committed an actual sin) and true guilt (feeling guilty after having done wrong) feel similar, they require different responses. Confront false guilt with the truth that humans are finite creatures. We all make mistakes—many every day. True guilt is forgiven by a loving God through confession. In the activity above I wrote F, T, T, and F.

🍂 **Have you experienced any of the following feelings of false guilt? Place a check mark beside any feelings you recognize.**

❏ Feeling responsible for the loss.

❏ Believing the other person was always right and you were wrong.

❏ Feeling responsible for your children's pain.

❏ Believing that other people are better than you.

❏ Accepting all criticism as valid.

❏ Not trusting your own decisions.

❏ Thinking of yourself as a bad person.

False guilt causes us to doubt our abilities, question everything we do or think, act indecisively, and deplete our energy supply. We overlook our strengths and concentrate on our weaknesses. Then fear sets in. We are afraid of mistakes because we want to please everyone. Read Mark 3:6 in the margin. Jesus was the only perfect person who has ever lived, yet some hated Him enough to kill Him. If our perfect Lord was unable to gain everyone's approval, what are our chances? We do not have to feel guilty because someone is displeased with us.

🍂 **Reflect on the guilty feelings you experienced after your previous marriage ended. Now that you've learned the difference between true and false guilt, in the margin list an example of each.**

The Pharisees went out and began to plot with the Herodians how they might kill Jesus.
—Mark 3:6

True Guilt:

False Guilt:

To what extent is guilt (both true and false guilt) interfering with your ability to be a good parent, or a good husband or wife? Mark the following line with a G for true guilt and F for false guilt.

None   A Little   Some   A Lot

Throughout our lives we will have many opportunities to forgive and seek forgiveness. Remember--a forgiven person is a forgiving person.

DAY 3

LETTING GO OF THE PAST

Martha's father was an alcoholic. As a child, Martha watched her father come home drunk and her mother lie to keep his behavior a secret from others. "Your father is 'not himself' today," she said. Although her mother tried to protect Martha, her father's abusive behavior left deep emotional scars.

When she married, Martha behaved very much like her mother. Although Martha's husband did not drink, if he yelled at the children she would send them out of the room and say, "Your father is 'not himself' today." Martha sought peace at any price and was always frightened whenever anyone became angry.

Do you see the pattern? Martha's frightened and protective actions resulted from the behaviors she observed and learned in her childhood. However, peace at any price did not produce the peace Martha desired. Martha's husband divorced her when she was 35 and left her with their three children.

Martha began to acknowledge the emotional scars of her childhood. Finally, she sought help from a counselor. The counselor helped Martha realize that she was not bound by the past. Though her childhood scars could not be erased, she could learn to recognize certain tendencies within herself and even use her experiences in a positive way. The past influences our lives in both positive and negative ways. If we were raised in loving homes, our early life experiences probably left us with positive influences. If we were raised in dysfunctional homes, we may struggle throughout our lives with negative influences. If we can discover the positive in the negative, the scars will not fester and bring destruction. Overcoming past pain may even be the ingredient that pushes us to greater accomplishment.

 If you still struggle with a particular emotional scar from your childhood, identify the degree to which it impacts your lifestyle. Put an X on the line below that best represents how often this particular pain influences your thoughts and actions.

Daily   Regularly   Occasionally

God's Purposes in Your Past

God can use those circumstances of birth to accomplish His will.

Did God know the family that would rear you? Of course He did! Why did He allow that? Although God never wills child abuse, poverty, or limited opportunities, He can use those circumstances of birth to accomplish His will.

The Book of Genesis contains a wonderful illustration of this truth. Jacob had 12 sons by 4 different women (see Genesis 30). Added to this very complex situation was the fact that Jacob had a favorite among his children–Joseph. Jacob had observed favoritism in his own parents. Jacob's father loved Esau best, while his mother loved Jacob. Jacob was simply passing along to his family the dysfunctional behavior he learned from his own past.

Jacob's favoritism provoked intense jealousy among his other sons. Joseph's brothers plotted to kill him. Ultimately, Joseph's life was saved because the brothers sold him as a slave instead.

Can you imagine how Joseph must have felt? He went from being the favorite son to a lowly slave, all in the blink of an eye. His self-esteem might have been destroyed by such an experience. Joseph could have felt sorry for himself, telling everyone he met what a terrible injustice he had suffered. Instead, he became the best possible slave to his master, Potiphar. The Bible says: "Joseph found favor in his eyes and became his attendant. Potiphar put him in charge of his household, and he entrusted to his care everything he owned" (Genesis 39:4). Not a bad life for a slave!

If that were the end of the story, Joseph still would be an inspiration. However, God had much more in store for Joseph. Having regained some measure of status following his brothers' betrayal, Joseph was thrown in jail because Potiphar's wife falsely accused him of rape. As Joseph's true character was revealed over time, the prison warden "put Joseph in charge of all those held in the prison, and he was made responsible for all that was done there" (Genesis 39:22). Once again, Joseph triumphed in a difficult situation.

While in prison, Joseph met a fellow prisoner, who was Pharaoh's cupbearer. He interpreted the cupbearer's dream. Later, when the cupbearer was restored to Pharaoh's favor, Pharaoh himself had a dream and Joseph was summoned to interpret it. In Pharaoh's dream God warned of an approaching famine. Miraculously, Pharaoh appointed Joseph to oversee Egypt's agricultural program–the one that ultimately prevented the starvation of Joseph's own family.

When Joseph's brothers came to buy grain from Egypt, Joseph revealed his identity. The brothers were overcome with shame. After Jacob's death, the brothers asked forgiveness. Joseph said, "You intended to harm me, but God intended it for good to accomplish what is now being done, the saving of many lives" (Genesis 50:20).

Biblical overcomers:

This story illustrates how someone reared in a dysfunctional family can break free and bless others. Emotional scars do not have to destroy us. Often the very process of overcoming such scars carries great rewards. God can use the pain of the past to equip us for a productive life.

Those who did not overcome:

In the margin list some examples from the Bible where persons successfully overcame their past. Then list some examples of Bible persons who could not overcome the influence of their past.

How did you do? I thought of David who repented of his sin with Bathsheba (2 Samuel 12:13) and went on to become Israel's greatest king. Peter denied he ever knew Jesus (Matthew 26:69-75) and yet became the leader of the church. Saul hated and persecuted Christians, yet he became Paul the missionary after an encounter with the Lord. He also wrote much of the New Testament.

Who are some Bible personalities that were unable to overcome their pasts? I thought of Lot's wife who, as she fled the burning cities of Sodom and Gomorrah, looked back and was destroyed (Genesis 19:26). The Israelites wandered in the desert, constantly complaining to Moses that they had it easier back in Egypt as slaves (Exodus 15:24; 16:3; 17:3). How about the rich young ruler who wouldn't give up his wealth to follow Jesus (Matthew 19:16-22)?

🐦 **The past need not cripple us. Everyone must overcome obstacles in his or her life—some put there by others and some of our own making. Circle the obstacles from your past you are trying to overcome.**

fear	anger	disappointment	jealousy	hurt
depression	distrust	habits	abuse	

Following my own divorce, I experienced the most difficult time in my life. The pain was more than I thought I could endure, and it lasted far longer than I expected. I look back on that time as a period of significant growth. God refined and redefined my faith. What I considered as faith before now seems very small. He taught me to rely upon His power and His love. He did it for me; He can do it for you.

🐦 **How has God used pain and struggle in your life to help you become a better person? Write one or more examples in the margin.**

Is there a source of pain that you have ignored? If so, check ways you intend to actively pursue resolution.
❏ write what I am feeling
❏ look into opportunities for counseling
❏ talk to someone I trust as a Christian friend
❏ read a book on the subject
❏ other? _____

The past is indeed past. However, the past shapes the present. God uses today as the foundation on which to build tomorrow. If we learn the lessons offered by the past, we will be better persons today and tomorrow.

🐦 **Write this week's Scripture memory verse in the space below.**

_____

_____

TRUSTING AGAIN

I often say to couples whose weddings I perform: "The vows you exchange today express something holy, tender, and beautiful; they are an expression of your love. Also, they are a commitment in which you willingly bind yourselves together for the benefit of both." Now, why would people willingly bind themselves together? What draws us to marriage? After all, we could simply live together. Today there is very little social consequence to cohabitation. Nevertheless, every day thousands of people freely enter into the covenant of marriage. Why? What is the attraction?

Although people marry for a variety of reasons, I have discovered many couples marry because they long for the security that comes from the commitment. Do you remember the emotional roller coaster of dating? You never knew how long a relationship would last. You were a little guarded in your words and actions. It was difficult to totally trust the relationship.

Trust and predictability are major reasons why marriage remains popular. While it is certainly true that no one should take the marriage relationship for granted, the ability to trust the partner's commitment to the relationship does allow a certain freedom. Couples living together can never completely relax, because they are never sure the other person will stay. The relaxation and freedom experienced in a truly committed relationship is the hope that propels a couple to greater levels of intimacy.

> **The relaxation and freedom experienced in a truly committed relationship is the hope that propels a couple to greater levels of intimacy.**

🌺 **Read the words of this wonderful hymn.**

> *Make me a captive Lord and then I shall be free.*
> *Force me to render up my sword, and I shall conqueror be.*
> *I sink in life's alarms when by myself I stand.*
> *Imprison me within Thine arms, and strong shall be my hand.*[1]

The song reveals a basic paradox of life. Binding ourselves to Jesus sets us free to live abundantly. In the same way, binding ourselves to another person in marriage sets us free. We worry less about the future. Basic security and trusting love allows us to direct our energies in creative ways.

 What are some things you are free to do as a married person that would be more difficult if you were single? For example: As a married person I have more time to write. When I was single, I spent a lot of energy seeking companionship.

_____

_____

Trusting Your Spouse

Marriage, freely entered between two people before God, family, and friends, involves some of the most sacred commitments known to humankind.

Marriage involves some of the most sacred commitments known to humankind.

 The following questions are often used in marriage ceremonies. Read each one and underline the commitment in each question.

> "(Name), will you have (name) to be your wife/husband? Will you love her/him, comfort her/him, honor and keep her/him, in sickness and in health; and remain faithful to her/him as long as you both shall live?"

The questions begin by asking if we want this other person to be our husband or wife. The second question asks for a commitment to love, comfort, and honor that person. It also reminds us that marriage is a lifelong commitment, to be honored in sickness as well as in health, and pledges fidelity as long as both are alive.

When a couple makes their vows to each other, they reiterate those commitments: "I (Name), take you (name) to be my wife/husband, to have and to hold from this day forward, for better, for worse, for richer, for poorer, in sickness and in health, to love and to cherish, till death do us part, and thereto I pledge you my faith."

Not only are these words a statement of love between two people, they are a strong commitment to permanency, a pledge to stay with that person throughout both good and bad. They are a promise not to leave when the going gets tough—and it always does. That's life.

A prayer I often use at weddings I perform sums it up: "Lord, we commend unto you the lives of (names). Help them to find in this marriage the true blessing that comes when two people really share their lives. May they discover rewards in this marriage not yet dreamed of as being possible and may they always recognize You as their companion and friend. When difficulties arise—as we know they must, for life is not all beauty and joy, but often involves struggle and work—may they find strength enough in each other to meet each task, and may they only grow stronger together, through Jesus Christ our Lord. Amen."

🌹 **Reflect on some of the difficult times you have encountered in your marriage. How has your commitment to the marriage helped you through those difficulties? Would you have stayed with your spouse without that commitment?**

Assessing My Trust Level

Couples in a second or subsequent marriage may have had their trust violated in a previous relationship. Trusting again is a major growing point. I must admit that I withheld trust for a long time after I remarried. I not only found it difficult to trust Betty (although she was worthy of my trust), but also I found it difficult to trust myself. Would I botch this relationship as well?

I began a Scripture search on the word *trust*. I am pleased to report that the Bible does not teach us to trust each other. Proverbs 3:5 says, "Trust in the Lord with all your heart, and lean not on your own understanding." Our trust should be in God, who is the only totally trustworthy Person. David admonished in Psalm 118:8, "It is better to take refuge in the Lord than to trust in man."

Because I trust God with my whole being, I can trust Him with whatever happens in my new relationship. People--even my spouse--will fail me at times. But I can choose to act toward my spouse with a trusting heart because my trust is in God. He and I can handle together whatever comes my way. This truth set me free from obsessing about whether or not I could give my heart completely to a new relationship. I was free to love because Someone loved me enough to die for me (John 3:16).

Is it possible to be too trusting? Persons deserve the benefit of the doubt when we have no valid reason not to trust. But there are untrustworthy people in the world who will use and abuse us. God expects us to use our assessment skills to be "fruit inspectors." If persons demonstrate by their actions they are not trustworthy, we should heed all the warning signals and withhold trust.

Most of us don't struggle with the issue of not trusting untrustworthy people. We do that quite well. What we struggle with is trusting those closest to us who have shown themselves to be trustworthy. To them we need to say a hearty, "I trust God and therefore I trust you."

🍃 **Where are you on the trust index? Place an X to represent your trust level.**

Not very trusting	Trusting	Too trusting

Living Out of Trust

Some of us may not know how a trusting person acts. Trust may feel like a new pair of shoes, confining and inflexible. We may long for the old comfortable pair. So perhaps that's where we should start. What does lack of trust look like?

🍃 **Circle the descriptors below that indicate lack of trust.**

suspicious   jealous   withhold love
withhold acceptance   apprehensive   gracious   accepting
confident   hopeful   committed

When I feel untrusting, I want to run for cover. I may think I'm protecting myself when I withdraw; but actually I am choosing to disengage from the relationship. I must confront my feelings; if unfounded, I must release them. Learning to trust is a matter of reprogramming the brain, much like we reprogram our computers. We must tell the new program to run this message: "I am in a new relationship. I must not transfer to my spouse issues that were true of my previous relationship. I can and will learn new patterns of thinking and behaving."

🍃 **What are some of these new patterns of thinking and behaving? Check the responses below that build trust.**

❏ 1. I check up on my spouse to see where he/she went.
❏ 2. I sneak a look at the check register each evening.
❏ 3. I assume my spouse is telling the truth.
❏ 4. I don't look for double meanings in my mate's words.
❏ 5. I reserve judgment until I have heard all the facts.
❏ 6. I'm never surprised when something bad happens.

I hope you were able to check 3, 4, and 5. When we choose to trust, we give up our right to leap to conclusions about the present based on the performance of others in our past.

 Write this week's Scripture memory verse in the margin. Think about why trust is an essential part of two persons working together to accomplish a goal.

D A Y 5

FOCUSING ON THE PRESENT AND FUTURE

I find it relatively simple to claim I am living in the present and not in the past--that is until a "trigger" prompts some memory that puts me right back in the past again! I've tried to identify my "triggers" so that I am better prepared to deflect them when I feel them coming.

For example, holidays are triggers. I recall happy holidays in my first marriage and the lonely ones when I was single again. In a matter of minutes I can sink into a depression just thinking about my first Christmas after the divorce. As I am writing this book, the holiday season is approaching. I remind myself that I have every reason to be happy this year. I can reject the "holiday trigger" because it no longer applies to my life.

Through the years other blended family couples have shared their triggers with me. For one it was finances. "When my wife would bring home a new dress or shoes, I panicked and thought only about my previous wife's overspending."

Another person shared that lack of affection was a trigger. "When my husband seems distant or cold, I feel I have done something wrong. Usually he's just preoccupied. I always assume it's because he's mad at me. My former husband was a rageaholic."

What are some triggers for you that bring up the past?

_____

_____

What positive messages can you give yourself when these triggers arise?

_____

_____

Focusing on the Present

Some of you may want to re-read day 3, "Letting Go of the Past," several times. When we have not adequately dealt with issues that affected previous relationships, these issues continue to play themselves out in our present relationships.

Once you feel you have dealt adequately with past issues, concentrate on the present and future. This process may require retraining the mind so that it remains focused on today. We can train our minds to be physically, mentally, and emotionally in the present. When a stray thought from the past haunts me, I can choose to keep the offending thought from settling in and making a nest.

Paul reminds us to think about "whatever is true, whatever is noble, whatever is right, whatever is pure, whatever is lovely, whatever is admirable" (Philippians 4:8). His list eliminates much of what I might otherwise focus on. It is not so much a matter of thought control as of Christ control. I'm too weak to consistently choose positive thoughts. As I allow Christ to mold me into His likeness, I find it easier to choose the good.

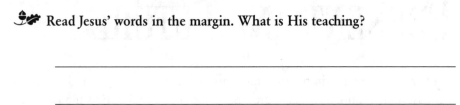 Read Jesus' words in the margin. What is His teaching?

_____

_____

If you were to "cast out" seven unhelpful thoughts, what thoughts would you put in their place? Write them in the margin.

You may have such deep wounds that stray thoughts will haunt you for a long time. God is the God who heals. He doesn't promise a quick fix to painful memories. I take comfort in David's reminder that weeping may come in the night, but joy comes in the morning (Psalm 30:5). You will again have cause for joy. Jeremiah the prophet was known as the weeping prophet, yet he experienced God's compassionate nature as "new every morning" (Lamentations 3:23). Each day you can awaken to His fresh supply of compassion for you and your situation.

 Imagine what God would say to you right now if you could hear His audible voice. Say those words aloud to yourself. Thank God for His tender mercy.

The Problem of Anger

Focusing on the present requires a heart that is freed from the bondage of anger. Being a slave to anger doesn't happen overnight. Anger about injustices from the past eat away at us slowly. When those angry feelings are not resolved, they collect in a pool at the bottom of our hearts.

This anger pool doesn't drain properly. When we put new sources of anger into the pool, it spills over with the excess. We find ourselves blowing our tops at insignificant events. We may even become known as an "angry person." The anger has a life of its own. We are angry, period. Not angry about something, just angry. Temper is extremely difficult to control when its source is an anger pool.

"When an evil spirit comes out of a man, it goes through arid places seeking rest and does not find it. Then it says, 'I will return to the house I left.' When it arrives, it finds the house unoccupied, swept clean and put in order. Then it goes and takes with it seven other spirits more wicked than itself, and they go in and live there. And the final condition of that man is worse than the first. That is how it will be with this wicked generation."
—Matthew 12:43-45

🌿 **Do you have an anger pool? What are some sources of your anger? List them in the margin.**

How do you drain an anger pool? Forgiveness is the key. Review page 27 that suggests steps to forgiveness. Forgiveness means that I choose not to hold another person accountable for the wrongs done to me. I give them to God. Justice belongs to Him and Him alone. Therefore, I choose to act as a loving person, who according to 1 Corinthians 13, doesn't keep the record of wrongs updated constantly and doesn't hold grudges. Forgiveness may not restore the relationship. I may need to keep an emotional or physical distance from abusive family members; however, I can forgive them in my heart and move beyond those feelings to live abundantly today.

When anger no longer controls me, I may still get angry for good reasons! But anger is like a thermostat. When the needle points to "hot," deal with the problem. The admonition not to let the sun go down on our anger implies that the cause of our anger must be investigated and resolved quickly.

🌿 **What would be a good way to drain your anger pool?**
- ❏ Forgive a person(s).
- ❏ Stop holding grudges.
- ❏ Stop keeping a record of wrongs done to me.
- ❏ Resolve new sources of anger quickly.

"In your anger do not sin": Do not let the sun go down while you are still angry.
—Ephesians 4:26

Focusing on the Future

By definition a focus keeps some things out and lets other things in. Consider a microscope or a telescope. You see the item on which the lens is focused. When we choose to focus on today, we keep out the parts of the past that de-focus us and allow in thoughts that point us in positive directions.

🌿 **Focus keeps the main thing the main thing. What is the main positive focus for your marriage right now? In order to answer that question, you may have to stop and state some goals you have set for your marriage. Write these in the margin. Focusing on goals enables you to concentrate on building a new life. Be prepared to share these goals during CoupleTalk.**

Goals point us to the future. Goals indicate direction and purpose. They guide our choices and keep us on the right path.

🌿 **Say the Scripture memory verse for this week to a family member. Notice the present tense of this verse. How does focusing on the present help us gain a good return on each day's investments?**

---

1. George Matheson, "Make Me a Captive Lord," *The Baptist Hymnal* (Nashville: Convention Press, 1991), 278.

COUPLETALK

For you to complete

1. What did you learn from the three lessons of grief? Phrase your answer as a goal for the future.

   _____

2. What source of false guilt are you willing to relinquish? If you did not identify a source, summarize the difference between false guilt and true guilt.

   _____

3. What do you need to let go of from your past? How do you plan to do so?

   _____

   _____

4. What would help you become a more trusting person?

   _____

5. List at least one goal for your marriage.

   _____

   _____

For you to share with your spouse

1. Sit down facing each other and take turns sharing how each of you completed the above section. If you are not comfortable sharing a response, you may pass.
2. Make a master list of your marriage goals on a separate piece of paper. Keep these where you can refer to them throughout this study. If possible, display them in your bedroom.
3. Decide on one goal to pursue this week. Make specific plans.
4. Tell one thing you love about each other.
5. Say together this week's Scripture memory verse.
6. Pray for each other, either silently or aloud.

BUILD COMMUNICATION SKILLS

Angela and Mark had known each other since fifth grade. They dated a few times in high school, but it was never serious. Eventually each married and had a son. Mark's wife died when he was 42. Angela and her husband divorced.

Mark and Angela met again at their 25th high-school reunion. They began dating, discovered they enjoyed many of the same activities, and decided to marry a year and a half later. Both sons appeared pleased with the decision.

Angela's pastor insisted on premarital counseling. He asked the couple to complete a premarital inventory relating to various aspects of the marriage relationship. After the minister reviewed their responses, he suggested that Mark and Angela work on their communication skills. Neither Angela nor Mark indicated the other listened very well, and both said they hesitated to express feelings when they were upset.

Over the next few weeks the minister worked with Mark and Angela to improve their communication, specifically the ways they shared personal information. Mark discovered he was more comfortable talking if they were doing something else as well, like walking or taking a drive. Angela realized her mind wandered when Mark was talking to her. She was preoccupied with her own response. She began to listen more intently.

Mark and Angela were building communication skills for a stronger marriage. A relationship is either growing or dying. Nurturing a relationship takes time and effort. In a blending family, the couple relationship must be a priority for the new family unit to survive. Without a strong commitment to this relationship, blending issues may drive a wedge between the couple. Prevention is better than a cure. This unit explores ways to build effective communication patterns.

What You'll Study
DAY 1
- **Valuing the Differences**
DAY 2
- **Talking and Listening**
DAY 3
- **Setting Boundaries**
DAY 4
- **Spending Time Together**
DAY 5
- **Establishing an Action Plan**

This Week You Will:
- identify differences between you and your mate;
- improve your own communication style;
- set boundaries for meaningful communication;
- determine ways to schedule couple time;
- establish an action plan for troubled times.

This Week's Scripture Memory Verse
"Over all these virtues put on love, which binds them all together in perfect unity" (Colossians 3:14).

VALUING THE DIFFERENCES

We are attracted to those who have skills and personalities that compliment our own weaknesses. Something within each of us says, "Here is a person who, unlike me, seems to have a handle on this area of life. I like that!" Perhaps we like knowing they easily accomplish tasks we find difficult. Maybe they are outgoing and we're shy, or we just jump right into a situation and they wait to consider all the angles. Unfortunately, the character traits that initially attract us to another person may be the same characteristics that eventually irritate us the most and that we try to change! Spontaneous persons tire of waiting on the planners, and the quiet introverts grow weary of the pace of the social butterflies. Differences become the enemy!

The character traits that initially attract us to another person may be the same characteristics that eventually we try to change!

When Samantha and Bill were dating, Samantha was impressed with Bill's punctuality. If Bill said he would be there at 6:00, the doorbell rang at 5:58. Although Samantha admired Bill and wished she were like him, she was seldom on time. It was not unusual for Bill to wait for her 15 minutes or longer. While the waiting irritated Bill, he recognized his own punctuality was compulsive and wished he could be a little more laid back. In fact, one of the things Bill liked about Samantha was her carefree nature.

After they married, Bill's compulsive punctuality drove Samantha crazy. If they were going to a party, Bill wanted to be there early. "No one wants guests to come early to a party," Samantha complained. "They probably won't be ready." On the other hand, Bill was constantly frustrated that Samantha did not care if they were late. He felt especially embarrassed when they were late for meetings.

Isn't it interesting that at first Bill and Samantha considered their opposite natures complimentary? After several years Bill and Samantha reached a compromise. Samantha worked at being ready early, especially for meetings and important events. Bill learned to adjust his expectations. He developed techniques, such as reading or watching television, to pass the time while waiting for Samantha. He stopped rushing her while she dressed, and eventually, even enjoyed arriving late for parties.

🌿 **What differences about your spouse did you find attractive at first but later became sources of irritation?**

_____

_____

Have you learned to live with these differences? ❑ Yes ❑ No
Is either of you still attempting to change the other? ❑ Yes ❑ No

Choosing Change

We do change through the years. We change because we learn some ways are better than others. We change because some things consistently fail and others succeed. We change because the Holy Spirit constantly works to help us become the persons God intended. Change is part of our spiritual pilgrimage.

Behavioral changes are never easy. We develop various patterns of behavior over the years and as a result of individual personality styles. Even when we want to change, we cannot easily abandon those patterns. Generally, we change when we are ready and willing; we change when we are convinced we should.

Compromises made out of consideration for our spouse, without giving up our own basic personality, are changes that hold us together as a couple rather than pulling us apart. Keep in mind if one partner succeeds in changing the other, part of what attracted them to each other in the first place disappears. While some people believe they might be happier if their partners were more like them, that is seldom the case.

> **We change when we are ready and willing; we change when we are convinced we should.**

🌿 **Identify a way you have changed to accommodate your present spouse.**

_____

_____

List some significant changes your spouse has made.

_____

_____

How have these changes improved your relationship?

_____

_____

Encouraging Change

Most of us would like to change *some* things about ourselves. A supportive marriage partner encourages us to change for the better. Expressing support demonstrates respect for each other as responsible adults in the relationship. Nitpicking often leads to a parent-child dynamic in marriage that reduces one or both partners to a child status.

John was a smoker. Although his wife insisted John smoke outside the house, she refrained from nagging him. Julie knew he wanted to quit. He had attempted to do so twice before they married. Both times John returned to smoking.

Julie told John: "I love you for trying to quit smoking. It must be very difficult. When you are ready to try again, let me know if I can help."

Because Julie's comments were not negative or accusing, John replied: "I will try again. I'm not sure when, but I promise I will. Thanks for understanding."

More than a year passed before John felt ready to try again. This time he succeeded. If Julie had constantly reminded John to quit smoking, he might not have succeeded in his attempt.

When you are genuinely convicted that a change is necessary for the health of your marriage, state your position in concrete action terms. Save the lecture. Don't insist you are right. Simply state what you want and need. "John, I will no longer pick up your dirty clothes. From now on, I will wash only the clothes in the hamper." Or, "Sheila, I will no longer be responsible for putting gas in your car. If you run out, there is an empty gas can in the trunk."

🌿 **Is there a certain change you would like your spouse to make? If so, ask yourself these questions:**

Would this change affect our family in a positive way? ❏ Yes ❏ No
Am I seeking this change out of selfish motivations? ❏ Yes ❏ No
Do I believe this change is in the best interest of my spouse?
❏ Yes ❏ No
Am I coming across as self-righteous (I am right, you are wrong)?
❏ Yes ❏ No

Affirming the Differences

Some people are shocked to discover their spouses choose to remain different—forever! All our efforts to the contrary may not succeed in making our mates perfect by our standards. When we finally realize our mates choose not to conform to the image we have determined as ideal, we accept a God-given opportunity to love them exactly as they are. Remember: Your individual differences are part of what attracted you to each other. Choose to value the differences in your mate.

One of my friends is married to a minister. She is quiet and shy. The minister is talkative and meets people well. My friend admires her husband's outgoing personality. However, she has spent many lonely moments waiting in the car for him to greet everyone on the church premises.

One day, as she again was waiting for her husband, she thought to herself: *I'm a lucky woman. Many men have difficulty talking to their wives. I can't get my husband to stop talking!* It occurred to her—really for the first time—that her husband was a package deal. She couldn't pick and choose only traits that pleased her and omit the rest. In order to have a husband who talked freely to her, she had to accept a husband who also talked to others.

When we accept our mates as a total package, choosing to love and accept them just as they are, we reach a new level of couple intimacy. Our spouses need not fear living life as our personal "repair project." They can open up without the threat of criticism.

The love that Jesus and His disciples said we are to have for one another is described in 1 Corinthians 13 as one that "keeps no record of wrongs." Faultfinders make poor lovers!

🌿 **In the margin read Colossians 3:12-14. Underline the virtues that love binds together.**

🌹 **Practice saying Colossians 3:14 from memory.**

Therefore, as God's chosen people, holy and dearly loved, clothe yourselves with compassion, kindness, humility, gentleness and patience. Bear with each other and forgive whatever grievances you may have against one another. Forgive as the Lord forgave you. And over all these virtues put on love, which binds them all together in perfect unity.
—Colossians 3:12-14

TALKING AND LISTENING

*F*rank and Harriet are quiet individuals. They love to take a stack of books to the beach and read—their idea of a great vacation. When they first met, Frank and Harriet talked constantly, exploring many interesting topics. Although this easy conversation was a strange new sensation to both of them, the sharing felt comfortable and right.

New love is often that way. Someone who seldom converses at length finds that with this special person he has all sorts of interesting things to share. After all, this new person has never heard any of his stories. She doesn't know the various details of his past life. They have so much to talk about.

As new love matures, partners usually slip back into their most natural behavior patterns. Quiet people are quiet once again. A successful marriage does not follow one "correct" pattern of communication. Our communication styles in marriage reflect our unique personalities.

Neither Frank nor Harriet were great conversationalists before they met. After they married, they talked much less than when they first started dating. Frank and Harriet's quiet style is normal for them. Some people simply talk more than others. Unlike Harriet and Frank, quiet people very often marry talkers, and talkers often marry quiet people. When people marry their opposites, the other's behavior frequently frustrates them. How do we maximize our particular blend of personalities so that the communication pattern in our marriage uniquely fits us?

A successful marriage does not follow one "correct" pattern of communication.

❧ **How would you describe communication in your marriage? On the line below, place an H for husband and a W for wife.**

Quiet	Moderate	Talker

❧ **How comfortable are you with your ability to talk and share both ideas and events with your spouse? Check the box to the left.**
❑ I can share events better than ideas. ❑
❑ I share ideas as well as events. ❑
❑ I'm not comfortable sharing, period! ❑

Now rate your spouse on the same questions, using the box at the end of each sentence.

If You Are the Quiet One

My wife Betty is more comfortable talking than I am. While I often share ideas and stories in public settings, one-on-one sharing is difficult for me. I would describe myself as a quiet person and Betty as a talker. Her description of a movie takes almost as long as actually viewing the movie. I summarize the plot in one or two sentences.

Naturally, Betty is often frustrated by my failure to share with her what has happened during my day. She wants to feel a part of my life. If I stretch myself, I can share daily occurrences, even if they seem insignificant to me. Let's face it, there is nothing insignificant about sharing life with a mate. The more we share, the better our relationship becomes. For some, such sharing may never be natural. In my case, I consciously work at detailed communication. When I do, my relationship with Betty grows. When I stop, our relationship suffers.

I learned to share more when one day I realized that prior to counseling sessions I pray the following prayer: "Dear Lord, if there is something You want to happen during this conversation, I will try to be open to Your Spirit. Use me as You desire. Amen." When I offer that prayer, incredible things frequently happen. I share insights that could come only from God.

I asked myself, *Why don't I say that prayer before going home to spend time with Betty?* I neglected to offer the same openness to God's Spirit at home that I offered at work. That afternoon as I drove in my driveway, I prayed: "Dear Lord, if there are things you want to happen here at home, I will try to be open to Your Spirit. Use me as You desire. Amen." From that point on, my priorities were different.

If you are the quiet one, determine ways to become more verbal. Talking is one way to learn about the other person. Although we glean some information through smiles, frowns, posture, mannerisms, and other nonverbal communication, most of what we learn about another person is through verbal communication. Also continue nonverbal communication that works for you—a back rub, a listening ear, sitting arm-in-arm on the sofa, or taking long walks together.

Realize the tremendous value of intentionally sharing with your spouse the circumstances and happenings of your day. At first, it may take considerable effort. Include more details than would be usual for you. The results will be very significant—the relationship will grow. Try it!

Which of the following would you be willing to try during the coming week?
- ❏ A note with an affirming message
- ❏ A call during the day just to say hi
- ❏ A personal message on his or her answering machine
- ❏ A greeting card with a special message
- ❏ Other? _____

If You Are the Talker

Talkers will readily share with their spouse what has happened throughout the day—probably in great detail! If both husband and wife are talkers, they may compete for time and attention. "Sharing time" is a potential combat zone. Two talkers may perceive each other as self-centered and controlling.

If you are the talker and your spouse is quiet, accept the fact that your partner may never be as comfortable as you are in communicating feelings. To judge your spouse by your communication style is a disservice to the relationship. Instead, evaluate the degree to which each of you meets the other's needs. The two of you may never share ideas equally. Differences are part of why you love each other.

Two talkers may perceive each other as self-centered and controlling.

If you are a talker, ask specific questions and listen for the answers. If an answer is not forthcoming, ask follow-up questions without judging the non-talker's willingness to share. Non-talkers seldom know what to say or how to say it. They need encouragement and time to process and present their thoughts. Focusing on the talker is a communication technique known as active listening.

Focusing on the talker is a communication technique known as active listening.

Rachel understood that Tom did not share easily. He was a quiet man who found it easier to read a book or watch television. He wanted her to be in the room with him, but he only talked when she asked him a question or commented directly. Even then he usually responded with only a few words or sentences.

Rachel was frequently frustrated by Tom's lack of communication. Rachel decided to take the initiative to bring about better communication. One evening while the children were gone, Rachel asked Tom, "How is Roger (a co-worker of Tom's)?"

Tom replied, "He's fine." Knowing to expect Tom's short reply, Rachel continued by asking, "Wasn't his wife expecting a baby?" Tom, who had been reading a book, looked up and said: "Their baby girl was born two months early, and the baby is still in the hospital. Everything seems to be OK. I think Roger said they were planning to bring the baby home next week."

"They must be exhausted," said Rachel. "What a frightening time!"

"You're probably right. I hadn't thought much about it; maybe that's why Roger was distracted at the meeting the other day. I wouldn't have my mind on work if one of our children were in the hospital." Their conversation continued several minutes because Rachel lovingly coaxed Tom with her gentle questioning.

Practice active listening in the next conversation with your spouse. Evaluate your success by asking these questions:
- Did I tune out distractions around me?
- Was I focused on my spouse?
- Did I ask appropriate questions to initiate further communication?
- Did I limit my responses to appropriate words of encouragement for my spouse to continue?

One of the reasons we fail to practice active listening is our habit of listening autobiographically. In other words, every comment another person makes reminds us of something that happened to us. And we share it! We do not appear to hear the other person. Why? We were listening for a spot to jump in or thinking exclusively about ourselves.

Perhaps you believe what you have to say will encourage your spouse. You think sharing a similar experience may comfort him or her. Don't be fooled by this reasoning. None of us knows exactly how another person feels, and no two experiences are exactly alike. Your spouse deserves the time to share his or her story and to have that experience validated. Only when your spouse is ready to move on should you share a similar happening. At that point, your spouse may be open to hearing your story.

Recall your most recent conversation with your spouse. Did you jump in with an example about yourself? ❏ Yes ❏ No
If so, determine to break this habit in your next conversation.

Assessing the Health of Our Communication Style

Thus far we've looked at communication styles in marriage where both partners are quiet, both partners are talkers, and one is quiet and the other is a talker.

Since there is no universally correct communication pattern in marriage, each of us is free to determine whether our communication style is working for us or against us. Generally, we can assess the health of our communication by evaluating how each person feels about the level of talking and sharing. You'll have opportunity during CoupleTalk to do just that.

You may feel defensive about the prospect of sharing your evaluation or hearing from your mate. The purpose of this exercise is not to criticize but to offer helpful ideas about how to improve your own unique style. All of us can improve. Make the decision to listen actively, respond prudently, and build up each other as you speak the truth in love (Ephesians 4:15).

A friend loves at all times.
–Proverbs 17:17

Over all these virtues put on love, which binds them all together in perfect unity.
–Colossians 3:14

Read Proverbs 17:17 in the margin. Compare it to this week's Scripture memory verse, which is also listed. How is your spouse like a friend? What does it mean to "love at all times," especially in a blending family? Jot some ideas beneath the Scriptures in the margin.

DAY 3

SETTING BOUNDARIES

*Y*ou've heard the expression, "Talk is cheap." Simply talking to your mate is not, in and of itself, growth-producing. Talking needs substance. Substance is achieved when partners exchange meanings, learn to communicate at deeper levels, and establish boundaries. When and where something is shared—even what is shared—is open for negotiation between the two of you.

What is a boundary? Boundaries are invisible lines between appropriate and inappropriate, timely and untimely, helpful and non-helpful communication. Consider a boundary as a fence. Just as a fence establishes property lines and keeps out intruders, communication boundaries offer guidelines for sharing information. In 1 Corinthians 6:12 Paul says, " 'Everything is permissible for me'–but not everything is beneficial." Concentrate your attention on beneficial speech.

Learning What to Share

Not everything we say is helpful. Some words only hurt and erect barriers between you and your spouse. Before speaking, always weigh the advantages against the disadvantages. An important part of good couple communication is learning not everything needs to be said, and not every question needs to be asked. Of course, simply stuffing your feelings is never a long-term solution. Stuffed feelings are held inside and often denied. They cause resentment and anger that eventually erupt like a volcano—usually over a trivial incident.

If this information or aggravation is important enough to warrant sharing, be as considerate as possible. Some thoughts, statements, evaluations, or questions may be difficult for your partner to hear and accept. Speak them with gentleness and understanding. James, the brother of Jesus, wrote, "Everyone should be quick to listen, slow to speak and slow to become angry" (James 1:19).

Jerry and Ann learned this lesson the hard way. Both of them believed the other one was lenient with his or her children. Ann believed that Jerry's kids had him wrapped around their fingers. Whenever they asked Jerry for money, he opened his wallet and gave it to them. Ann believed her kids could do no wrong, or so Jerry thought. If they stayed out past curfew, Ann accepted any excuse as legitimate. Both Jerry and Ann seemed to take great pleasure in pointing out the faults of each other's children. Neither parent was grateful for the other's insights. In fact, most of the time the biological parent ignored any insights offered and rushed to defend his or her children.

After a long year, Ann and Jerry finally learned that criticism of one's children must be tempered with grace. Criticism is always difficult to swallow, even when the biological parent knows there is a problem. Defending our children is both natural and normal. As a stepparent, present any criticism with love and care.

As a stepparent, present any criticism with love and care.

🌿 **In your own blending family, how often do you argue over children's behavior?**

Rarely	Some	Often

As a biological parent, circle which feelings you have when your partner criticizes your children.

anger   guilt   fear   doubt

worry   bitterness   despair

As a stepparent, circle which feelings you have when you see your stepchildren misbehave.

anger   guilt   fear   doubt

worry   bitterness   despair

Our blending family group practices this motto: "Choose your battles carefully." If you find your family preparing for a necessary battle, remember you cannot improve everything at once. The Serenity Prayer may need to be prayed many times during your blending family experience: "God, grant me the serenity to accept the things I cannot change, the courage to change the things I can, and the wisdom to know the difference."[1]

God, grant me the serenity to accept the things I cannot change, the courage to change the things I can, and the wisdom to know the difference.

🌿 **What have you found to be a helpful "rule of thumb" regarding information to share with your spouse?**

_____

Learning When to Share

Do you and your spouse spend an exorbitant amount of time discussing children? Probably you didn't get married to talk only, or even mostly, about the children. Children do demand a great deal of attention and can detract from your ability to communicate about other issues. Limit discussions about the children and related problems to just as few hours each week as possible.

One couple I know decided to set aside couple time on Saturday mornings to discuss problems that occurred during the week. Unless the situation needed immediate attention, they agreed to wait until Saturday morning to discuss it. While this technique for solving problems did not change this couple's differences about raising children, it did free them from talking as often about child-related problems. Delaying problem-solving allowed them time to talk about themselves and activities at work, at church, and in the community.

Do you think couple time set aside to solve problems would be helpful in your family? ❏ Yes ❏ No

If your partner agreed, when would be a good time?_____

Learning How to Share

We've looked at setting boundaries concerning what and when to share. Boundaries help us think before we speak. Words can be lethal, and once said, they cannot be retracted. Learning to share information that is both important and timely is a lifelong skill developed through trial and error.

From the list of words below, circle those that describe conducive attitudes for communication.

> gentle   brash   compassionate   tender
> judgmental   loving   hurried   harsh
> kind   sarcastic   thoughtless   understanding

Make a practice to pray about the what, when, and how of sharing with your spouse. Ask God for wisdom and guidance. Ephesians 4:29 summarizes good principles to build on. Read it in the margin.

The Book of Proverbs gives practical life principles for communication. List the key communication tip in each verse below.

❏ Proverbs 12:15 _____

❏ Proverbs 15:1 _____

❏ Proverbs 17:22 _____

❏ Proverbs 21:9 _____

❏ Proverbs 22:24-25 _____

Do not let any unwholesome talk come out of your mouths, but only what is helpful for building others up according to their needs, that it may benefit those who listen.
—Ephesians 4:29

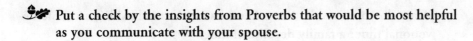 Put a check by the insights from Proverbs that would be most helpful as you communicate with your spouse.

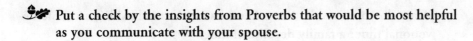 Say this week's Scripture memory verse to at least one family member.

SPENDING TIME TOGETHER

*I*n a nuclear family, children usually are a unifying force through whom the couple share a common identity. In a blended family, children represent a history not shared. Rather than being a unifying force, they often seem to divide and provoke resentment. Children in a blended family represent:
• potential jealousy of your time and attention;
• lack of freedom to say certain things;
• discipline problems;
• unfamiliar communication styles and personality differences.

Time Alone

Many blending family couples discover they had more time alone when they were dating. Couples need time each day to spend together, apart from the children. But couple time will not just happen—it must be planned. Time together does not have to involve a lot of expense. Spend time simply sitting together, holding each other, and talking. You might also try walking, riding bikes, or working together in the yard.

Martha and William had three children who lived with them all the time. Alone time for them was precious and limited. They tried to plan time with each other after the kids went to bed, but evening chores took priority.

Finally, William and Martha decided to get up earlier in the mornings. They spent 30 minutes every morning drinking coffee together, catching up on the previous day, reading the Bible or a devotional book, and praying. This small change helped them begin their day at peace and with each other.

William and Martha so enjoyed their time together that they initiated an evening devotional time with the children. Schedules sometimes prevented the family time, but they met as often as possible. As a result, the family grew closer!

Consider sharing a devotional time together at the beginning or end of each day. If you include the children in this time, set aside another time to pray together as a couple.

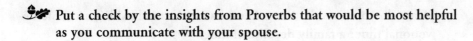 Do you and your spouse share a devotional time? ❑ Yes ❑ No
If not, would you like to? ❑ Yes ❑ No

Couple time will not just happen—it must be planned.

What do you consider the greatest barrier to establishing a couple devotional time? a family devotional time?

_____

Date Night

Joan and Stephen have been married two-and-a-half years. Their four children live with them most of the time. From the beginning, Stephen and Joan decided their relationship with each other mattered as much as their relationships with the children. If something happened to them as a couple, the whole family would suffer. Therefore, they take time each week just for the two of them.

Every Friday night is date night. The children expect a baby-sitter and pizza. Every Saturday night is family night. Joan and Stephen plan an activity or outing with the children. Initially the kids were not delighted with this arrangement and expressed their displeasure. Now, because they know Saturday night is their night, they accept date night as part of the weekly family routine. Where Joan and Stephen go on Friday nights is not important; why they go is very important. Friday night is their time alone together. They religiously follow one rule: They do not talk about the children.

Every husband and wife needs time to explore, develop, and enhance their couple relationship. The whole family needs them to be a healthy couple. Often I say to remarried couples: "One of the very best things you can do for your children is to have a healthy marriage. Your children and stepchildren will have your relationship as a model for the rest of their lives."

How much couple time each week do you and your spouse take now? Circle the hours.

| None | One or Two | Three to Five | Six or More |

Do you think the amount of time you circled is adequate? ❑ Yes ❑ No

How much time each week would you like to spend with your spouse?

___ hours

What are some things you would like to do during that time?

_____

_____

Planning Ahead

Family planning helps to prioritize alone time for couples. Every blended family couple needs time alone; how they accomplish it varies.

As soon as they returned from their honeymoon, Peter and Susan discovered the difficulty of finding time to spend alone. While they were dating, Peter lived in an apartment. His two children visited every other weekend; but most of the time, Peter's apartment was a quiet place for him and Susan to spend time alone,

> One of the very best things you can do for your children is to have a healthy marriage.

watch television, and share a quiet meal while Susan's three children were with a sitter.

After they married they had no such retreat. Susan's three children lived with them and Peter's two visited every other weekend. Alone time was scarce. Peter and Susan spent nearly six stress-filled months trying to figure out the difference.

One night while the kids were seeing a movie, Susan said to Peter: "You know, I really miss your apartment. Do you remember how peaceful it was there without the kids?"

"Boy, do I," replied Peter. "I thought maybe it was just me. I feel guilty for being so selfish."

"We need to find a way to be alone more often," said Susan. "I love my kids, but I love you, too. Do you have any ideas?"

Susan and Peter reached a turning point when they scheduled couple time. Unlike Joan and Stephen, they did not plan a weekly date night. Instead they retreated to their bedroom at nine o'clock every night. Two of the children had a nine o'clock bedtime, and the oldest was instructed to study or read in his room between nine and ten o'clock. At first, the oldest child complained about the change; but when Susan and Peter stood firm, the complaints ceased and they settled into the new routine.

🍂 **You've read examples of ways two couples achieved time alone. For the next few days, record your daily activities. Ask your spouse to do the same. Compare your logs to discover when and where you might schedule some alone time. Discuss it during CoupleTalk.**

Of course, regular alone time does not guarantee closeness. Even when a couple truly wants to share, talking may be difficult. To avoid this problem, Susan and Peter devised several techniques to direct their conversation. One was to read a book aloud together. Many nights they read just a few paragraphs before discussing what they read. Other nights they would finish a chapter. Peter and Susan considered their alone time an important part of their blending family process.

🍂 **How would you like to structure the time alone with your spouse? Mention several things you both like to do.**

_____

_____

🍂 **Write this week's Scripture memory verse in the margin. In the space below tell how spending time together contributes to the "perfect unity" you seek in your marriage.**

_____

_____

ESTABLISHING AN ACTION PLAN

*A*ll families experience troubled times. The degree of trouble is the only variable. Frequently in a blended family, trouble comes quickly. The couple barely settles in from the honeymoon before major obstacles arise.

Learning to handle such difficulties in a positive way is the secret of successful family living, whether it be in a nuclear family or a blended family. Time is precious. Deal immediately with any obstacles, major or minor, before they cause emotional separation within the family unit.

Commit to Seeking Help

When I conduct premarital counseling, I ask couples to agree in advance to seek marital counseling if either of them feels the need for it. I ask them to agree to this as a love gift to each other. Making this commitment early almost always guarantees a lasting marriage.

Some people shy away from counseling because they view it as a long-term, expensive endeavor. Although long-term therapy may be the answer for some families, others may find that only a few visits can turn what appears to be huge brick walls into solvable stumbling blocks. Twice Betty and I have benefited from a single session with a counselor. Because of his expertise and outside perspective, he helped us identify workable solutions.

🍂 **Have there been times when you felt your marriage was in trouble?**
❑ Yes ❑ No

What did you do about it?

_____

Did this approach solve the problem?

_____

Would you be willing to seek counseling in the future? ❑ Yes ❑ No

Michael and Vivian never dreamed they would be sitting in a marriage counselor's office. Recently all of their marital difficulties seemed to relate to the ongoing conflict between Vivian's daughter Robin and Michael.

Robin was 14 years old and in many ways a typical teenager exercising her independence. She decided she did not want or need another father. She had a father, and she wanted to live with him. There was only one problem. Robin's biological father also was remarried, and Robin did not particularly like his new wife. She was extremely angry and acted out of her anger. Since Michael was the nearest culprit, he bore the brunt of Robin's anger.

Nothing Michael did seemed to have any positive effect on Robin. Finally, Michael gave up; he "laid down the law." He insisted that Vivian ground Robin until she could relate to him without being rude and disrespectful.

While she recognized Robin's behavior as being unacceptable, Vivian did not agree with grounding Robin indefinitely. She feared it would increase Robin's frustration. She even worried Robin might run away. For two weeks, the entire family lived in turmoil. Vivian and Michael argued constantly. Robin sulked and spoke to no one. The other two siblings fought with each other. Finally, in desperation, Michael and Vivian scheduled an appointment with a counselor.

The counselor asked to spend time alone with Robin before meeting with the whole family. "Oh, Robin will never come," Vivian replied.

"See," Michael quipped. "That's the problem. She gives her a choice."

"Well, I can't just make her come. She's 14," cried Vivian.

"This time I agree with Michael," the counselor interrupted. "Don't give Robin a choice. Tell her she must come. A teenager usually will not want to visit a counselor. You don't have to be belligerent, Vivian, but you do have to be firm. Let Robin know you came to me because you want your family to work. Explain to her that the entire family is scheduled to meet after she shares her perspective. But don't give her a choice. This is not something a 14 year old is wise enough to choose."

As expected, Robin snapped, "I'm not going, and you can't make me."

"You are going," Vivian firmly stated.

"Well, I'm not going to talk. You can't force me to talk." With that comment Robin stomped off to her room.

True to her word, Robin gave the counselor the silent treatment. However, the counselor was not intimidated: "I just thought you might welcome a chance to tell your side of the story. I've already heard what your mother and Michael think is the problem. I thought you might have a different opinion. If you don't want to talk, I suppose I'll have to assume everything they told me is true."

"What did they tell you?" asked Robin.

"Well, I'm afraid that's confidential, just as everything you tell me is confidential. I can't tell you what they said, and I can't tell them what you say." The counselor continued, "That's the way counseling works."

"Oh, well, I guess I can tell you what I think is going on. And you won't tell them, right?" asked Robin.

"That's right," assured the counselor. "I won't tell them anything without your permission. Agreed?"

Convinced she was safe emotionally, Robin shared her feelings about her parents' remarrying. They both married people she didn't like, and she felt it was unfair to her. Many of Robin's pent-up feelings exploded in the safe, neutral zone of the counselor's office.

The situation did not have a storybook ending. Everything did not improve immediately. However, it was the beginning of a new relationship between Michael and Robin as they continued to work through the blending process. That was God's miracle. The family did not give up on itself.

🍂 Do you remember our Scripture verse for this week? Love requires us to do all we can to make our marriage and family work. For your family's sake, ask God to reveal any part of yourself you are not willing to improve. Confess it to Him and ask Him to give you the desire to grow as a mate and parent.

You Are Not Alone

Not every problem needs a trained therapist. Sometimes talking with a friend or a minister, reading a book, or attending a seminar can work wonders. Keep in mind that when we are open to His Spirit, God can use a wide variety of resources to provide help. The weekly support group you attend is comprised of other couples who understand. You are not alone—even if you feel like it at times.

First Kings 19 tells a wonderful story. Elijah destroyed the prophets of Baal on Mt. Carmel and fled from King Ahab and his wife Jezebel because they wanted to kill him. At the end of verse 14 he cried out to God, "I am the only one left, and now they are trying to kill me too."

Do you think Elijah was surprised when God said to him, "Yet I reserve seven thousand in Israel—all whose knees have not bowed down to Baal and all whose mouths have not kissed him" (v. 18)? Elijah thought he was alone, but he wasn't. You, too, may feel completely alone at times. You aren't. Not only is God with you, but there are others who understand and can help.

When we are open to His Spirit, God can use a wide variety of resources to provide help.

🍂 What will you do the next time you face trouble as a couple or as a family? Establish an action plan using any of the following suggestions. Begin this process during CoupleTalk.

- talk to my mate
- talk to my minister
- seek counseling
- talk to my support group
- talk to another family member
- read an appropriate book
- attend a marriage/family enrichment event
- Other? _____

🍂 Read Ephesians 4:15 in the margin. How does "speaking the truth in love" contribute to the perfect unity we are trying to build into our marriages?

_____

Instead, speaking the truth in love, we will in all things grow up into him who is the Head, that is, Christ.
—Ephesians 4:15

🍂 Say this week's Scripture memory verse to at least two family members.

---

1. Reinhold Niebuhr, "The Serenity Prayer," (St. Meinrad, IN: Abbey Press)

COUPLETALK

For you to complete

1. How would you describe the communication style in your marriage? Check one:
   - ❑ We are both talkers.
   - ❑ We are both quiet.
   - ❑ One is a talker and the other is quiet.

2. Is this style working well for you? Check the statement that best represents your answer.
   - ❑ working well
   - ❑ working adequately
   - ❑ not working so well

3. Look back at day 3. Write one idea for each of the following:

   What to share _____

   _____

   When to share _____

   _____

   How to share _____

   _____

For you to share with your spouse

1. Sit down facing each other and take turns sharing how each of you completed the above section.
2. Discuss time possibilities for scheduling couple time alone. Talk about ways to use the time. Plan a date night or other alone time.
3. Begin to establish an action plan for troubled times. Share ideas.
4. Tell one thing you really love about each other.
5. Say together this week's Scripture memory verse.
6. Pray for each other, silently or aloud.

LEARN TO LIVE TOGETHER

When Marsha and Daniel moved into their new home, they believed they knew each other very well. They had dated for two years before a year-long engagement. After only one week their bubble burst. Daniel didn't consider himself a "neat freak," but Marsha called him one. Marsha didn't think of herself as a slob, but according to Daniel she should be living in a barn. Then there was the problem of the checkbook. *How did she ever balance her checkbook when she was single?* Daniel wondered. He had already ordered checks with carbons so Marsha would have a record of her expenditures. Marsha and Daniel didn't notice these differences while they were dating. Now that they were married, these became real issues calling for their best negotiating skills.

Much of what Marsha and Daniel experienced occurs in every marriage. Couples go through a stage of learning to share space, holiday traditions, and finances. Every couple must adjust their conflict resolution skills to fit the personality and style of their partner.

Learning to live together requires many compromises and changes. How we handle these issues affects our attitude toward our mates and other family members. Many couples are locked in a power struggle over some of these changes. Who will prevail and who will give in? Add to that children from a previous marriage who are also resisting change from a former way of life. The results often resemble chaos!

God took chaos and created a new and better world. In the first chapter of Genesis we read, "Now the earth was formless and empty, darkness was over the surface of the deep, and the Spirit of God was hovering over the waters" (v. 2). Whether over the world or in our lives, His Spirit hovers over the chaos—and creates. When we are open to that creative Spirit, good things happen.

What You'll Study

DAY 1
• **Sharing Space**
DAY 2
• **Establishing Routines**
DAY 3
• **Planning Celebrations**
DAY 4
• **Handling Finances**
DAY 5
• **Resolving Conflicts**

This Week You Will:
• identify issues that present problems in learning to live together;
• establish routines and traditions that fit the lifestyle and make-up of your blended family;
• model responsible money management;
• practice problem-solving skills that will lead to resolving conflicts.

This Week's Scripture Memory Verse
"The Lord is with me; I will not be afraid" (Psalm 118:6).

SHARING SPACE

*B*lending differences into a common pattern of living is not easy. Each of us follows a particular way of doing things. Learning a new way takes time. Even when we decide that change is necessary, we may easily slip back into the old way. After all, the old way is a comfortable rut.

Mentally walk through your house and list differences you have encountered in the way you share space with your mate and his/her children.

❑ bedroom _____

❑ bathroom _____

❑ kitchen _____

❑ living area _____

How did you resolve these differences? Check one or more.

❑ compromise   ❑ held my ground

❑ did it his/her way   ❑ the kids won

❑ other? _____

Put a check by the differences that remain unresolved.

Develop a Win-Win Mentality

What is perfectly normal in one home may often be unacceptable in another. Unfortunately, we may turn personal preferences into moral issues. When we pass judgment on others' styles and preferences, we are saying in effect, "My way is right and your way is wrong." Our Lord Jesus instructed us: "Do not judge, or you too will be judged. For in the same way you judge others, you will be judged, and with the measure you use, it will be measured to you" (Matthew 7:1-2).

When we insist on our way of doing things, we set up a win-lose mentality in which the family loses, no matter who wins. Family members take positions and hold fast to their viewpoints until a winner is declared. This competition sets up a reward system for the loudest, the one who complains the most, the one with the most persistence, or the one who best manipulates the system. Success, or winning, is achieved at the expense of someone else. Hurt feelings and loss of pride may linger for hours or days.

When we insist on our way of doing things, we set up a win-lose mentality.

How do you feel when a power struggle develops in your family? Would you like to avoid power struggles in the future?

A win-win spirit reinforces the value of cooperation. Instead of "me first," it's "we first." This spirit seeks solutions which are mutually beneficial. Win-win is achieved by allowing all family members to participate in determining change. Once a decision is made, everyone commits to the action plan.

Think about an immediate issue facing your family in which you would like to see a win-win solution. In the margins or on a separate piece of paper write what would be considered a "win" from the other person's perspective. Then write what would be a "win" for you. Look for points of connection between the two. Plan a time when you and the other person(s) can negotiate until you reach a mutually beneficial solution. See day 5 for a problem-solving format.

Practice the Art of Compromise

Compromise is good news and bad news. The good news is that we reach a decision. The bad news is that each person has to give up a little of what he or she wants. Compromise requires us to take half a loaf, rather than the whole loaf. If there is a win-lose competitive atmosphere in our families, compromise is often a last resort. When we practice a win-win mentality in our families, compromise is a natural part of decision making.

Paul and Jan had argued for months over formal and informal dining. Paul and his two boys enjoyed the camaraderie of eating together in front of the television. Jan insisted that the family eat together at the table—with no interference from the TV or radio.

While Paul agreed in principal that eating meals together would be a better family practice, he found enforcing the rule difficult, especially if Jan were not present. One night Jan worked late. When she arrived home, she found dishes on the coffee table, a sure sign of eating in the living room. When she confronted Paul about it, he said, "Well, you weren't here, so I thought it would be OK this one time."

"It's not OK," said Jan. "Either we have rules that we live by all the time, or the rules just don't mean anything."

"But it's fun to eat in front of the TV. You should try it sometime."

"I don't want to try it," said Jan. "Eating together and talking about our day was always important in my family. I want that for us, too. If we start giving in now and then, it might become a habit. I don't want to take the chance."

In this situation did Paul have to win while Jan lost, or vice versa? Eventually the couple realized compromise was the best alternative. When Jan is home and prepares the meal, the family eats in the dining room. When Jan is away or they have take-out food, the family has the option of eating in the living room.

Although Paul's boys were not enthusiastic about this arrangement, gradually they adjusted. Interestingly, when both boys were grown and had families of their own, each established a rule that eating in the living room while watching TV was not allowed except for special occasions.

🍃 **What compromise has your new family reached? In the margin explain how you arrived at the compromise and why.**

In family life compromise is not always possible. Let's suppose the family is trying to decide which video to watch. Because of children's age differences, there may be no consensus. A win-lose position would force some of the children to view a movie they don't want to see or holds no interest for them. A win-win would mean finding that elusive video that appeals to every age group. In such a case a win-win situation may be impossible. The family may be better served to give up the video idea and go bowling or take a picnic lunch to the park.

Learn from the Experiences of Others

When Darlene and Fred attended their first premarital session, their pastor encouraged them to take advantage of their church's mentoring program. Nearly married couples were assigned to older married couples who would meet with them several times before and after the wedding. Darlene and Fred reluctantly agreed, mostly to please the pastor. As it turned out, their mentoring couple was also in a second marriage and had much to offer. The first session focused on adjustments during the first two months of marriage.

🍃 **If you were a mentor, what advice would you give to an engaged couple about adjustments they would likely face in their first months?**

_____

_____

All of us could benefit from the insights of others who have gone before us. Your *New Faces in the Frame* group provides an opportunity for learning from others who face similar challenges. God delights in giving us second chances. Now is a perfect opportunity to improve family relationships.

🍃 **This workbook, the CoupleTalk time, and the group process are all tools that God can use to teach you how to be a better family member. List some things you have already learned from your group about adjusting to your marriage partner.**

_____

_____

_____

🍃 **Write this week's Scripture memory verse in the margin. Underline the promise in the verse. How is the Lord's presence a comfort to you as you learn to share with other family members?**

If you would like to mentor engaged or newly married couples, Marriage Mentors by Bob and Yvonne Turnbull is a wonderful resource. The mature couple helps the new couple work through the inevitable problems and tensions of the marriage relationship. Order Marriage Mentors by calling the Customer Service Center at 1-800-458-2772 and ask for item 0-8054-9852-4.

ESTABLISHING ROUTINES

*R*elinquishing control over your own schedule is one of the trade-offs of marrying again. When you were single, you came and went without checking in. Bedtime was whenever you wanted or needed it to be. No one squabbled with you about when to set the alarm or what time to eat dinner. Now routines must be coordinated with another person's preferences, personalities, work schedules, and habits—and they may not match your own.

Routines help us function efficiently and accomplish tasks without much thought. Deciding the best way to complete every action in a day's time would be time consuming. Consider your bathroom routine in the morning or getting dressed. Most of us perform such tasks on automatic pilot, never consciously considering the steps to completion. If I were to stop and think about how to put on my tie, it would be much more difficult!

Describe the route you travel to work. Does it vary? If so, why?

_____

_____

Routines, while useful, are powerful habits and difficult to change.

Most of the week I travel the same route to the church where I work, turn at the same streets, and park in the same place. On Sundays, however, I vary my route because I park in a different lot. Unless I concentrate, I often turn the wrong way—heading straight to my week-day parking spot. Routines, while useful, are powerful habits and difficult to change.

Offer Your Mate a Love Gift

A routine is followed without much thought until such a time as it becomes unnecessary or nonproductive. I find that when I want to change a routine, I must concentrate to do so. Because a routine is engrained, the pattern is hard to break.

Bob and Gloria shared much in common. However, Bob was a morning person who loved to get up at 5:00 a.m., jog three miles, eat a big breakfast while reading the paper, and arrive at work with twenty minutes to spare. On the other hand, Gloria hated to get up early. She enjoyed evenings, and her personal clock only began ticking in the late night hours. Obviously, their routines clashed.

In the early months of their marriage, each spent considerable energy trying to force change on the other. When Bob and Gloria finally stopped trying to change each other and began to look for solutions, they developed a routine that worked for the two of them. Bob accepted that Gloria was probably always going to prefer the evenings, and Gloria conceded that Bob would always enjoy sunrises.

The compromise called for Bob to intentionally stay up a little later on Thursday night, sleep later on Friday morning, and sacrifice his early morning jog in order to have energy to spend a late Friday night with Gloria. On Saturdays, Gloria got up a little earlier, went to bed earlier on Saturday evening, and rose to watch the sunrise with Bob on Sundays. This compromise was their love gift to each other.

The new routine worked well for Gloria and Bob. They respected each other for who they were and what they liked. At the same time, in their love they sought to be accommodating.

✿ What routine have you altered in order to please your new mate?

_____

_____

Are there any routines that are still in conflict?

_____

_____

New Faces in the Frame allows you and your spouse the opportunity to talk through areas of conflict and come to some satisfactory conclusions. In week 5 we will look at problem-solving techniques. Think about how you will approach a discussion of routines during CoupleTalk.

Blending Children's Patterns

Blending the unique routines of children and stepchildren can be equally stressful. Children accustomed to home life with a single parent must adjust to the routines of a new adult in the family, not to mention step-siblings.

Bob and Gloria had three children living at home, each with their own unique routines. Gloria's children practiced their mother's routine of sleeping late and rushing off to school at the last possible moment. Bob's son Jason never was comfortable with his father's early morning energy. Jason quickly adopted the routine of Gloria and her children.

After a while, Jason found the last-minute rush difficult. He developed his own compromise between his father's and Gloria's routine. Jason set his alarm to rise a half hour earlier than Gloria and her children. Then he and his dad had a few minutes together before Bob went to work.

Unlike Jason, many children cannot arrive at their own solutions to dilemmas over routines. When routines collide, you must make decisions about whose routine will be followed or what new routine will be established. If one family is accustomed to getting up late on Saturday morning, while the other family's routine involves getting chores out of the way, conflict may result. If the routine in one family requires all homework to be done before play and the routine of the other allows for homework to be done before bedtime, someone must decide whose rule will prevail in the blending family.

Blending the unique routines of children and stepchildren can be equally stressful.

When, in the interest of an entire family's needs, a child is asked to change a routine, explain the logic as best you can. Don't expect him or her to like the change or to agree with your reasoning. As a loving parent, be willing to set rules. The child's responsibility is to obey and trust the parent's decision.

Follow-through is essential. Some children are experts at making a decision so difficult to enforce that parents give up and return to the previous routine. That pattern sends children the wrong message. The world will not change to meet their demands. The earlier children learn this essential truth, the better prepared they are to face adulthood.

🍂 Has one of your children or stepchildren developed a new routine to meet the needs of the blended family? If so, thank him or her for being flexible and creative. Tell about this family member in your next group meeting.

Develop Two Virtues

Develop the virtues of patience and flexibility.

Most routines are neither right nor wrong. They are simply our way of functioning. Blending routines requires work, but solutions *are* possible. Jesus said, "Seek and you will find" (Matthew 7:7). The problem for most of us is deciding too quickly that a solution does not exist. We give up, believing we must simply learn to live with the situation or force the other person to change.

One of the primary virtues in any blended family is patience. To coin a phrase, Rome wasn't built in a day. If you are having problems meshing routines, continue to work toward creative solutions without expecting a quick fix.

A second virtue is flexibility. Conformity is not necessarily the goal of family life. Every person operating on the same schedule may sound appealing, but individual styles, ages, and backgrounds make that impossible. Learning to live with one another means learning to value and respect one another's differences.

🍂 Describe one individual difference you have chosen to respect and leave intact between you and another family member.

_____

_____

Now stop and pat yourself on the back—literally! You have offered a love gift.

🍂 Write this week's Scripture memory verse in the margin.

List several reasons you may be fearful of change. How does God's presence help you deal with change?

_____

_____

_____

PLANNING CELEBRATIONS

Celebrations, like routines, vary widely. Throughout the world people love holidays; however, they practice them in multiple ways. Families celebrate according to customs that have been handed down from previous generations.

Even holiday menus vary from family to family, especially if those families come from different regions of the country. Before moving to Georgia, I had never heard of cornbread stuffing cooked outside of the turkey. I thought everyone ate sage stuffing cooked inside the turkey, made just like my mother's and her mother before her. In my wife's family, the turkey's liver and heart were cooked and added to the stuffing beforehand. Now, many years and Thanksgiving dinners later, it still "feels" more like Thanksgiving when I eat foods prepared my mother's way.

Make Holidays "Holy Days"

If one family always celebrates Christmas at Mom's house, while the other likes to have a Christmas mini-vacation, a struggle is inevitable. As part of a blended family, I've learned to adapt my holiday traditions. One concept that helped me change is thinking of holidays as "holy days"–days that honor the Lord Jesus Christ. When Christ is the center of a "holy day," the celebration takes on more meaning. I am less tied to details and more willing to consider the newness in Christ.

Celebrating "holy days" (holidays) began in Old Testament times. God established holy days throughout the year so that Israel would recall His blessings. The New Testament records holidays Jesus and His family observed in Nazareth and Jerusalem. Jesus traveled with His parents to the temple in Jerusalem to celebrate the annual Passover (Luke 2:41-52).

When Christ is the center of a "holy day," the celebration takes on more meaning.

List as many of the ancient holidays as you can remember. If you need help, check the Old Testament Book of Leviticus, chapter 23.

_____

_____

Did you find the *Sabbath* (Lev. 23:1-4)? One of the Ten Commandments instructed, "Remember the Sabbath day by keeping it holy" (Ex. 20:8). Others include: *Passover* and *Feast of Unleavened Bread* (Lev. 23:5-8)–a time for celebrating the Israelites' deliverance from slavery; *Firstfruits* (Lev. 23:9-14)–a festival offering God the first of the harvest; *Feast of Weeks* (Lev. 23:15-22)–a feast which took place 50 days after Passover (also known as Pentecost) and celebrated the ingathering of the wheat harvest; *New Year Festival* (Lev. 23:23-25)—a celebration marked by a blast of trumpets; *Day of Atonement* (Lev. 23:26-32)—a special day set aside for renewing relationship with God; and *Feast of Tabernacles* (Lev. 23:33-44)—another harvest festival held in the fall.

🕊️ **Which of these holidays or customs are celebrated by Christians? What additional holy days do Christians celebrate?**

_____

_____

Christians today practice the observance of Sabbath; however, we changed Sabbath Day to Sunday in honor of the Lord's resurrection. Pentecost is also a Christian celebration, but in a new sense. At Pentecost the Holy Spirit came on the Christians gathered in Jerusalem (Acts 2:1-41). While Thanksgiving is not specifically a Christian holiday, in many ways it is like the Hebrew Feast of Tabernacles, a day set aside to thank God for the harvest.

Christmas is decidedly a Christian holiday, designated to celebrate Jesus' birth. Most other Christian holidays are related to Easter and Jesus' last week of life on earth. We refer to that week as Holy Week. It includes Palm Sunday, Holy Thursday (or the last supper), Good Friday, and Easter, when we celebrate our Lord's resurrection.

🕊️ **Would thinking of holidays as "holy days" enable your blended family to be more open to changing traditions?** ❏ Yes ❏ No

🕊️ **In what ways do you honor Christ with your holiday traditions? Write one or more in the margin.**

Tackle the Christmas Dilemma

Both you and your spouse may encounter a certain amount of depression as you recall Christmases past. Expect your children and stepchildren to do the same. Acknowledge your own grief and allow your children to acknowledge theirs. Recognize moodiness or acting out as visible signs of inward pain. When we share our pain and hear someone else's, we no longer feel isolated or different.

Along with those very real emotions, Christmas brings new delimmas for the blending family: When and where will we open presents? How will we get children/stepchildren back and forth between ex's and grandparents? Will we decorate outside or just inside the house? Who is getting gifts and from whom?

Shirley and Dale were not prepared for their first Christmas together. While they thought they knew each other well, their first Christmas made them doubt they knew each other at all. In Shirley's family, gifts were exchanged only between parents and children. Shirley planned to buy gifts for their three children, Dale, her parents, and Dale's parents. Since most of the gifts would be for the children, she expected to spend a considerable amount of money.

Dale's experience was very different. In his family gifts were given to brothers, sisters, cousins, even friends. The gifts were inexpensive tokens of love; the best

When we share our pain and hear someone else's, we no longer feel isolated or different.

ones were handmade. The children's gifts were never costly. As you might expect, Dale and Shirley also had different ideas for decorating and opening presents. What was the problem? They each had traditions and neither wanted to abandon the traditions they had grown up with and practiced for many years.

🍂 **What are some holiday traditions you and your spouse found difficult to blend?**

_____

_____

How did you finally resolve the differences?

_____

_____

What differences remain unresolved?

_____

_____

Develop New Traditions

While the purpose of "holy days" is to focus our attention on something holy, it is easy to miss the true meaning and get caught up in traditions and celebrations. If those old traditions and celebrations are a source of conflict, consider establishing new ones for your family. If everyone involved is invited to give input, including the children, the process can happen smoothly. When parents make a decision without any input from the children, the children almost never appreciate the decision, even when it is a good one.

Shirley and Dale, whom you met earlier, found blending their Christmas traditions difficult. For a while no one wanted to let go of the past. When the family tried to include a little of both traditions, no one was happy. Finally, Shirley and Dale called a family meeting to plan next year's Christmas.

After much discussion, they decided to celebrate the true meaning of Christmas by having a birthday party for Jesus. Instead of focusing on presents for each other, they determined the best gift they could give Jesus. One year it was a special offering for a mission project at church. Another year, they "adopted" a homeless family, had Christmas dinner together, and gave them all presents. Christmas became a very special time because of their new tradition.

🍂 **What new traditions has your blended family established?**

_____

_____

Consider developing new traditions for your family.

What are some possible new traditions that might nurture your blending family's process?

_____

_____

Say this week's Scripture memory verse to another family member.

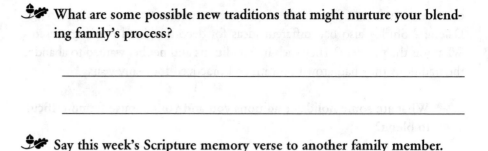

HANDLING FINANCES

_B_lended families deal with finances in various ways based on the history of the people involved. Couples remarrying usually have accumulated possessions and have definite thoughts about their personal finances. Divorced persons may be wary of relinquishing control over finances. Some blending families combine all possessions and income; others maintain separate checking and savings accounts for years. Most couples fall somewhere in between.

A woman once told me that while she loved her husband and knew that their marriage would survive, she could not sell her appliances even though they had decided that they would use his. The appliances represented giving up some of her independence. What if she needed them again? It was more than a year before she could sell them.

Recently I attended a seminar on finances in blending families. The leader asked how many attending had merged income and possessions. Of the 10 families represented, no one had done so completely, although most of us had been married between 6 and 10 years. Often, finances are the final blending component in a blending family.

Often, finances are the final blending component in a blending family.

Which of the following is true for you?
- ❑ All income is deposited into joint accounts from which all bills are paid.
- ❑ Each spouse pays certain bills after which leftover money is strictly his or hers.
- ❑ Bills are paid from a joint account, but each person has an individual account as well.
- ❑ Other: _____

Be Willing to Discuss Finances

How you and your spouse deal with the finances in your home is probably not as important as your willingness to talk together about money. In too many homes, money is seldom mentioned except in an argument. Couples may include a spender and a saver. What one person considers a luxury, the other views as a necessity.

Both you and your spouse need to know your total income, financial obligations, and the plan you have to meet those obligations. Each of you can still have money that is totally your own to spend as you desire. You should, however, come to some agreement about family financial goals.

Mark and Brenda both worked outside the home. They had not discussed finances prior to their wedding. Since Brenda had moved into Mark's house, she assumed that Mark would continue to pay the mortgage and she would contribute to food and utilities. Brenda wanted her name added to the deed in the event something happened to Mark.

When the deed was mentioned, Mark suggested that Brenda help with the mortgage payments since it would be her house, too.

"But you earn more than I do," said Brenda.

"That's true," Mark answered, "but I have to pay a big chunk of my income for child support. After that, our salaries are about equal."

"Well, they're your kids," said Brenda. "I shouldn't have to pay for them."

For several months, Mark and Brenda argued about this issue. What seemed fair to one did not seem fair to the other. Both wished they had discussed finances prior to the wedding.

Eventually they compromised. Brenda agreed to deposit half of her pay into a joint account from which all household expenses were paid. Mark did the same with what remained after paying his child support. Each was responsible for their own car expenses, clothes, and personal matters. As time passed, some adjustment to the initial plan was necessary, but it was the beginning of a unified effort.

 When was the last time you sat down with your spouse and talked (not argued) about finances?

_____

_____

On the scale below, indicate your rate of satisfaction with how your family handles finances?

Not Satisfied   Moderately Satisfied   Completely Satisfied

Regard Finances as a Spiritual Issue

Money represents many things: power, independence, security, and dreams for the future. Finances—the allocation of our money—is a spiritual concern of the highest order. Jesus talked about money and possessions throughout the Gospels.

Remember the rich man whom Jesus invited to give away his possessions and follow Him (Luke 18:18-25)? The man could not bring himself to part with his wealth. Jesus remarked that it was easier for a camel to pass through the eye of a needle than for a rich man to enter the kingdom of God (v. 25). Money and possessions can easily become a spiritual shackle which keeps us from enjoying the riches of fellowship with God.

Money represents many things: power, independence, security, and dreams for the future.

🍃 What are some ways money and possessions pose difficulties for families trying to blend?

_____

_____

Which of these are spiritual problems? _____

_____

_____

Since God created everything that exists and labeled it good, in some way everything is spiritual. Jesus taught that we are stewards of what God has entrusted to us. Jesus told a parable about three servants who were given a sum of money—the first, $5,000; the second, $2,000; and the last, $1,000. The servants were not only to spend their money, but also to use the money in a constructive way until the master returned (Matthew 25:14-30).

In many ways, our attachment to money and possessions is directly related to our spiritual growth. It also is related to our happiness. In my book, _Single and Growing_, I relate the following story in a chapter called "Happiness is a Choice."

While visiting the seashore recently, I saw a magnificent house for sale. Located right on the beach, it seemed to have everything I could ever want in a dream house. I thought, _If I could only have that house, I could be happy for the rest of my life._ But that house cost $499,000, far beyond anything I could afford. But I could dream. I imagined that somehow I bought that house and was happy.

For more than a week, I traded the happiness I already was experiencing for make-believe happiness I would never experience. In doing so, I concentrated on what I saw as need rather than on God's abundance. I became fretful about my present house. I failed to recognize that God already was giving me everything I needed in order to be happy.

The danger of all fantasies is the focus on want and need rather than God's gracious provision. The moment I thought, _If I had that house, I could be happy,_ I forgot that prior to that time, I had been happy. God's blessings were all around me. I did not need more in order to be happy. Happiness was at hand. It disappeared only when I perceived that I needed something else in order to have it.

When we submit ourselves to God's plan of stewardship we truly find happiness and contentment with what we have. I have yet to meet someone who feels he does not have more after he has tithed. While the mathematics do not add up, the truth remains.

Model Responsible Money Management

Most children who see their parents deal with finances responsibly will grow up to treat money with the care it requires. Linda used to get angry at how Harold's daughter Beth constantly asked him for money and he always gave it to her. Linda asked Harold to keep track of how much money he gave Beth in one month's time. Harold was shocked to discover he had given his daughter $137.50.

Our attachment to money and possessions is directly related to our spiritual growth.

Harold and Linda devised a creative way to teach money management. They asked Beth to write down how much money she needed each month—including spending money. They gave her that much as an allowance, with instructions that when her money was gone, she could not ask for more.

Of course, Beth ran out of money the very first month. To her credit, she did not ask for more. The second month Beth was more frugal. At the end of four months, Beth had saved $75, which she proudly added to her college fund. She had also learned a valuable lesson that would benefit her the rest of her life.

🌿 **What kind of role model are you when it comes to teaching the children in your household about finances? Check as many answers as apply:**
❑ I don't talk about money, but I spend it wisely.
❑ I frequently talk with my children about how to deal with money responsibly.
❑ My mate and I share with the children our financial ups and downs. They always know where we stand financially.
❑ I need to demonstrate more financial responsibility.

🌿 **What lessons about money would you like for your children to learn before they leave home?**

_____

_____

🌹 Part of responsible money management is trusting God to provide for our needs. Repeat the Scripture memory verse to yourself. Take a moment to thank God for ways He has provided for you materially.

DAY 5

RESOLVING CONFLICTS

Conflict is normal and essential to a growing relationship. Learning to resolve conflict in a way that allows each partner to feel like a winner takes patience and determination.

Conflicts About the Children

In a blended family, conflict is often about the children, or at least one of them. One child almost always assumes the position of "problem child." The other children gladly step back and allow the conflict to revolve around him or her. This pattern is observed and repeated in many family systems studies (how families organize themselves).

Of course, conflict over a child sets up conflict between the couple. Biological parents feel torn apart by conflict concerning one of their children. Stepparents feel like outsiders with no right to an opinion. The biological parent and stepparent may end up being more upset with each other than with the child. When children observe this conflict between spouses, they often, and deliberately, add more fuel to the fire. Finally something erupts!

While conflict in any home is normal, conflict in a blending family just beginning to bond is very disruptive. Couples frequently disagree about discipline. Because each spouse was reared differently, they *could* learn much from each other, but that will happen *only* if they choose to respect their mate's opinion.

What is your biggest area of conflict with the children or a child?

_____

What do each of you do when a conflict arises?

_____

_____

Does the conflict ever get resolved? How?

_____

_____

Schedule a Time to Talk

Conflict is usually handled best when emotions are calm. In the heat of an argument, very little is likely to be resolved. In fact, when emotions are turbulent, people often make statements and accusations they later regret. Couples should schedule a time when both are calmer to sit down, talk about the problem, and seek a solution. Scheduling a conflict resolution time keeps the problem from being swept under the carpet, yet gives each partner time to cool down. Parents know how helpful "time out" can be with children. It's also good for adults.

Once you have scheduled a time to talk, pray about what to say. Ask God to show you the best way to confront issues. Ask Him to guide you when you speak so that your words will be spoken in love and not hostility. Ask God to help you listen to your spouse and to be flexible. Finally, ask God to help your entire family learn to live together in peace and harmony.

I don't like to discuss problems when I am rushing off to work, and Betty doesn't like to discuss them at bedtime. When is a good time for you to talk over issues? Share this information with your spouse during CoupleTalk.

Agree to Disagree

Couples do not have to agree on everything. Total agreement is next to impossible. People really are different and differences are acceptable. Agree to disagree. Appreciate the other person's opinion even when you cannot buy into it. Having different thoughts and opinions does not mean you don't love each other.

How does a couple coexist with disagreements? In some cases, you buy two tubes of toothpaste! One can squeeze the tube from the bottom, and the other can squeeze it from the top. Other decisions are not so simple. If Betty and I can't find a solution that benefits us both, we agree to disagree. Neither of us forces our own agenda on the other one. We respect each other's opinions.

Sometimes we think that if only our partners would listen, they would understand and agree. Not so. A person can totally understand and still disagree. Agreement is not the backbone of a marriage. Love is. Real love is a decision to love a person, even when he or she disagrees with you. Respect is the commitment that holds a marriage together.

> **Real love is a decision to love a person, even when he or she disagrees with you.**

 Our human nature desires control. But the desire to be right, to be agreed with, does not promote a peaceful home life. Spend some time thinking about your relationship style. Ask God to help you as you relinquish control appropriately.

Use a Problem-Solving Process

Use this time-tested formula for resolving conflict:

1. *Define the real issue by writing it down.* Try to get beyond the details of the last incident. Peel off the layers of the conflict like you would peel an onion, until you have gotten down to the basic issue.
2. *Take responsibility for your part in keeping the conflict going.* What causes this issue to surface? What does each of you do that aggravates the problem? No issue is completely one-sided.
3. *Brainstorm several possible solutions to the problem.* Don't evaluate them as you go, just write them down. All options are allowed at this stage. Do not stop until you have listed at least five solutions.
4. *Try one of the solutions.* Make sure you have been clear about your expectations. Who will do (or not do!) what? Be specific. "I will not get mad over ..." is not a specific solution. "I will count to 10 before I speak" is more specific.
5. *Set a time to evaluate your solution together.* If the first solution is not working, be willing to try another solution from your list.
6. *Thank each other for wanting to solve the problem.* It is much easier to fight over issues than resolve them. If the issue surfaces again (and it probably will), remember that you and your mate are on the same team. Consider your mate an ally, not an adversary.

Practice this problem-solving approach by working through a problem at work or at church in the margin. Sometimes situations away from home are not as volatile. Be prepared to share a family problem that you and your spouse can work on during CoupleTalk.

Write this week's Scripture memory verse in the margin.

CoupleTalk

For you to complete

Look over the notes you wrote for each day. Beside each of the topics listed below jot down some ideas you want to discuss with your spouse.

Sharing Space _____

_____

Establishing Routines _____

_____

Planning Celebrations _____

_____

Handling Finances _____

_____

Resolving Conflicts _____

_____

For you to share with your spouse

1. Share the ideas you listed above. Listen actively to each other. Try to hear what your mate is saying, regardless of whether you agree or disagree. You may want to repeat what you hear your spouse saying to make sure you understand. Keep asking for clarification until you can repeat it accurately.
2. Of the ideas presented, choose no more than three that you agree to work on.
3. Follow the problem-solving method in day 5 for each issue.
4. Tell one thing you love about each other.
5. Say together the unit Scripture memory verse.
6. Pray for each other, silently or aloud.

MINIMIZE INTERFERENCES

Vernon and Patricia each brought two children to their marriage. While all four children live with Patricia and Vernon, they still spend weekends part of the time with their other parents, both of whom have remarried. As a result, both sets of children live in two blended families, only one of which they share together.

None of the children care for the back-and-forth arrangement very much, but they can do nothing about it. The children frequently complain they feel like outsiders in their other homes. Not surprisingly, the stepsiblings in those other homes feel their space has been invaded.

At a recent family reunion, Patricia's two children felt even more like outsiders. It was a family reunion of their father's new wife. At the reunion their stepmother's parents made a big fuss over their biological grandchildren, but hardly said more to them than, "Hello. We're glad you could come."

Vernon and Patricia listen to these frustrations with empathy but helplessness. They continue to work on relationship problems with their ex-spouses, but the children's frustrations on top of theirs is sometimes too much to bear.

In a blended family the list of issues that intrude on the blending process is extensive. New spouses add new relatives. Busy careers result in time away from children and stepchildren who may not have accepted the authority of the stepparent left in charge. Friends from a previous marriage may represent assets or liabilities to the blended couple.

How blended families handle these interferences will determine their rate of progress in the blending process. In this unit we will examine ways to minimize the negative aspects of these influences.

What You'll Study

DAY 1
• **The Former Spouse**
DAY 2
• **The Couple's Parents**
DAY 3
• **Friends**
DAY 4
• **Work**
DAY 5
• **Outsiders**

This Week You Will:
• recognize influences that detract from your blending process;
• learn behaviors and attitudes that limit the effect of these influences;
• seek to bring family members who feel like outsiders into the family unit.

This Week's Scripture Memory Verse
"Make sure that nobody pays back wrong for wrong, but always try to be kind to each other and to everyone else" (1 Thessalonians 5:15).

THE FORMER SPOUSE

Whether living or dead, the former spouse(s) will be a factor in your present marriage, at least as long as their children remain under your roof. Occasionally, I hear reports from blended couples of pleasant--or at least cooperative--relationships with former spouses. More often I hear of disruptive relationships. A living spouse can seem like a specter–present but unseen–in blended family interactions. A deceased spouse may become increasingly virtuous as time passes. It is hard to compete with a saint!

Impact of a Deceased Spouse

Deceased spouses remain alive in our memories. New mates often discover that simply moving a picture or a piece of furniture can have major repercussions. "I like that picture where it was. Mary (or Jim) always kept it there." Years may pass before a widow or widower lets go of the various "shrines" dedicated to a deceased spouse. Even when a more realistic picture of the deceased is present, grief issues and various household matters related to the former spouse continue to surface. There may be stocks to manage, estates to settle, bills to pay, or businesses to sell.

The children of the deceased may openly or covertly resist the parent's remarriage. When Bob married Teresa, his daughter Laurie told him: "You didn't really love my Mom. You couldn't marry again if you did." Bob was crushed. He had been by her mother's side constantly for three years while she was dying. He told Laurie he would always love her mother, but he loved Teresa too. Bob's argument was reasonable and authentic, but it fell on deaf ears. Laurie was not ready to have her mother replaced as Dad's wife. She needed time to adjust.

If you are in a marriage where the deceased spouse's presence is still prominent, here are a few ways to minimize the effect.

1. *Refuse to feel threatened when the deceased spouse is mentioned.* Allow appropriate grieving to occur. Pretending the deceased person never lived will trap your marriage in an unrealistic time warp. Acknowledge the implications of the previous marriage on your present relationship with your spouse.

2. *Encourage healthy mourning.* Acknowledge family members' grief and express appropriate words of comfort. If you feel the fine line between appropriate and inappropriate expressions of grief has been crossed, seek professional advice.

3. *Don't try to replace the deceased mate.* If Dad was a fisherman, don't take up fishing to make up for the loss. If Mom was a great cook, share her children's pride, but don't attempt to compete in the kitchen. Work at creating your own unique place in the family.

4. *If you are the widow or widower, be sensitive to your new mate's feelings when you reminisce.* When you feel the need to talk about your deceased spouse, sharing with family friends and relatives may be more appropriate.

5. *Ask yourself, "What am I holding on to that I need to let go of?"* Whether it's furniture arrangement, family routines, or mementoes, determine to what extent these items or issues tie you to the past rather than promoting a new and rewarding future.

Impact of a Living Ex-Spouse

When I am leading a blended family group that begins to talk about former spouses, I ask them to picture a group in the next room also talking about former spouses--only *we* are the spouses they are discussing! Many of us don't get along with our former spouses. (Perhaps that is why we are no longer married to them!) While some wonderful exceptions to this statement exist, most divorced persons dread dealing with their ex's. You cannot control your ex-spouse's attitudes or behavior. You are only accountable for your actions. Minimizing interferences from a former mate requires:

1. *Solving problems.* Allowing a situation to get out of control or become an ongoing problem teaches your children that solutions are impossible. Model problem-solving skills. Refer to unit 11 for a problem-solving model.
2. *Being proactive.* Don't wait for problems to arise. Anticipate situations and plan ahead so that your reaction is measured and appropriate.
3. *Being assertive without being aggressive.* An assertive person states succinctly what he or she needs in definite behavioral terms. Assertive persons tell who, what, how, when and where in direct communication. An aggressive person conveys the attitude that he or she is looking for a fight, often with veiled threats.
4. *Follow-through.* Determine a course of action if former spouses do not follow instructions for pick up, return, etc. Nagging, threats, or tears will not make irresponsible persons responsible. Allow them to deal with the consequences of their actions. For example, offering to pick up the children from your ex-wife's house because she is always late simply reinforces her pattern of irresponsibility. Instead, phone your attorney and ask him to reaffirm with your ex-spouse's attorney the terms for visitation.

Model problem-solving skills to your children.

🌿 **What other words of advice would you give persons dealing with deceased or divorced spouses?**

_____

_____

The Problem with Paybacks

Wayne's former wife always sent his six-year-old daughter to visit without appropriate clothing. Even when Wayne alerted her in advance about specific outings or events, his daughter inevitably arrived without the necessary items. Wayne and his wife then had to take his daughter shopping. They complained all weekend about his former wife's actions.

After repeating this cycle for months, they asked me for advice. I suggested they buy some clothes for Wayne's daughter and keep them at their house. Then they would not be dependent upon his former wife's clothes selection.

"I provide adequate child support. She's supposed to buy clothes using that money," Wayne replied. He continued to rage over what he considered an injustice. Most of us, like Wayne, would rather hang onto our anger than seek solutions. For the price of a few clothes for his daughter, Wayne could experience peace. Instead, he chose to remain angry.

Remember our memory verse from 1 Thessalonians? Paul shares this advice in an effort to free us from personal turmoil. Paybacks only lead to alternate paybacks. We break the cycle only when we heed Paul's advice.

Make sure that nobody pays back wrong for wrong, but always try to be kind to each other and to everyone else.
—1 Thessalonians 5:15

❤ **Can you think of a time when you practiced payback? How do you feel thinking back on that incident? Children in a blended family usually reap the result of payback between divorced parents. Read 1 Thessalonians 5:15 in the margin. Then pray, making the verse your commitment as a parent and spouse.**

First Thessalonians 5:15 does not mean we should become doormats for someone else's bad behavior. Blended family couples often need to be assertive and proactive when it comes to dealing with former spouses. I remember a couple who expressed confusion when I made this statement in a blended family group.

Don and Michelle were dealing with Harold, Michelle's first husband, who used his child support payment as a weapon.

"Weren't you the one who said that Christians weren't supposed to do paybacks?" Don asked.

"That's true," I replied. "We're not supposed to return wrong for wrong. There is a big difference between paybacks and standing up for what is right and demanding justice. An example of paying back wrong for wrong might be to let the air out of Harold's tires or refuse to let him see his children. I suggest that you contact a lawyer and force Harold to meet the terms of the divorce agreement."

"Really?" asked Michelle. "Is that not an example of payback?"

"Not at all," I answered. "Even Jesus stood up for Himself—countless times. Refusal to defend yourself only invites people to misuse your goodness."

🌿 **Before I conclude this story, read Mark 2:13-28 in your Bible. Write a brief descriptive phrase identifying three times Jesus stood up to people who were trying to harm His witness.**

1._____

2. _____

3. _____

Jesus defied evil without returning evil. The Pharisees and priests quickly learned not to trifle with Jesus.

Interestingly, Michelle and Don never even returned to court. A letter from their attorney stating the complaint and informing Harold of a court date prompted him to action. The child support checks arrived on time. Unfortunately, ex-spouses may return to court more than once. Protecting your children's interest and your new family requires courage and appropriate boundaries.

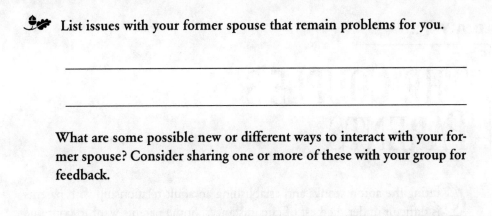 List issues with your former spouse that remain problems for you.

_____

_____

What are some possible new or different ways to interact with your former spouse? Consider sharing one or more of these with your group for feedback.

_____

_____

Effects on the Children

When dealing with a former spouse, remember that children consider themselves as one half of each biological parent. When we criticize their other parent, children may interpret those as negative statements about themselves. Evaluate the impact of your words on the children. When you need to discuss your ex with your spouse, talk in private.

Often children will listen in on phone calls between their parents. Even though it hurts them to hear their parents argue, they are always interested in the interaction between these very important adults in their lives. Unfortunately, the children can't help but get caught up in some of the negative feelings that exist between divorced parents. A former spouse who attempts to poison the children's relationship with the other parent is one of the most difficult situations a blended family faces. Retaliation is tempting.

Margaret's former husband, Jack, was an attorney who used the law to his advantage. Not only did she lose the custody fight, but she also was forced to pay child support though she barely made enough to pay her own living expenses.

One day Margaret's son told her in anger: "I'm never coming back to your house. Dad says you don't want me anyway. That's why I live with him."

Margaret said: "I don't know why your dad told you that, but it is not true. I would give anything to have you live with me. Although I don't think it is fair, the court decided your father could provide a better home than I can. I love you very much. I want to spend as much time with you as possible."

Margaret's son was relieved. He was carrying a heavy weight, believing that his mother did not want him.

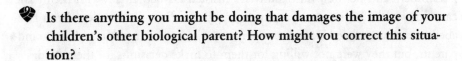 **Is there anything you might be doing that damages the image of your children's other biological parent? How might you correct this situation?**

How does this week's Scripture memory verse help you to deal with criticism from an ex-spouse?

> **Children consider themselves one half of each biological parent.**

THE COUPLE'S PARENTS

Cutting the apron strings and establishing an adult relationship with parents is difficult under the best of circumstances. Some parents want to continue their parenting role indefinitely. It is especially likely to occur if you lived with them during your single-again days.

Parents can pose obstacles in a blending family in at least three ways. First, they offer well-meaning but unwanted advice. Second, they give material possessions to the children without your permission. Third, they may play favorites among your family and ex-family members. The frustrations caused by these factors must be tempered by the biblical admonition to honor parents.

> ❧ Do any of these obstacles exist in your relationship with parents at this time in your blending family? What other factors are difficult to resolve? List them in the margin.

Unwanted Advice

Parental advice may seem welcome to you because you are longing for solutions to difficult problems! The problem is that *unconsciously* we may revert to childlike status and perceive the advice as command. We may think: *I must do this. Mom and Dad feel it is the best approach.* Once begun, this pattern is difficult to break.

Most of us dislike parental advice, especially when it is uninvited. We must inform parents firmly but lovingly that we appreciate their intentions; however, we are responsible for making our own decisions.

Gift-giving

Elizabeth, a widow, had one 15-year-old son named Daniel. Elizabeth had remained close to her husband's parents after he died. When Elizabeth remarried, Daniel's grandparents were polite enough at the wedding, but it was obvious they believed their son and Daniel's father had been replaced. They suggested Daniel come and live with them. They also offered him a car when he turned 16.

Elizabeth and her new husband Mark insisted Daniel remain with them. The car offer was the beginning of a power struggle for Daniel's affection. Both Elizabeth and Mark wanted Daniel to experience a loving relationship with his grandparents, but they were not willing for them to make decisions for their child.

Finally, Elizabeth and Mark confronted her former in-laws. They promised they would receive Elizabeth's approval before giving Daniel anything that cost more than 50 dollars. Daniel was allowed to drive the car as long as he obeyed Elizabeth and Mark's rules.

In a blending family, parents must establish guidelines for acceptable gifts from relatives before children see or hear about them. If the guidelines are violated, use your best judgment but be willing to return the gift. Inform the gift-givers that, although the sentiment is appreciated, you cannot accept it at this time. Be gracious; avoid a lecture. You can show respect for their position even when you cannot agree with their decision.

🐟 **What would you like to say to your relatives about advice and/or gift-giving? What keeps you from sharing your feelings?**

_____

_____

_____

Favoritism

Carl's mother was very close to his first wife, Fran. When Carl remarried, his mother was polite to Brenda but kept a picture of Carl and Fran on her piano in the living room. The picture made Brenda uncomfortable.

When Carl spoke to his mother about the picture, she replied: "I like that picture. After all, it is my home. Do you expect me to hide a picture that I like?"

When Carl and Brenda sought my advice, I said to them: "It *is* Carl's mother's house, and she does have every right to display the picture. However, if she insists on making Brenda uncomfortable, you also have the right to choose not to visit. Carl, I suggest you ask your mother to place that particular picture in her bedroom or some other place, and that you and Brenda will not visit until she agrees. You might consider giving her a picture of you and Brenda to put in its place."

Carl followed my suggestion and within one month, Carl and Brenda's picture stood on the piano, and the old picture was moved to his mother's dresser.

When favoritism is obvious and hurtful, confrontation is necessary. Parents may not realize the hurt they are causing. Even if they do, confrontation demonstrates your commitment to your spouse and family.

Parents might also play favorites among the grandchildren, especially toward their own son or daughter's children. While biological ties cannot be ignored, favoritism still hurts the children. Consider Andrew's plight.

Andrew was the only grandchild of Barbara's parents. When Barbara married Wesley, her parents totally ignored Wesley's children. They were polite to them, but Andrew was the only one ever invited to outings and the only one who received gifts.

Barbara was hurt by her parent's actions. She told them that Wesley's children felt left out.

"Oh my," replied her mother. "We never intended to hurt them. It's just that Andrew is our own. They're, well, they aren't really related to us."

"They are through me. We are a family. What you do, or don't do, is making that difficult. Please try to include them—for my sake."

That discussion made a world of difference. Their favoritism toward Andrew was far less noticeable. All the children were happier, and Barbara and Wesley relaxed when her parents visited.

Confronting favoritism demonstrates your commitment to your spouse and family.

Do not allow parents, in-laws, and former in-laws to interfere with your family's blending process. When or if they do, the person closest to them should confront. Most of the time, parents understand.

🌿 **Is favoritism a problem with your parents or in-laws?** ❏ Yes ❏ No
If so, think of one specific step you can take to initiate change. Plan to share it with your group for feedback.

Honoring Parents

Ignoring the wishes of parents is very difficult for most people. Some even suggest that it violates God's law. After all, the fifth of the Ten Commandments says, "Honor your father and your mother."

🌿 **Read Exodus 20:12 and Deuteronomy 5:16 in the margin. What is the blessing promised to those who honor parents?**

_____

Obviously, the Scriptures teach us to honor and care for our parents. The Bible is clear that when we marry, our first priority is to the marriage partner.

🌿 **Read Genesis 2:24 and Ephesians 5:31 in the margin.**

When the apostle Paul wrote to the church at Ephesus, he quoted the Genesis passage (Ephesians 5:31). He went on to say, "However, each one of you also must love his wife as he loves himself, and the wife must respect her husband" (Ephesians 5:33). In the story of Carl and Brenda, Carl was firm with his mother with respect to Brenda's feelings, while at the same time he honored his mother's feelings with respect to Fran. True honor exhibits respect.

🌿 **Disrespect begins with the letter *D*. What other *D* words can you think of as synonyms for disrespect?**

_____

_____

Did you list *discounting, demeaning, demanding, dismissing, disregarding,* and *dishonesty?* Respect acknowledges the benefits of parents' age, wisdom, and experience without our own regression to child-like obedience.

🌿 **If you have experienced a turbulent relationship with your parents or your parents-in-law, how does this week's Scripture memory verse relate? What might you do to treat them with respect?**

_____

_____

Honor your father and your mother, so that you may live long in the land the Lord your God is giving you.
—Exodus 20:12

Honor your father and mother, as the Lord your God has commanded you, so that you may live long and that it may go well with you in the land the Lord your God is giving you.
—Deuteronomy 5:16

For this reason a man will leave his father and mother and be united to his wife, and they will become one flesh.
—Genesis 2:24

For this reason a man will leave his father and mother and be united to his wife, and the two will become one flesh.
—Ephesians 5:31

FRIENDS

When I am counseling about-to-be-married couples, I always ask about their friends. Whenever they respond that their fiancee is their one and only friend, I know they are in trouble. A spouse cannot fulfill all our friendship needs. Men need men friends, and women need women friends. Together, the couple needs couple friends. Without a combination of all these types, the marriage relationship is strained.

Friends as Assets

Church is a great place to develop solid friendships. Many churches have sports teams where men can enjoy the camaraderie of other men. Some churches have women's sports teams, and some churches even offer couple teams. Bible study and discipleship groups provide a wonderful environment for study and social interaction. Within the organizational structure of most churches, there are men's groups, women's groups, and couple groups. Friendships develop naturally with regular attendance. Meeting friends in a healthy place usually results in healthy friendships.

🌿 **Can you think of some close personal friendships between Bible personalities? Read one example from 1 Samuel 18:1-4 in the margin.**

Jonathan and David were of one mind and loved each other as they loved themselves. They made a covenant and sealed it with gifts. In 1 Samuel 20:4 Jonathan promised, "Whatever you want me to do, I'll do for you." Now there's a friend! Jesus' relationship with the disciples was certainly more than that of teacher and students. In many ways their relationship was that of friends (John 15:15). Paul's relationship with Barnabas was more than simply a co-worker (Acts 9:27; chs.13-15).

🌿 **What are some key actions that describe friendship?**

_____

🌿 **List your friends in the following categories:**

Couple friends _____

Husband's male friends_____

Wife's female friends_____

Encourage your mate to have friends! It is beneficial to you both as individuals and as a couple.

After David had finished talking with Saul, Jonathan became one in spirit with David, and he loved him as himself. From that day Saul kept David with him and did not let him return to his father's house. And Jonathan made a covenant with David because he loved him as himself. Jonathan took off the robe he was wearing and gave it to David, along with his tunic, and even his sword, his bow and his belt.
—1 Samuel 18:1-4

Friends as Liabilities

Not all friendships are good for the family. Some friends interfere with the blending family process. Joe loved sports—any sport. He loved playing them, watching them, and talking about them. Almost every weekend Joe and his friends were off somewhere attending a game. Stephanie, Joe's new wife, frequently found herself watching Joe's kids while he went off with his friends to a sporting event. Stephanie often felt used. Joe did not seem to understand. "You do things with your friends," he said. "I don't object."

"But you ask me to watch your kids while you're gone. I don't have children. I don't mind you going when the kids aren't here, but I do mind your expecting me to be your babysitter. I didn't get married to babysit your kids all the time."

Joe and Stephanie argued over this problem for some time. Finally, Joe realized that if he was going to remain married (which was something Joe really wanted), he was going to have to be more considerate of his wife. Also, Joe realized he was not spending much time with his children, nor were he and Stephanie enjoying alone time as a couple.

Joe was not a bad person. He was more caught up in doing things with his friends than he was with his family. While friends are vital to a person's well-being, we must establish priorities, and family must always come first. When friends begin to take precedence, our priorities are out of line.

While friends are vital, the family must always come first.

When Friends Become Advisors

Often we turn to friends for advice with family problems. Their advice can be helpful, since they are more objective and have a different perspective. However, even good friends sometimes give poor advice, especially if they have never experienced blending family living. What works well in a nuclear family may not work well, or at all, in a blended family.

When Polly and Richard experienced some problems, Polly talked with her best friend Beth. Polly always dealt directly with her ex-husband concerning their three children. After all, they were the biological parents and matters concerning them did not involve Richard, her present husband. At least, that is how Polly reasoned, and her friend Beth agreed.

"You should handle all the arrangements with Allen," Beth stated. "You've had to work with him for years. I think you know what is best."

What Polly and Beth forgot was that if Polly and Allen decided to change weekend visitation, Richard's plans were disrupted as well. Also, Richard's non-involvement made him feel like an outsider. While Beth was being supportive of Polly, she reinforced an opinion that was detrimental to Polly's blending family.

Eventually, Polly and Richard did agree that Polly would discuss her decisions with Richard before she and Allen finalized them. Beth meant well. She just did not live in a blended family!

> Have you ever received bad advice from a friend? What guidelines should you keep in mind before taking a friend's advice?

When Friends Represent the Past

A final way friends can distract your new family involves the time frame of the friendship. If they were friends prior to your present marriage, they represent history not shared with your current spouse. Often long-time friends still maintain loyalty or concern for a former mate. They may inadvertently cause the present mate to feel unaccepted.

A new spouse may interpret visits with old friends as shared secrets about a time and place unknown to him or her. Be sensitive about bringing former friends to your new life and home. Make inclusion comfortable for both you and your mate. Work on developing new couple friends.

🍂 **What good principles for friendships are included in this week's Scripture memory verse? List them in the margin.**

DAY 4

WORK

While work interferes to some degree with all families, those families with children from previous marriages do encounter special problems. When two families blend, the new family needs time to develop relationships, establish routines and traditions, and set guidelines. Children and stepchildren need time to get used to another authority figure in the home. Spending quality time at home while spending necessary time at work requires advance planning and commitment.

🍂 **In what ways do work or career demands pose a problem for time with your blended family?**

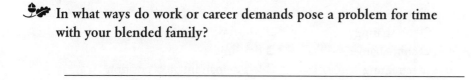

When Work Takes Priority

🍂 **In the margin, list your top three priorities. Then, beside each one, list the amount of time it requires during a given week.**

I'll guess that you listed work as one of your three priorities and that your time at work represents the majority of your waking hours during a week. Priorities don't always equal the amount of time they require. For example, did you list God as a priority? Very few of us spend 40 hours a week in prayer, Bible study, or church. Yet, God influences every waking hour.

You probably listed family in your top three. How much time does family take? Are you committing a sufficient amount of time? If not, do you see any alternatives? Many of us feel trapped without any options. Phil was such a person.

Phil had three children from his first marriage. Helen had never been married, but she had always wanted children. Now she had a husband and three children, all at once. Because Phil's work required him to travel twice a month, Helen spent more time with Phil's children than he did. At first, the scenario was great! Helen and the children experienced wonderful family times when Phil was gone. When he returned home, they recounted stories of the activities Helen and the children did together.

The fun lasted several months. Then the routine turned into work. Eventually, Helen felt used and taken for granted. Helen felt the children didn't even appreciate her. She resented the kids; she resented Phil's work. This marriage was not at all what she imagined or expected.

When Helen attempted to talk about the problem with Phil, he became defensive. Sometime later Phil said to Helen: "I am considering a change in positions at work. It's not a sales position and would require very little travel. Most of the time, I could be home for dinner with the family. I would, however, earn less money. What do you think?"

Helen was delighted. "Oh Phil, take it. I've been praying that something would happen to allow us to be more of a family."

"As I said," interrupted Phil, "we probably won't have as much."

"I don't care. I'd even be willing to move into a less expensive house just to have you home more," offered Helen.

Phil did take the new job, and they did end up moving to a smaller house. The strain on their marriage and family lessened considerably. Sometimes work must be examined in the light of other priorities.

Phil and Helen's solution may not work for you. However, a little creative effort often reveals a variety of possibilities.

Check any of the following options that might work for you in your situation.

❏ job sharing   ❏ part-time work
❏ shift change   ❏ flex time
❏ retraining   ❏ less demanding job position
❏ career plateau   ❏ work out of the home
❏ other? _____

When Work Equals Worth

If status and the amount of money earned is our standard, climbing the ladder of success will always be more important than family time. Although work contributes significantly to a person's identity and self-esteem, work cannot be the primary issue in making family decisions.

Our culture advertises wealth and possessions as keys to happiness. Remember the house at the beach? Even thinking that I could somehow be happier if I owned that house blocked the happiness I had previously experienced. God already had given me everything I needed to be happy, but I stopped trusting Him. I began to think I knew more about what would make me happy than God did.

Did you ever explain to a child that he could not have a particular toy he wanted because it was dangerous or inappropriate? Most likely the child threw a tantrum of sorts—right? Maybe he sulked, pouted, and made himself (and you) miserable for a while. He did not like to be told no. Neither do adults! We often make ourselves and others miserable when we don't receive all that we want.

While the world rewards workaholics, remember that addictions of any sort are still addictions. As such, the workaholic often uses work to escape from something considered unpleasant. We enforce the mind-set of the workaholic through praise by saying, "Isn't she a hard worker?" or "Isn't he industrious?" However, if working too much is hurting the family, how is that different from the alcoholic who hurts his or her family through drinking?

🌿 **In the margin read Matthew 6:25-27, 31-33. Summarize what Jesus taught about work and worry.**

_____

_____

This Scripture passage speaks to one of the Christian's most difficult spiritual struggles: *trust*. Do we trust God to take care of us? Most of us want to, but we aren't convinced He will take care of us in the manner we desire. Letting God set the agenda and trusting that He really does want good things for us is difficult. Nevertheless, I am convinced that the only people in the world who are ever truly happy are those who trust God completely with their lives—and that includes work, money, and families.

A Balancing Act

Few of us have the option of choosing not to work. Since work is a factor in every blended family, let's look at ways to balance work and family life:

1. *Communicate to your family that they are priority.* A blending family is like a tender plant. It needs more than adequate time, attention, and nourishment. Family life cannot be nurtured with only a couple of week-day hours and a weekend outing. Ask yourself: *Does my family know they are important to me? How do I show them they are a priority? What have I sacrificed of my own time, hobbies, and professional advancement to give family members my undivided attention?*

2. *Set reasonable expectations for your standard of living.* If you and/or your spouse is paying child support, you probably operate on a tight budget regardless of your income. Be willing to say no to the latest gadget or costly toy. Pressure to keep up with the neighbors robs you of peace of mind and drives you to overtime or even a second job. Ask yourself, *What do I want my children to most remember about our home? Its size or its atmosphere?*

3. *Keep disruptions to a minimum.* Pass up the promotion. Choose to get on the career plateau track where you stay at your present level in the company rather than moving to a position with more responsibility. Forego moving across the country every two years or traveling extensively if doing so would put your family's blending at risk.

🌹 **What work adjustments do you need to make in order to give adequate time to your blending family? Set a specific goal related to work and family and then share it with your mate during CoupleTalk.**

🌿 **Say this week's Scripture memory verse to a family member.**

"Therefore I tell you, do not worry about your life, what you will eat or drink; or about your body, what you will wear. Is not life more important than food, and the body more important than clothes? Look at the birds of the air; they do not sow or reap or store away in barns, and yet your heavenly Father feeds them. Are you not much more valuable than they? Who of you by worrying can add a single hour to his life?

"So do not worry, saying, 'What shall we eat?' or 'What shall we drink?' or 'What shall we wear?' For the pagans run after all these things, and your heavenly Father knows that you need them. But seek first his kingdom and his righteousness, and all these things will be given to you as well."
—Matthew 6:25-27, 31-33

OUTSIDERS

When we were children, most of us experienced being chosen last (or nearly last) for a school team. I still remember that hurt today. All of us want to be accepted. We want to be on the team. It hurts to be on the outside of any group in which we would like to be included. During this week's study we've looked at people and issues that pose interferences to a blending family. Today let's consider how feeling like an outsider in your blending family interferes with the blending process. Then let's determine ways to bring the outsiders inside.

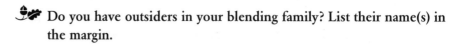 Do you have outsiders in your blending family? List their name(s) in the margin.

When a Parent Is Outside

One obvious outsider in a blended family is the stepmother or stepfather. An adjective often linked with those words is *wicked*. We will consider the wicked stepparent syndrome in week seven. At some point, most stepparents end up feeling like the wicked stepparents referred to in childhood fairy tales, or at least believing that the children regard them in that manner.

Stepparents never begin with the intention of being wicked. They want to love their spouse's children so much that the children will love them in return. Unconsciously, the stepparent believes he or she can control what and how the children think. When children shut out a stepparent, they do so out of their own pain, without regard for the stepparent personally. Most of the time, it has nothing to do with the identity of the stepparent. The children do not want ANY stepparent.

When the stepparent's love is unreciprocated, they feel even more an outsider than before the marriage. It is painfully obvious they cannot share the close bond between biological parent and child. Most stepparents long for the day when they will be a part of that closeness. They may, but it will not come quickly or painlessly.

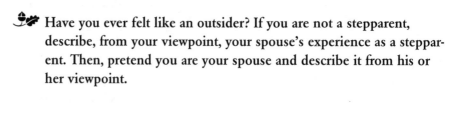 Have you ever felt like an outsider? If you are not a stepparent, describe, from your viewpoint, your spouse's experience as a stepparent. Then, pretend you are your spouse and describe it from his or her viewpoint.

_____

_____

Helping the Outsider In

If you are the outsider, you may be feeling disheartened at the situation. If you're not the outsider, but are the biological parent, you still may be feeling disheart-

Who is an outsider in your blending family? Any family member who does not feel included.

ened for your mate. Take heart! The biological parent can contribute to the bonding process between stepparent and stepchildren.

Every day Jane felt more and more like the wicked stepmother. Nothing she did seemed to matter. Her husband Gerald felt increasingly torn emotionally. Daily, Jane told him about something hurtful the children said or did and daily the children complained to him about Jane. Gerald pictured himself as being in one of those ancient torture chambers being literally pulled apart.

At a stepfamily support meeting, someone suggested that Gerald build up Jane's position in the family to the children. He decided to try it. When his son Tom asked Gerald if he could spend the night with a friend, Gerald hesitated. It was the weekend, he knew the friend and his family, and the boys had spent many nights together. "I don't know," Gerald told Tom, "you've been gone a lot lately. I don't think it's a good idea tonight, but let me ask Jane what she thinks."

When Gerald talked with Jane, her answer was exactly what he expected. "Sounds fine to me," she said.

Gerald then told Tom, "Well, I didn't think this was too good an idea, but Jane said she thought you should be allowed to go to your friend's house. Go ahead!"

"Whoopie!" shouted Tom. On his way up to his room to pack his clothes, Tom poked his head into the kitchen and said, "Thanks, Jane."

Gerald could just as easily have told Tom, "Sure, you can go." His checking with Jane allowed her to be a hero for Tom. Gerald also began to praise Jane in front of the children. He gave her credit for wonderful cooking, complimented her for how she decorated a room, and told her over and over what a difference she made in the house. Gerald never asked the kids to agree with his comments because he knew they might not agree. He simply wanted the children to hear his feelings about the positive contributions Jane made to their family.

The children's attitude toward Jane did not change quickly, but it did improve over time. Jane began to feel less "wicked," and the children complained less often. It was years before Jane stopped feeling like an outsider with Gerald's children, but it did happen—one small step at a time.

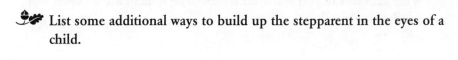 **List some additional ways to build up the stepparent in the eyes of a child.**

_____

_____

When Children Feel Like Outsiders

In a blending family, children may feel like outsiders to the relationship between their biological parent and the stepparent. Mom or Dad's new spouse seems to have taken their place and stolen the parent's affection. Young children find these feelings hard to articulate but their actions speak volumes. When the married couple sits down on a couch, a young child will attempt to sit between the adults. Older children may not be as obvious with their actions, but their feelings are basically the same.

During the five years Kevin and his mother Catherine lived alone, they developed a very close relationship. At first Kevin was delighted when his mother mar-

Children's actions speak volumes.

ried Mitch. Mitch took him fishing, and they played ball together. However, something changed in Kevin's relationship with his mother. Before, Kevin seldom had a babysitter. When his mother wanted to go out to eat, Kevin went with her. When they watched TV, his mother usually sat with her arm around him. Now, she and Mitch sat arm-in-arm on the couch.

Catherine noted several behavioral changes in Kevin. Kevin became withdrawn. Usually an active, outgoing boy, when Kevin came into the house after school, he only wanted to watch television. He was sick more often, and Catherine would stay home from work to care for him.

On a weekend hike with Mitch and Catherine, Kevin seemed determined *not* to have a good time. He tripped over a log, limped around for the rest of the day, and persuaded his mother to cut the hike short and go home. Mitch suspected the limping was fake and told Catherine. Later in the day when she saw Kevin riding his bike with one of his friends, Catherine began to wonder.

What Kevin experienced is very common. Children have difficulty expressing what they feel, especially to a parent. Therefore, many children act out their feelings, often in destructive and negative ways. Children fear they will lose the relationship they have with their biological parent.

While it is perfectly normal for people in love to spend time alone with each other, hold each other, and be close, it is important to realize how such behaviors affect blending family children. Take action as a new blending couple to include the children rather than making them feel like outsiders. Avoid excessive physical affection in front of the children, especially in the early years of the relationship. Such moments of intimacy may breed resentment in children who feel threatened by the couple relationship. Include the children as often as is healthy for your couple relationship instead of leaving them with a babysitter.

Children may feel threatened by the couple relationship. Spend some quality time with each child individually.

Verbally affirm your love for each child. Express the importance of him or her as a family member, and spend some quality time with each child individually.

🌿 **Have you noticed signs that indicate your children feel like outsiders? What actions can you and your spouse take to help the children feel more secure?**

The blending family can only function as a unit when outsiders are allowed inside. However special you may feel in the tug-of-war between your spouse and your children, do not revel in it! "One for all and all for one" is a healthy family slogan.

🌿 **Write this week's Scripture memory verse in the space below. Say a prayer asking God to keep you accountable.**

COUPLETALK

For you to complete

1. Look over the notes you wrote for each day and list significant insights you want to share with your spouse.

_____

_____

_____

2. What strategies did you devise as ways to minimize outside interference by the former spouse, parents, friends, and work? List them below.

_____

_____

_____

3. What thoughts or ideas have you had about including persons who feel like outsiders in your blended family? Write them here:

_____

_____

For you to share with your spouse

1. Share your responses to the activities above.
2 Tell one thing you really love about each other.
3. Say the Scripture memory verse together.
4. Pray for each other, either silently or aloud.

RELY ON GOD

*T*erry and Lisa knew they needed a spiritual dimension in their blended family if it was going to become what they desired. Both of them had friends who were going through their second divorce. They wanted their marriage to last. Since both had been active in church when they were young, they believed God could make a difference in their lives. They also wanted their children to grow up in a godly home.

With 7 children in their blended family, ranging in age from 3 to 12, Lisa and Terry wanted to be effective role models as godly parents. Did they have to be perfect Christians around the children? What if they couldn't live up to their own expectations?

What does a "Christian family" look like? Is a spiritually strong family problem free? Will Jesus make blending your family easy? Probably not. God doesn't work that way. He knows that easy lessons seldom teach us very much. Peter assures us that trials come so that our faith, which is worth more than gold, "may be proved genuine" (1 Peter 1:7).

We are spiritual beings as well as physical, mental, and emotional ones. For any family to fulfill its potential, the spiritual framework surrounding the family must be more important than the physical house in which they live. Jesus is the Rock upon which a blending family can stand and survive (Matthew 7:24-27).

Strong spiritual roots in a family begin with the couple's covenant relationship, both with God and each other. The covenant relationship is nourished through prayer, Bible study, worship, and service. This week's study will challenge you to demonstrate your reliance on God by discovering ways to make His presence an evident framework in your home.

What You'll Study

DAY 1
- **The Covenant Relationship**

DAY 2
- **Praying as a Couple and Family**

DAY 3
- **Using the Bible as Our Guide**

DAY 4
- **Worshiping Together**

DAY 5
- **Practicing Our Faith**

This Week You Will:
- evaluate your covenant with your spouse and children;
- make plans for enhancing prayer, Bible study, and worship in your home;
- determine ways to practice your faith as a family.

This Week's Scripture Memory Verse

"Since we live by the Spirit, let us keep in step with the Spirit" (Galatians 5:25).

THE COVENANT RELATIONSHIP

*B*randon gazed expectantly toward the center aisle as Joy stepped into view. He was as proud and happy as any man who had ever lived. When Joy was halfway down the aisle, Brandon walked to meet her and the two of them returned to stand before the minister.

The minister spoke these words: "Dearly Beloved, we are gathered here in the sight of God and in the presence of family and friends to join together Joy and Brandon in holy matrimony; which is an honorable estate, instituted of God; which holy estate Christ Himself adorned and beautified with His presence in Cana of Galilee. It is therefore not to be entered into unadvisedly, but reverently, discreetly, and in the fear of God."

Brandon and Joy chose a church wedding because they wanted to acknowledge God as a partner in their marriage relationship. Each had a personal relationship with the Lord, and they wanted their individual commitments to God to be a part of their commitment to each other.

Marriage is a covenant between two people and God. God does not just witness the vows made by the couple—God actively participates in the covenant.

God's Covenant with His People

The word *covenant* is mentioned frequently in the Old and New Testaments. In fact, the word *testament* is another word for covenant. God's covenant with Noah illustrates the distinct nature of a covenant relationship.

🌿 **Read Genesis 9:8,11-13 in the margin. State the covenant in your own words.**

_____

_____

What was the sign of this covenant? _____

In making this covenant, God placed limits on His own power on behalf of all creatures on the earth. He promised never again to flood the earth, and He provided the rainbow as a sign of the covenant. In Genesis 12–17, God made a covenant with Abram, eventually changing his name to Abraham. God told Abram His descendants would outnumber the stars and possess the land of Canaan. As a sign of their covenant with God, all the males were circumcised.

After delivering His people from Egypt, God made another covenant with them through Moses when He gave them the Commandments. The covenant

God said to Noah and to his sons with him: "I establish my covenant with you: Never again will all life be cut off by the waters of a flood; never again will there be a flood to destroy the earth."

And God said, "This is the sign of the covenant I am making between me and you and every living creature with you, a covenant for all generations to come: I have set my rainbow in the clouds, and it will be the sign of the covenant between me and the earth."
—Genesis 9:8,11-13

promised that if the people were obedient, God would bless them. If they broke the covenant, they would suffer. In Deuteronomy 30:19-20, God said: "This day I call heaven and earth as witnesses against you that I have set before you life and death, blessings and curses. Now choose life, so that you and your children may live and that you may love the Lord your God, listen to his voice, and hold fast to him. For the Lord is your life."

The New Covenant

Through Jesus, God established a New Covenant that goes beyond the more narrow covenant with the Hebrew people. Through this New Covenant, God provides salvation for all who trust in Jesus.

Read Hebrews 9:15 in the margin.

For this reason Christ is the mediator of a new covenant, that those who are called may receive the promised eternal inheritance—now that he has died as a ransom to set them free from the sins committed under the first covenant.
—Hebrews 9:15

Has there been a time in your life when you entered into this covenant relationship? Have you acknowledged that Jesus died on the cross to pay for your sins? Has God forgiven you and accepted you as a child of the New Covenant?

If you have not yet taken this step of faith, now is the time. Receive Jesus Christ as your Savior and Lord; invite Him into your life. If you desire to trust Christ and accept His payment for your sins, use this simple prayer to express your faith.

Lord Jesus, I realize I have sinned, and my sin has separated me from you. I accept Your death on the cross as payment for my sins. I invite You to be Lord of my life. I commit myself to love You, to honor You, and to serve You as long as I live. Please help me grow in my understanding of Your love and power. Thank You for forgiving me and for giving me a new life. Amen.

Signature _____ Date _____

If you confess with your mouth, "Jesus is Lord," and believe in your heart that God raised him from the dead, you will be saved. For it is with your heart that you believe and are justified, and it is with your mouth that you confess and are saved. As the Scripture says, "Everyone who trusts in him will never be put to shame."
—Romans 10:9-11

If you have just made this life-changing decision, or if you have questions, call your group leader, pastor, or a Christian friend whom you trust. Share your decision with him or her. Telling others about your decision confirms your faith and allows them to share your joy.

If you made this decision some time ago, pause and thank God for accepting you as a part of His covenant community.

Marriage as Covenant

God's covenant promises provide a glimpse of God's intent and design for marriage. A covenant marriage demonstrates to a watching world the transforming power of God's love in human relationships. As married partners live in covenant with God, they also live in covenant with each other.

The heart of the covenant is not rights and responsibilities; it is steadfast love which never ceases (Lamentations 3:22). Covenant partners express love to each other, whether or not it is earned or deserved, just as God loves us. Caring for each other in marriage mirrors God's care for us. The promises of a covenant marriage are made possible by God's mercy and grace which enables us to overcome our weakness and sinfulness as marital partners. Covenant marriage is not possible without God.

✿ Put a check beside qualities in your marriage that are modeled after God's covenant with you. Put a star beside those you want to develop more fully.

❑ unconditional love   ❑ forgiveness   ❑ mercy
❑ comfort   ❑ hope   ❑ faithfulness

Family as Covenant

In a blended family, the covenant involves husband, wife, children, and God. During weddings involving couples with children, I usually say something similar to this: "You enter this marriage with children. These children will have a profound effect upon your marriage. Your commitment today is not only a commitment to each other, but also a commitment to each child as well. Only with patience, effort, and love will your family become what you desire.

"To the children, let me say that this marriage will also have an effect on you. It is a wonderful opportunity for you to embrace another adult person in your life. This relationship will not just happen, however. It will take hard work. You are part of a new family, and I urge you to commit yourselves to this family, as (names of couple) commit themselves to each other and to you. May the Lord God bless you all."

✿ Look again at the list of covenant characteristics. Check those characteristics you want to develop in relation to the children in your blending family.

❑ unconditional love   ❑ forgiveness   ❑ mercy
❑ comfort   ❑ hope   ❑ faithfulness

The covenantal relationship is clearly established on our behalf and for our blessing. Jesus instructed us to call God, "Father" (Luke 11:2). Parents desire good things for their children, and as Matthew 7:9-11 states, God wants good things for us. However, receipt of those good things is conditional upon lifestyle. God is in control. What would happen in a family if the children were in control? Chaos would reign. Children do not have the maturity to run a home. Nor do we, as God's children, have the maturity to control our homes or our marriages. We must relinquish control to God. As Head of the family, we entrust decisions—major and minor—to His care.

"Which of you, if his son asks for bread, will give him a stone? Or if he asks for a fish, will give him a snake? If you, then, though you are evil, know how to give good gifts to your children, how much more will your Father in heaven give good gifts to those who ask him!"
—Matthew 7:9-11

✿ List some ways you demonstrate that God is Head of your family.

_____

_____

✿ In the margin read this week's Scripture memory verse. Underline the words you feel are keys to living in a covenantal relationship.

Since we live by the Spirit, let us keep in step with the Spirit.
—Galatians 5:25

PRAYING AS A COUPLE AND FAMILY

*U*nderstanding the importance of God as Head of our lives and our families and then actually relinquishing control to Him are two completely different concepts. As a couple, you can affirm God as priority in your family. Practice faith disciplines before your children. Allow them to see in your lifestyle the importance of prayer, Bible study, worship, and service. This week focuses on the couple relationship as you lead in providing spiritual growth opportunities for the family.

Praying for Each Other

Terry and Lisa, mentioned in this week's introduction, talked specifically about their desire for God to guide them in blending their family. They asked the minister who married them to include such a request in their wedding prayer. Lisa hung a wooden plaque in their dining room that read, "God Is the Head of This Home."

Nevertheless, Lisa and Terry were frequently overwhelmed by the complexities of blended family life. Family prayer time was one of the casualties of their hectic lifestyle. Although both of them wanted to spend time praying as a couple and as a family, they often ate at different times and kept different schedules.

Perhaps you share Lisa and Terry's dilemma. Start where you are. Begin individually to pray regularly.

 How important in your life is prayer? Put an *X* on the scale.

Not very important	Important	Very important

Very early in the morning, while it was still dark, Jesus got up, left the house and went off to a solitary place, where he prayed.
—Mark 1:35

Jesus often withdrew to lonely places and prayed.
—Luke 5:16

One of those days Jesus went out to a mountainside to pray, and spent the night praying to God.
—Luke 6:12

God hears your prayers and responds in love. Prayer is our means of communicating with God. Jesus Christ, our High Priest, tore down the wall of separation between us and God when He died on the cross for our sins. We have complete and free access to God! (See Hebrews 10:19-22.) We can talk to the God who created the universe!

Jesus not only made it possible for us to "approach the throne of grace with confidence" (Hebrews 4:16), but also He modeled the importance of prayer in His own life.

 Read the Scriptures in the margin that describe Jesus in a time of prayer. Underline when and where He prayed.

If Jesus, the Son of God, needed prayer to know and do God's will, how much more do we need prayer to live consistent Christian lives? Your spouse and your children need to know and observe that decisions in the home are matters of prayer. They need assurance that you seek God's will in your life. They benefit from knowing that you pray for them daily. Whether these prayers are voiced silently and alone or as a couple or family, praying for one another is foundational to a family who relies on God.

Do your mate and children know you pray for them?
❏ Yes ❏ No

Praying with One Another

Praying *for* your mate and children draws your family closer together. Praying *with* your mate and children adds yet another spiritual dimension to your family.

Put an *M, C* or *B* in the blanks below to indicate times you could pray with your mate, children, or both:
___ before meals
___ before bedtime
___ before major decisions
___ other? _____

Even the youngest family members can voice simple prayers. Some families join hands around the table as they pray. Others kneel at their bedsides to pray. Some fathers place their hands on a child's head as they pray, reminiscent of the Old Testament blessing. Regardless of your family traditions, children appreciate and look forward to family prayer times when you model their importance.

Some family members are more comfortable praying aloud than others. Don't force someone to pray aloud. Pausing for silent prayer is appropriate in this situation.

Prayer time is especially meaningful to a couple when they can pray with each other openly and honestly before God. There are, however, hindrances to a couple's prayer experience. Arguments and conflict, criticism, or a superior attitude all will interrupt meaningful prayer. Also, if one or both partners enter the prayer time with a private agenda, especially as it concerns the other partner, sincere prayer is hindered. For example, "Lord, help (name of spouse) to lose weight," may be ill-advised unless he or she has asked for prayer regarding this issue.

Can you think of any reasons why your mate would hesitate to pray with you? What can you do to encourage couple prayer times?

_____

_____

The Substance of Prayer

In a blended family prayer can easily become crisis praying and revolve around the latest family conflict or problem situation. Imagine for a moment that your only contact with your child involved that child coming to ask you for a favor. Soon you would feel used.

Is it possible God sees our prayers as a laundry list of needs and wants? Although Scripture teaches us to take everything to God in prayer, prayer is primarily a relationship. The Bible instructs us to spend time in prayer getting to know the One who loves us unconditionally. Quality prayer time includes praise, thankfulness, and intercession for others outside our family unit.

There is another inherent danger when prayer centers on needs. We present God only as a giver or withholder of blessings. We imply that on a particular day God is good because He grants our requests. On another day He is bad because He said no or didn't seem to hear us.

Children must learn that God's will is not always accomplished on earth. He grants us free will to make choices that please or displease Him. He chooses not to jump in and straighten out all our messes. We live with the consequences of our actions and learn from them. That choice does not make God bad; it makes us responsible. We are accountable for our actions. Prayer is not a quick fix; it is a request for patience, faithfulness, peace in the midst of a storm, joy that transcends circumstances, and love for persons who are often unlovely.

A balanced prayer life includes praise, thankfulness, intercession, and supplication. Modeled as such, it will help family members to build a relationship with God strong enough to support them during times of crisis.

 Repeat this week's Scripture memory verse. Consider how prayer keeps us in step with the Spirit.

Prayer is a request for patience, faithfulness, peace in the midst of a storm, joy that transcends circumstances, and love for persons who are often unlovely.

DAY 3

USING THE BIBLE AS OUR GUIDE

🌿 **In the margin read the parable of the houses built on sand and rock.**

*B*lended families need strong foundations. It's quick and easy to build a foundation on sand. On a sunny, dry day, a foundation built on rock may not seem so essential. However, when the crises come, and they will, a foundation built on Jesus Christ, not sand, is the only answer.

🌿 **Reflect on your current marriage. What kind of spiritual foundation are you building?**
   ❑ sand—the easy way out
   ❑ mud—soft and squishy
   ❑ shale—looks solid but is slippery to walk on
   ❑ solid granite—good for a lifetime
   ❑ other _____

"Everyone who hears these words of mine and puts them into practice is like a wise man who built his house on the rock. The rain came down, the streams rose, and the winds blew and beat against that house; yet it did not fall, because it had its foundation on the rock. But everyone who hears these words of mine and does not put them into practice is like a foolish man who built his house on sand. The rain came down, the streams rose, and the winds blew and beat against that house, and it fell with a great crash."
—Matthew 7:24-27

I hope you have chosen to build your blended family on Jesus Christ, the solid Rock. The Bible is the family guidebook for building a strong spiritual foundation to endure a lifetime.

🍂 Read Psalm 119:105 in the margin. In your own words, explain why the Bible should be your family's guide.

_____

_____

Your word is a lamp to my feet and a light for my path.
—Psalm 119:105

Read the Bible Together

Do you know the history of how the Bible came to be translated into English? Many courageous individuals paid with their lives for translating the Bible from its original languages. Their reasoning was simple: Every Christian should have access to the Bible in his or her own language. I've asked myself, *Has their sacrifice been worthwhile based on my Bible reading?*

The Bible teaches that the home is the primary environment for Christian education. "Talk about them [God's commands] when you sit at home and when you walk along the road, when you lie down and when you get up" (Deuteronomy 6:7). This verse encourages the modern-day family to quote Scripture, sing Scripture songs, and read Bible verses at mealtimes, on family outings, as we ride in the car, and at bedtime.

🍂 Underline phrases that motivate you to read the Bible.
1. Teaches practical truths for living a Christlike life.
2. Provides solutions for problems.
3. Draws me closer to God.
4. Strengthens me against temptation.
5. Comforts and encourages me in times of trouble or unhappiness.

There are many ways to make Bible thoughts a focal point in your home. Consider decorating rooms with Scripture plaques and pictures. Write Scripture verses and post them in obvious places around your home such as on the refrigerator or the bathroom mirror. If you have small children, invest in several Bible picture and storybooks. Play Bible games. A family I know plays "Bible Alphabet." One family member secretly chooses a Bible character and then calls out the beginning letter of his or her name. Family members take turns guessing until they identify the Bible character.

Participate in the "Read the Bible Through in a Year" plan printed in Bible study literature or in devotional magazines such as *Open Windows*. As a couple, alternate reading verses of Scripture until you have read through a complete Bible book. If you read separately, discuss what you read with each other.

🍂 Underline the above ideas you will seek to implement in your family. Write additional ideas in the margin.

"The Spirit of the Lord is on me, because he has anointed me to preach good news to the poor. He has sent me to proclaim freedom for the prisoners and recovery of sight for the blind, to release the oppressed, to proclaim the year of the Lord's favor."
—Luke 4:18-19

You have laid down precepts that are to be fully obeyed. I will praise you with an upright heart as I learn your righteous laws. I will obey your decrees.
—Psalm 119:4,7-8

Commit the Bible to Memory

We know Jesus was educated in the Scriptures. When Jesus went to the synagogue in Nazareth and they asked Him to read from the scroll of the prophet Isaiah, He unrolled it to a familiar place. See Luke 4:18-19 in the margin.

When Jesus was tempted in the wilderness by Satan (who also quoted Scripture), Jesus countered with three Scriptures from the Book of Deuteronomy. His knowledge of the Scriptures was amazing. He could not take the synagogue scrolls home with Him so He memorized them. Jesus made the Scriptures a priority in His life because His parents made God a priority in their home. One of the reasons God chose Mary and Joseph to be Jesus' parents was their commitment to "train a child in the way he should go" (Proverbs 22:6).

On the continuum below, mark with an X how you relate to this verse: "I have hidden your word in my heart" (Psalm 119:11).

Not true of me   True of me

Does memory work bring thoughts of school to your mind? Scripture memorization is intended for our personal growth, not for a passing grade on God's exam! It has several purposes, one of which is stated in Psalm 119:11: "I have hidden your word in my heart that I might not sin against you."

Read Psalm 119:4,7-8 in the margin. Find these other reasons to hide God's Word in our hearts and underline them in the verses.
to become more obedient
to praise God with a pure heart
to learn God's laws

Have you made the Scripture memory activity each week a priority? If not, ask God to help you commit to hiding His Word in your heart. Write this week's Scripture memory verse in the space below.

_____

_____

Study the Bible

In addition to reading and memorizing portions of the Bible, Christians grow by studying selected passages or themes. Study goes beyond simple recall or recognition. Study implies that we understand the meaning of verses and can paraphrase them in our own words. Study enables us to apply Bible truths to life issues.

If you are a part of an ongoing Bible study group, tell at least one way studying the Bible in a group has helped you grow as a Christian.

_____

_____

Studying the Bible as a couple can help you to cultivate a spirit of unity in your home. Seeking God's truths together builds your partnership and teaches reliance on God.

🕊 **Here are some resources you may use for couple Bible study. All of these are suitable for group study. As you read the list, put a check by any you would like to consider.**

❑ *Building Relationships: A Discipleship Guide for Married Couples* by Gary Chapman. This 12-unit course teaches married couples sharing and communication skills vital to the marriage relationship. The course also guides couples into a deeper relationship with God by teaching how to spend daily time with Him. Couples develop skills and learn how to establish routines that encourage discipleship both as individuals and as a couple. Item 0-8054-9855-9.

❑ *Communication and Intimacy: Covenant Marriage* by Gary Chapman and Betty Hassler. This workbook equips couples to achieve responsible communication and intimacy in their marriage. Couples will identify God-given processes and develop skills to stabilize and strengthen their relationships. Item 0-8054-9934-2.

❑ *Making Love Last Forever* by Gary Smalley. This 12-session interactive workbook leads married couples to understand happiness as it relates to them individually and to their relationships. Dr. Smalley's material reveals how to develop the best kind of love and to balance your happiness with your mate's. Item 0-8054-9791-9.

❑ *I Take Thee to Be My Spouse: Bible Study for Newlyweds* compiled by David Apple. This 26-week inductive Bible study and Bible commentary is based on the interests and needs of newlyweds, such as finances, communication, conflict resolution, and husband and wife roles. Item 0-7673-2552-4.

❑ *Experiencing God: Knowing and Doing the Will of God* by Henry Blackaby and Claude King. This 12-week interactive Bible study helps Christians discover God's will and obediently follow it. Daily learning and devotional activities help individuals develop an intimate relationship with God so they can hear when God is speaking and respond in obedience. Item 0-8054-9954-7.

Order these resources by calling the Customer Service Center at 1-800-458-2772 or by visiting A Baptist Book Store or LifeWay Christian Store.

In addition to individual and couple Bible study, your family can participate in family Bible study. Read a Bible passage to the family. Ask a question or lead children to paraphrase the verses. Act out a Bible parable or event. Calling for response moves us beyond reading the Bible to understanding its message.

🕊 **Would you be willing to lead a family Bible study?**
❑ Yes ❑ No

If so, be prepared to discuss plans during CoupleTalk.

🌸 **Say this week's Scripture memory verse to a family member.**

WORSHIPING TOGETHER

*O*rthodox Jewish children grow up celebrating their history with God. One of Judaism's most meaningful traditions is the Friday evening meal at the beginning of the Jewish Sabbath. The entire family gathers to recall God's goodness and deliverance. Christian families do not traditionally observe a time such as this for worship in the home. As a result, worship occurs primarily at church.

Making Church a Priority

Families establish routines and priorities around personal, school, and work schedules. These factors also may determine the importance of church. For instance, many families attend Bible study and worship every Sunday. They do not decide from week to week if they will attend. Other families make this decision each Saturday night or Sunday morning.

Jeffrey grew up in a family that attended church every week. His parents were active church members and he was expected to attend. He had no choice. Jeffrey's first wife did not attend church regularly before marrying him. While they attended occasionally, church on Sunday was not a routine in Jeffrey's new family. After his divorce, he often wondered if church attendance might have made a significant difference in his marriage. Jeffrey determined that if he ever married again, they would attend church together as a family.

Therefore, when Jeffrey began dating Linda, one of the first things he determined to learn was the importance of church in her life. Linda attended both Bible study and worship every Sunday. Jeffrey felt comfortable that if their friendship progressed and they married, they would experience a compatible Sunday routine.

Does your blended family have a compatible Sunday routine?
❏ Yes ❏ No

What would make it more compatible?

_____

_____

When Jesus was a child, His family life revolved around synagogue worship and observance of the feasts. Luke 2:41 says, "Every year his [Jesus'] parents went to Jerusalem for the Feast of the Passover." Attending Passover meant walking for days from Nazareth to Jerusalem. It was a priority! We model Jesus' example in His family when we set aside regular times for worship.

Insisting that children attend church against their will is a difficult issue for blended families. If you are the stepparent, you may feel awkward about enforcing such a decision. If you believe church attendance is a critical ingredient in your blended family's foundation, and if all of the family is expected to participate, then the question becomes not "do I have to go?" but "when do I need to be ready?" Some decisions are best made by mature parents, not immature children.

🕊 **Check ways you can make Sunday morning church attendance an enjoyable experience for your family.**

❑ go to bed earlier on Saturday night
❑ help other family members
❑ prepare breakfast
❑ eat breakfast or lunch in a restaurant
❑ prepare to leave at a scheduled time
❑ choose clothing the night before
❑ maintain a positive attitude
❑ other? _____

Avoiding the Spectator Syndrome

Some families go to church like they go to concerts or ball games--as spectators. After-church conversation may include superficial comments about the music, sermon, someone's attire, or sanctuary decorations. Such behavior teaches children that the preacher or singer is a performer and they, as part of the congregation, are the critics.

Encourage your family to be active worship participants by asking questions that lead them to examine their own spiritual responses. Examples are: Was God pleased with my worship? Did I truly praise Him today? Was my heart touched by God's Word as it was read and taught? Share insights you gleaned and commitments you made. Modeling sincere worship provides your family with a sense of its importance and nurtures respect for that time spent at church.

Spectatorism can infect our Bible study classes and church-related activities, also. Have your teenagers complained that the pizza was cold at the after-game fellowship? Does your child think his Bible study teacher is boring? Perhaps you've expressed the opinion that your Bible study class is too social, or not social enough. These attitudes imply that the church's function is service to us.

How can you avoid spectatorism? Assume a leadership position in the church. Volunteer to teach, lead singing, care for the bed babies, welcome visitors. There are any number of positions available for a faithful worker. Often we use lack of talent or ability as an excuse. God placed you in your church to fill a vital role, and He has given you the ability to carry out that function through His strength. The apostle Paul told the church at Corinth that "God has arranged the parts in the body ... just as he wanted them to be" (1 Corinthians 12:18). This is as true for us today as it was for the Corinthians.

Serving in your church says to your children, "church is important to me." On the other hand, attempting too many tasks at church says to your children, "church is more important to me than spending time with you." Find a balance and set boundaries for your involvement. But by all means be involved!

Encourage your family to be active worship participants.

List one church responsibility you presently have or one you would be willing to prayerfully consider.

_____

Home Life is a monthly magazine dedicated to the family. Home Life contains many helps for the family worship experience as well as solid advice, fresh ideas, and timely suggestions to benefit your family. You can order Home Life through the Customer Service Center at 1-800-458-2772.

Worshipping at Home

Are the words _worship_ and _church_ synonyms? For most families worship happens only if the family attends church on Sunday. But worship is not restricted to the church building! In fact, in today's society, many parents and older teens work on Sundays and/or Wednesdays. Worship can—and should—happen at home.

What is worship? Here's a simple definition: Worship is complimenting God. It is time set aside to praise God for Who He is and what He does on our behalf. It is affirming His right to be Lord of our lives. Worship is gratitude for His many blessings.

 Below are some suggested family worship activities. Put an asterisk by those you would like to pursue.

1. Take a nature walk. Thank God for specific trees, flowers, and birds that you observe. Praise Him for His creation.
2. Bring reminders of God's handiwork from nature into your home and display them where the family gathers.
3. Take turns praising the Creator. Name a characteristic of God that begins with each letter of the alphabet, such as A for almighty.
4. Sing Scripture songs and other praise hymns.
5. Take turns reading selected psalms of praise. Begin with Psalm 100.
6. Compose a poem to God and read it to the family.
7. Draw a picture symbolizing one of God's qualities. Display it on the refrigerator or in another prominent place.
8. Make love gifts for family members. Present them as tokens of God's love.
9. Conduct a "blessings" ceremony. Take turns laying hands on each family member and saying a blessing. Use Ephesians 3:16-18 or Numbers 6:24-26.
10. Act out a parable that portrays the qualities of God such as the prodigal son or the good samaritan. Talk together about those qualities.

 Write this week's Scripture memory verse below:

_____

_____

I pray that out of his glorious riches he may strengthen you with power through his Spirit in your inner being, so that Christ may dwell in your hearts through faith. And I pray that you, being rooted and established in love, may have power, together with all the saints, to grasp how wide and long and high and deep is the love of Christ.
—Ephesians 3:16-18

"The Lord bless you and keep you; the Lord make his face shine upon you and be gracious to you; the Lord turn his face toward you and give you peace."
—Numbers 6:24-26

 This week's Scripture memory verse implies that we draw our very breath as a result of the Spirit. Pause and thank God for the breath of life and each day's opportunities to celebrate His goodness.

DAY 5

PRACTICING OUR FAITH

Read Hebrews 11:6 in the margin.

Faith is believing God! We demonstrate that belief when we act in obedience. Abraham was obedient, even though he did not live to see all of God's promises come true (Hebrews 11:13). True faith obeys even when the result is not obvious or is slow in being realized.

Without faith it is impossible to please God, because anyone who comes to him must believe that he exists and that he rewards those who earnestly seek him.
—Hebrews 11:6

Think of a time when your faith was tested. What motivated you to obey without knowing the outcome?

For the sake of the combined four children in their blended family, Carol changed to the night shift to be home with the children after school. Her new supervisor was impossible to please. After three months of intense stress, Carol had still not adjusted to sleeping during the day. She and her husband Hal had little time together. After praying about it, Carol quit her job. Spending quality time with her husband and children was more important to her than the extra money she earned. Carol explained to her family the reasons for her decision. "Let's see how God provides," she said.

Carol's family was in a position to observe God's activity. Often we carelessly label God's provisions for us as "luck," "being in the right place at the right time," or "circumstances." When we claim our blessings as a result of God's initiative and care, our children learn to depend on His trustworthiness.

The Object of Faith

Who is safer? The person who possesses a lot of faith on thin ice or the person who possesses little faith on thick ice? Jesus said the size of our faith is insignificant because the Object of our faith is very significant. Our faith is in God—not our job, circumstances, fate, or our own abilities.

Learning to trust God is a progression of faithful encounters with Him. Just as in human relationships, we learn to trust those who are trustworthy. In order to nurture trust in God, find a way to mark faithful encounters with Him. One family I know displays a "faith wall" in their home. One hallway is covered with written accounts of answered prayer.

 Would you like to build a "faith wall" in your house? Begin by recalling some ways or times God has been faithful to you and your family.

Share one or more of these "faith markers" at your next family gathering. Consider making it a regular family practice.

Rely on God   **103**

The Evidence of Faith

James wrote that faith without action is dead (James 2:17). I may say I believe airplanes will fly, but until you see me get on an airplane, you do not know if I truly believe. Faith is validated by the way we live our lives.

One way to demonstrate faith is by doing good deeds. James said, "I will show you my faith by what I do" (James 2:18). How do you model good deeds before your family? Caring for the bereaved or ill, counseling co-workers after work, repairing the home of an elderly person, writing notes to someone who is discouraged—all represent ways to model good works. In addition, we can encourage faith by participating as a family in short-term or long-term ministry activities.

> **Put a check by any of the following activities in which your family could participate as a way of evidencing your faith.**
> ❏ giving canned food to a food shelter
> ❏ giving used clothing to a charitable organization
> ❏ volunteering time at a charitable organization
> ❏ saving money and donating to a charity
> ❏ short-term community mission project
> ❏ short-term overseas mission project
> ❏ other? _____

The Practice of Faith

In two of Paul's letters he references "the church in thy house" (Philemon 2 (KJV); also Romans 16:5). In early church history the only churches were "house churches,"—churches meeting in individuals' homes. What a wonderful concept! Consider that you have a church in your house, a body of believers fellowshipping together, holding one another accountable, offering comfort and encouragement. You are a "family of faith." Make your home a mission station for the Lord.

You are a "family of faith."

As you welcome neighbors and friends into your home, think of the implications. Do they view your home as a dwelling place for God? When friends visit your children, consider their visits an opportunity to demonstrate Christlike virtues. Many children have never offered grace before a meal or participated in devotional times or bedtime prayers. Gentle words, acts of kindness, apologies, consideration for one another's feelings, and affection are all ways to practice faith at home. Encourage your children to be consistent Christians and to use every opportunity to plant seeds in others' lives.

> **Think of one or more non-Christian friends, neighbors, or relatives who are frequent visitors to your home. List several ways you can use your home as a positive witness.**
>
> _____
>
> _____

> **How will you encourage your children to practice their faith more consistently at home? How will your example reflect that desire?**

A Faithful Family

We began this week's lesson by asking: "What does a Christian family look like? Is such a family perfect, problem-free?"

I am encouraged by Jesus' example. He did not live in a perfect family. His siblings thought on one occasion that He had gone mad and tried to take Him home (Mark 3:21). Even among His brothers there was confusion as to His real identity. Jesus was misunderstood by those closest to Him.

The distinction of a Christian family is not whether you have problems, but how you handle problems. In a blended family, problems can be a major characteristic. Blended family life often is crisis-centered. In the middle of seemingly endless problems, remember to ask which is more important: getting the right solution or reaching solutions in the right way?

What advice does Paul give for handling Christian family problems? Read Ephesians 4:32 in the margin. Underline Christian family characteristics.

Be kind and compassionate to one another, forgiving each other, just as in Christ God forgave you.
—Ephesians 4:32

A faithful family practices the laws of kindness and love. "If it isn't kind, it isn't said," is a good family rule. Be considerate of one another; consider how actions and attitudes affect other family members. Express love to one another and exercise a forgiving heart, remembering God's forgiveness to us.

The law of kindness does not insist that we ignore negative feelings and stuff our emotions. Rather, it encourages us to express emotions in appropriate ways. For example, shouting is not an acceptable way to express anger. A more acceptable way is to count to 10 before speaking.

Determine the family character qualities you want your family to demonstrate. Discuss ways to implement these ideals in practical terms. Consider compiling and posting a list of family rules, such as "no hitting" and "no insults." Establish appropriate and inappropriate ways to express feelings in your home.

A faithful family relies on God to nurture His character within each person. God's character is not achieved through wishful thinking. Christian character-building requires prayer, Bible study, worship, and service.

From the list of Christian characteristics named above, identify ways you will lead your family to develop one of them.

Characteristic:_____

_____

_____

Write this week's Scripture memory verse below.

_____

_____

COUPLETALK

For you to complete

1. Rate your family on the following topics where 1 is never, 2 is sometimes, and 3 is often.

My marriage demonstrates a covenant relationship.	1	2	3
We evidence a covenant relationship with the children.	1	2	3
My spouse and I pray together.	1	2	3
We pray as a family.	1	2	3
The Bible is a guide for family behavior and decisions.	1	2	3
Church is a priority for our family.	1	2	3
We worship at home as well as at church.	1	2	3
Our home is a place where we practice our faith.	1	2	3

2. List at least one idea from this week's study that you would like to implement in your family.

_____

_____

For you to share with your spouse

1. Sit down facing each other and take turns sharing how each of you completed the above section.
2. Decide which ideas you plan to implement from this week's study. Make specific assignments and determine a date for follow-up.
3. Tell one thing you really love about each other.
4. Say together this week's Scripture memory verse.
5. Pray for each other, either silently or aloud.

UNDERSTAND THE CHILDREN

*P*aula couldn't believe her mother was getting married. "Why?" Paula asked. "Who needs him? I thought the two of us were getting along just fine."

Twelve-year-old Paula instinctively knew her mother's marriage to Keith would dramatically affect her life as well as her mother's. When her mother and father divorced three years earlier, Paula thought she would die. She didn't, of course, but the divorce certainly changed her life. She and her mother moved to another house in a different school district, and Paula saw her father only a couple of times each month. Now her mother was planning to marry a man Paula considered a stranger. When would the turmoil in her life end?

At the wedding Paula was an unhappy junior bridesmaid, frowning as her mother walked down the aisle. As the minister, I saw her pain and made a mental note to follow up with this newly blended family.

Blended family weddings offer me the opportunity to observe the children and make assessments regarding their reactions to the marriage. Once I performed a marriage ceremony where both the bride and groom had three children from their previous marriages. There was an enormous contrast between the two sets of children. The groom's children were older, and their smiling faces revealed pleasure at their dad's remarriage. However, there were no smiles or shared laughter among the bride's children. They stood beside their mother with very long faces and made no efforts at even make-believe smiles.

Think back to your own wedding. Do you recall your children's expressions? What do you think they were feeling? Have those feelings changed? Even if you have been a blended family for some time, your children may still need to work through some issues that keep them from fully entering in to the new family. This week we will look at reasons children often are unhappy about a parent's remarriage and how children act out their unhappy feelings. You will determine ways to support your children during times of loss and grief as they deal with changes.

What You'll Study

DAY 1
• **Grief**
DAY 2
• **Fantasy**
DAY 3
• **Manipulation and Anger**
DAY 4
• **Teenagers**
DAY 5
• **Adult Children**

This Week You Will:

- discover grief issues which your children still need to resolve;
- determine whether fantasies are retarding your blending process;
- establish guidelines for dealing with manipulative and angry behaviors;
- identify ways to help teenagers and adult children blend.

This Week's Scripture Memory Verse:

"Jesus said 'Let the little children come to me, and do not hinder them, for the kingdom of heaven belongs to such as these' " (Matthew 19:14).

GRIEF

Grief is the period of adjustment following any loss. When a favorite toy gets misplaced, or a pet dies, or a neighborhood buddy moves away, children must adjust their lives to loss. The death of a parent or a divorce demands major adjustments by all family members.

Sadly, people within our culture do not know how to grieve. Many adults attempt to numb the pain of loss with drugs, sex, work, or new relationships. Since most adults do not know how to grieve in a healthy manner, it should not surprise us that children are overwhelmed when they experience loss. The old sayings, "Children are resilient" and "They'll bounce right back," may ultimately be true, but not without healthy nurturing through the grieving process.

How Children Grieve

Consider these characteristics of children during a grief situation. Before the age of five, children possess little understanding of permanence. To explain, "Daddy has died and will not come back," makes as much sense as "Dad doesn't live here anymore, but he'll pick you up on Friday." From ages five to eight children begin to develop a sense of permanence. Through television, movies and perhaps even real life, children are exposed to death. They ask questions about death that may seem irreverent to an adult, or they may role-play someone dying. They are attempting to make sense of an event they do not understand. Children eight and younger may assume they are somehow responsible for the loss. Children under the age of 10 do not have the verbal skills to fully articulate their feelings after losing a parent to death or divorce.

Between the ages of eight and twelve, most children grieve in what looks like an adult manner. Don't be fooled by this pseudo-adult behavior. They are still developing rational, analytical skills and often revert to child-like interpretations. Preteens may express what they prefer to believe: "Dad is coming back. I just know it." Disagreeing with these feelings proves ineffective.

Allow children to grieve as children.

As a caring adult, allow children to grieve as children. Do not force them into adult modes. If children giggle during a funeral, remember that they do not understand the event and cannot match your mood. Be patient as you answer questions again and again. Children need time to process their grief.

When Children Feel "Divorced"

When children talk about their parent's divorce they often say, "When I got divorced … ." Children typically respond like Matthew in the following story.

"When the teacher heard I got divorced, she told the whole class they would have to be nice to me for a while. I was embarrassed. Why did she do that?" Matthew asked his mom.

"I suspect she was trying to be helpful," his mother answered. "Matthew, you didn't get divorced. Your father and I did. You're still my son, and you're still your father's son. You always will be."

"OK, Mom. But it feels like I got divorced," explained Matthew.

His mom agreed. "Yes, I suppose it does."

Imagine yourself as a child. You are hearing one of your divorced parents criticize the other. How might the criticism make you feel? How do you feel when people you love don't get along?

While we expect the grief a child experiences following the death of a parent, we often fail to comprehend the loss children feel when there is a divorce. Even when both parents remain deeply involved in their children's lives, the children still experience the loss of a home and the loss of a parent. Accepting parents as individuals rather than as a couple, visiting between homes, dividing possessions and in some cases moving are all grief issues to children.

Most divorced parents observe that children become sullen, irritable, or withdrawn prior to and following visitation with the noncustodial parent. This period of adjustment before and after visits can last from several hours to several days. Children frequently decide they do not want to visit dad or mom anymore. The other parent may conclude that the visits are bad experiences, but the truth may be that it is too painful. Leaving one parent to return to another hurts. Of course, refusing visitation is not the solution to the pain. The pain of grief is only alleviated by learning to live with the present situation.

Check the evidences of grief you have observed in your children since your divorce or the death of your mate? Write each child's initials in the blanks that apply.

___ sadness	___ "acting out" behaviors
___ withdrawal	___ insecurity
___ anger	___ restlessness
___ inattention	___ apathy
___ other? _____	

What has been the most difficult aspect of your children's grief for you personally?

_____

Guilt and Grief

Guilt is a frequent symptom of grief. As adults, we know that our children are not to blame for our divorce, and certainly they are not responsible for the death of a parent. However, children often believe they are to blame. Read how one person described her feelings at the time of her parents' divorce.

Children often believe they are to blame.

"When I was 15, my dad told me he was leaving. He hadn't told my mother, so this was her first time to hear it also. I remember thinking that it was my fault because earlier that day I had a huge argument with my father. I told him: 'I don't want to live with you anymore. I'm tired of living with you.' I believed the argument pushed him over the edge. I don't know if it was coincidence or not, but I felt guilty. I remember being unable to sleep because I felt totally responsible for his actions."[1]

Did your children express feelings of guilt about the death or divorce?
❑ Yes ❑ No

We can sympathize with our children and validate their right to have feelings, even if the feelings are troublesome or based on false assumptions. We should assure children they are not to blame for the loss. Remind children that adults are responsible for their own behavior. Since younger children are egocentric and think they have magical powers to control the world around them, telling children they are not to blame won't totally resolve your children's feelings of guilt, but the message needs to be conveyed. Repeat this message as often as necessary.

Helping Children Deal with Loss

One of the great Beatitudes is "Blessed are those who mourn, for they will be comforted" (Matthew 5:4). The word *blessed* in this instance literally means "how happy." Isn't it incredible that Jesus suggests that people who mourn might one day be happy again? While the process is always painful, and certainly not easy or short, it is magnificent to watch someone move from despair, to hope, to new life, and finally joy.

Children also can receive this blessing. However, they need the help of caring adults. Often, adults are involved in a support group to aid in recovery after a divorce or a death. Support groups are helpful tools for people moving through the stages of grief. Numerous churches and schools offer support groups for children whose parents are divorced, or for children who have had a parent die. If no such group exists in your community, consider starting one with the help of your church. *KidShare: What Do I Do Now? Helping Children Deal with Divorce* is a resource designed specifically to be used with children in a small-group setting. Produced by LifeWay Press, *KidShare* follows the same interactive format you've been using in *New Faces in the Frame*.

Encourage your children to talk with you about their loss and to share their feelings. If you and other adults model personal and honest sharing, children will usually share also.

What are some positive steps you have taken or can take to help your child(ren) with the grief process? Check the ones that apply.
❑ We talk about our grief openly.
❑ The child(ren) are in a support group.
❑ The child(ren) are/have been in counseling.
❑ Other significant adults provide a listening ear.
❑ Other?_____

Jesus was a friend to children. They felt comfortable with Him. This week's Scripture memory verse reminds us that those with childlike qualities will inhabit the kingdom of heaven.

What childlike qualities do you think Jesus was referring to in this passage? Thank God for the childlike faith to believe in Him.

To order KidShare: What Do I Do Now? Helping Children Deal with Divorce, call the Customer Service Center at 1-800-458-2772. Ask for item 0-8054-9887-7.

Jesus said "Let the little children come to me, and do not hinder them, for the kingdom of heaven belongs to such as these."
—Matthew 19:14

FANTASY

Children easily confuse reality with make-believe. Sometimes, in spite of the facts, children desperately cling to their fantasies. In this lesson we will examine some common childhood fantasies related to parents who die or divorce.

"My Parent Is Not Dead"

Children who have had a parent die will pretend that the parent is alive. A young girl in our children's support group would relate stories about places she visited with her father, who was dead. It was a victory when, after several weeks, she told her group about her father's accident. Since the other children in her group also had a parent who died and understood her feelings, she was able to face reality.

If a parent has died, children consider loving—even liking—a stepparent as betrayal to the memory of their deceased parent. Children often have difficulty being vulnerable to a new relationship. In such circumstances, stepparents are wise to move slowly and constantly assure children they do not plan to take the biological parent's place. Say: "I know I'm not your mom (or dad), but since I live here, I would like to be your friend."

"My Absent Parent Still Loves Me"

Many custodial parents are frustrated when children idolize the non-custodial parent, especially if that parent fails to maintain a consistent relationship with the children. These same children may express anger and rudeness to the custodial parent. While it seems unfair, remember that when children are hurting, they are not concerned about how their behavior affects their parents.

When children are hurting, they are not concerned about how their behavior affects their parents.

As you read the following story underline words that remind you of circumstances you have faced.

Perry was five when his parents divorced. Although his dad promised that he would see him often, he did not. In fact, there were many times when Perry's dad cancelled their plans or did not even show up. Perry made excuses for his dad. "My dad is very busy," he would say. "His job is important."

More often than not, when Perry's dad failed to show up for visitation, Perry acted out his pain and anger. Once his dad cancelled a weekend outing. Later, Perry dismantled a puzzle and threw the pieces all over the room. When his mother made him pick them up, Perry screamed at her, "I hate you."

Privately, Perry was convinced that his dad left because of him or something he had done. Sometimes, Perry asked his mom, "Why doesn't dad love me?" At other times, Perry talked of his father in the most flattering terms. "My father is great," he said. "He's the smartest man in town." Perry invented trips and activities with his father and bragged about them to his friends. Another time he told his friends about going to baseball games with his dad. While none of these events occurred, Perry, in his grief, believed they did.

The need to boost a parent who fails to accept parental responsibilities stems from a child's strong desire for both parents. A child views himself as a combination of both parents. When one parent leaves, he is torn in half. To be whole again, he invents another half that cares. At the same time, the child is angry because of broken promises. Since he cannot express anger at the absent parent without risking a deeper rift in that relationship, the child often strikes out at the parent with whom he feels safe—the custodial parent. Thus, the responsible parent receives the least appreciation, and the irresponsible parent reaps devotion.

"My Stepparent Will Leave Too"

Another reason children are slow to develop a relationship with stepparents is that children frequently do not believe the stepparent is permanent in their lives. Margo and Scott observed their dad and mom date several people following the divorce. At first, they were close to those mom and dad dated and became friends with their children. After a while, as they repeatedly watched these relationships end, they began to ignore the people their parents dated. Subconsciously they said, "We don't want to be hurt again."

Children whose parents died sometimes experience these same feelings. At first, they fear this new person may die also. They wonder if they should get close. From their viewpoint, emotional attachment hurts.

In order to protect themselves from such hurts, children sometimes build a defensive wall around their emotions to remain detached. Thus, when their parent remarries, the children are convinced it won't last and they maintain their detached position several years into the new marriage. Children do not consider this relationship different simply because this time there was a marriage. After all, their mom and dad were married, and their relationship didn't last.

Blended couples must reassure their children that this relationship is permanent. It will, however, require more than words. If they see mom (or dad) arguing with the stepparent (and sometimes children provoke these arguments as a test), it only confirms what they already suspect: This relationship will end soon.

🌿 **Have any of the children in your blending family seemed reluctant to develop a relationship with the stepparent because they do not trust your marriage to last? ❏ Yes ❏ No**

What are some ways you and your spouse might demonstrate your commitment to each other? Write your ideas in the margin.

Learning to trust a stepparent is complicated by an insecure noncustodial parent who fears being replaced. Frequently biological parents tell their children, "I don't want you to call [your stepparent] Dad (or Mom)." Children hear this as a warning: "Don't get too close to this other person." Although you have no control over your ex's attitudes, understand that such expressions hamper the child/stepparent relationship.

"Mom and Dad Will Get Back Together Again"

I suppose the number one fantasy of most children whose parents are divorced is that their parents will get back together again. This fantasy can survive for years, perhaps forever in some children. Even adult children may harbor the hope that their parents will remarry.

When a parent marries someone else, the fantasy is disrupted. Without conscious intention, many children attempt to sabotage the new marriage in order to maintain the fantasy. Fighting between a biological parent and stepparent is a sign of progress. Even when fighting is a result of the child's actions and ultimately ends in punishment, the hope that the fighting might lead to a divorce continues to feed the fantasy.

When her father married Nancy, Megan began to deliberately disobey Nancy. Megan knew exactly what she was doing. She wanted Nancy to get upset and tell her father. She knew her father would defend her, and then Nancy and her father would fight. If they fought enough, Megan reasoned, Nancy surely would leave.

Many children attempt to sabotage the new marriage in order to maintain the fantasy.

🍃 Check the degree to which your child(ren) might be trying to manipulate your relationship with your …

	None	Some	A lot
spouse	❑	❑	❑
ex-spouse	❑	❑	❑

Whenever the above scenario occurs, children must hear from you: "We assure you that no matter what happens, we are not getting a divorce. We may argue sometimes, because no two people agree on everything, but we will stay married." Children must hear the depth of the couple's commitment. This verbal assurance encourages children to abandon this fantasy that is so destructive to a blending family.

🍃 Place an *X* on the line to indicate how fantasies affect your blending family.

not at all	somewhat	a lot

Reality Will Win in Time

Perhaps you may be asking, "What hope is there?" Do not be discouraged. Actually, there is tremendous hope. Many have traveled the road before you and reached their destination with a healthy blended family. But be alert and be armed. Although some days battles run rampant, what appears hopeless is not!

At first you may see little or no progress. Remember that as children mature, their capacity to understand matures also. True maturity is a life-long process. In time, fantasies give way to reality, and children move on with their lives. Fantasies attach us to the past—letting go frees us for the future.

Fantasies attach us to the past— letting go frees us for the future.

🛡️ In what ways does looking back (even at a past that was not so good) keep us from realizing a better future?

🛡️ Repeat this week's Scripture memory verse. Thank God for your future with your children and stepchildren.

MANIPULATION AND ANGER

Children are experts at manipulation. From birth, infants attempt to control the world in which they live. Babies believe themselves to be the center of the universe. Just as they learn to manipulate their fingers, they learn to manipulate other people. At first, they don't even realize that the other people are separate beings. Babies cry and someone feeds them. They cry again, and someone changes their diapers. They smile and someone picks them up and holds them. The system works perfectly.

Of course, what children believe at this stage is only an illusion. What they perceive to be infinite power is actually total dependence. Gradually, reality shatters their illusions of power and control. The terrible two's are a perfect example of frustrated children who realize they are not in charge. Tantrums are expressions of frustration. Children want what they want when they want it. "No," is not a word they want to hear. Therefore, they attempt new methods of manipulation.

As they grow older, children do not abandon their attempts at control. They change tactics. One tactic induces parental guilt. The method might include a show of jealousy, or it might involve wearing a sad face. Because children want their own way, they try whatever works.

Manipulation

Children bring their manipulative powers into the blending family. Since children know their biological parents' buttons to push, they seek to manipulate and control them. Two teenagers learned to play their divorced parents against each other. Each parent gave them thousands of dollars worth of electronic equipment and vacations because they told the other parent about the expensive gifts and trips. These two teenagers learned that their parents were afraid of losing their affection and would give them anything to keep that love. It took the parents about two years to recognize the manipulation.

🌿 **In what ways have your children or stepchildren tried to manipulate you or their biological parent(s)?**

_____

_____

Have they been successful? ❑ Yes ❑ No

What have you tried to do about it? What worked and what did not? List a couple in each category. Use the margin.

Children do not have the maturity or wisdom to be in control of a family. Control is a parental responsibility. When a parent senses a child is being manipulative, there are ways for parents to respond and maintain control. Confronting the child with his or her behavior is a good place to start. Letting the child know you are aware of the manipulation and that it will not work helps the child to give up ineffective tactics. Instead, teach a child to ask for what he or she wants and needs in a straight-forward way. Reward honest requests.

Cory and Mike discovered that to win their approval their stepfather would permit them to do almost anything. If they wanted to go to the movies, they "buttered him up." He didn't seem to notice they only called him "Dad" when they wanted something. And it worked—for a while. Finally, the stepfather caught on. He announced to them: "When you two boys can stop the games and ask both your Mom and me, we'll consider it. Until then, the answer is no." The boys got the message. They began asking both parents for permission in a straight-forward way. Their parents responded with reasonable boundaries and restrictions.

 If you are tired of manipulative behavior, check the ways you can deal with manipulation more effectively.
- ❏ be prepared spiritually
- ❏ understand the motives of others
- ❏ pray in advance for guidance
- ❏ seek God's control in all you do
- ❏ have an appropriate response ready
- ❏ refuse to give in to manipulation

Anger

Along with frequent attempts at manipulation, children in blending families often express anger. Anger is a gift from God. Without anger, we would not recognize personal hurt, nor would we have the appropriate energy and capacity to take care of ourselves. Expressed in a healthy manner, anger is a blessing, not a curse.

Still, many of us do not understand anger. We're afraid because anger sometimes causes us to act differently and say hurtful things. Some folks believe that anger is a sin. Expressed properly, it is not. When we hold anger inside, we endanger our physical, mental, and spiritual health.

In the margin, read what the Scriptures have to say about healthy expressions of anger.

"In your anger do not sin": Do not let the sun go down while you are still angry, and do not give the devil a foothold. —Ephesians 4:26-27

Children who have experienced loss harbor considerable anger. That anger results from their hurt. Appropriate anger can speed the healing process. Anger is a subconscious cry for care and protection. However, children don't understand their anger and frequently allow it to lead to self-destructive action. If another child had hurt them, they would understand better how to protect themselves. But when their parents cause the hurt, how do they protect themselves from the people they love most?

Edgar was 10 when his parents divorced. Because his parents hid their marital problems from him, Edgar could not begin to comprehend what he was feeling when his father simply didn't come home. At first, Edgar felt guilty. Surely, if he had been a better boy, his father would have stayed. Alone in his room at night, Edgar often cried himself to sleep. As time passed, everyone assumed that Edgar had adjusted to his circumstances. He was quieter than before, but other than that, Edgar seemed to be coping very well.

When Edgar was 12, his grades plummeted. Edgar's mother checked with the school and learned he was not turning in his homework assignments. At first, his mother thought it was simply a phase. After all, 12-year-olds face many hormonal and emotional changes. Then Edgar began hanging out with a rough bunch of older boys. Edgar also ignored curfew and stayed out late. He was out of control.

Edgar was fortunate. A teacher at school recognized the problem and befriended Edgar. His teacher's parents also had divorced, and he understood Edgar's anger. He told Edgar how angry he had felt. He confessed that he, too, had done some inappropriate things, but soon realized he was only hurting himself. His teacher encouraged Edgar to share his deepest feelings about the divorce. He allowed Edgar to express his anger at his father and to understand that he was not responsible. In time, Edgar again gained control over his life.

Like Edgar, many children express their anger in inappropriate ways. Although anger is a healthy emotion when used properly, when expressed improperly, it is extremely destructive. Anger can easily consume our lives. If you see children behaving in inappropriate ways, look for anger behind those actions. Help children deal with anger in constructive ways.

Place an *A* or an *I* in the box to indicate appropriate or inappropriate expressions of anger.

____ throwing things	____ cursing
____ talking about feelings	____ spending time alone
____ being disrespectful	____ disobeying parents
____ sulking, pouting	____ yelling, screaming
____ tears	____ vigorous exercise to vent emotions

Read this week's Scripture memory verse in the margin. During times of anger, remind your children that Jesus is available to them for guidance, self-control, and comfort. Model His example.

Jesus said "Let the little children come to me, and do not hinder them, for the kingdom of heaven belongs to such as these."
—Matthew 19:14

DAY 4

TEENAGERS

*T*he teenage years offer an opportunity to communicate with children in new and positive ways. With teenagers, explanation and reasoning are increasingly possible through conversation and sharing. As children grow, their potential for friendship grows as well. Normally children desire independence during the teenage years. This fact is important to blending families with teenagers. Just as the new family is trying to bond, the children are pulling away.

The Need for Independence

While establishing a separate identity from one's parents is a healthy goal, in the early years of a blending family, the contrasting goals of unity and independence work against each other. Blending couples want their families to become close, to discover common interests, and to like one another. Biological parents want their children to at least like—if not love—the stepparent. Likewise, stepparents desire to be a positive influence in the children's lives.

However, teenagers want to be independent. Even in a nuclear family, teenagers pull away from their parents. They want to make their own decisions and try out their wings. Therefore, the family's goals are in conflict. Who will win? The teenagers desire for independence is so strong that it usually succeeds, and it should. Children need to grow up and separate from their parents.

The contrasting goals of unity and independence work against each other.

Can you think of a time in your teenage years when you experienced conflict with your parents because of your desire for independence? What was the conflict about?

_____

From the occasion you just described, what did you learn that could help you understand your teenager(s)?

_____

_____

As a blending family couple try to understand and work with the process rather than against it. Teenagers want less and less family togetherness. They do not love their parents less. They are expressing a God-given desire for independence.

At the same time, teenagers do not possess the maturity for total freedom. They need restraints and guidelines. Even though many teens request complete freedom to make decisions, most teenagers are uncomfortable with such freedom. They interpret too much freedom as lack of caring by the parents. Balance between freedom and restraint is the art of good parenting during the teenage years.

Larry married Nanette when her daughters were 14 and 16. Nanette was a single mom for eight years, and both girls seemed ready for their mother to marry again. They liked Larry and accepted him as a second father

But Larry wanted more family life than Nanette's daughters did. They wanted their own time for school activities, friends, and boys. The girls liked Larry, but they were frustrated by his attempts to curtail them. Larry thought, *If the girls saw their friends at school, why did they need to talk with them on the phone? Why couldn't they spend weekends with Nanette and me?* He understood that they needed to visit with their father, but on alternate weekends the girls never planned time at home.

🍂 **If you have teenagers in your blending family, what are some ways you see them seeking their independence?**
❏ clothes   ❏ friends
❏ music   ❏ toying with philosophies and ideas
❏ questioning authority   ❏ pushing boundaries
❏ other _____

When Larry tried to limit their activities outside the family, the girls rebelled. Fortunately, Larry talked with a friend who also lived in a blending family with teenagers. Larry's friend helped him to understand that Nanette's daughters were behaving normally. They needed time with their friends more than they needed time with him right now. The best help that Larry could give the girls was to watch out for the dangers inherent to the teenage years and to steer them away from those pitfalls. If he insisted that they spend more time at home, they probably would not listen to Larry when they truly needed his advice.

🍂 **Larry had unexamined expectations regarding his teenagers. Have you taken the time to examine your expectations of your teenager(s)?**
❏ Yes ❏ No

If so, which of these do you consider realistic and practical? Which expectations may set you up for conflict.

realistic: _____

impractical: _____

Being a stepparent to teenagers is never easy. Generally, teenagers do not believe they need another parent. They might welcome a supportive friend, but on their own terms. Consider your teens' desire for independence. Learn to talk with them. Ask for their ideas and opinions and then listen when they respond. They need a safe place to test their thoughts, and it may cement you as a refuge in times of need. A stepparent offers friendship without history—a real benefit to teens.

A stepparent offers friendship without history—a real benefit to teens.

🍂 **If you do not yet have teenagers, what are some things you can do now to prepare both your younger children and yourselves for this critical period of life?**

_____

_____

Anger in Teenagers

Yesterday, we looked at anger in children. Not surprisingly, much of the anger children feel concerning their parents' divorce or death is not expressed until they become teenagers. Many children do not have confidence in their own perceptions prior to their teen years. Generally, they believe there is something wrong with them, not their parents. When children reach the teenage years, however, they begin to question their parent's judgment. Consequently, many teenagers act out their previously bottled-up anger.

Norman is a good example. His parents divorced when he was nine. On the surface, he adjusted very well, visiting between parents as scheduled. He remained obedient to both and appeared to have weathered the situation. When Norman turned 14, everything changed. Suddenly this quiet, obedient boy talked back to his mother and father. Neither understood the change in behavior. Finally, through family counseling, Norman talked about his devastation during and since the divorce. His parents and stepparents asked him why he had waited so long to express his anger. "I was just a kid before," he told them. "I couldn't do anything then. I'm not a kid anymore."

 Review the appropriate and inappropriate ways to express anger you checked in day 3. Discuss the appropriate ways with your teenagers. Encourage them to express their feelings rather than burying them inside.

The Threat of Losing Custody

Parents and stepparents of teens face an additional frustration—the fear of losing custody to the other parent. The possibility of a teenager choosing to live with the noncustodial parent is a real concern. For noncustodial parents, this possibility is often viewed with anticipation. Unfortunately, too few consider the teenager's best interests.

Most children do a decent job of choosing. When they have lived with one parent for years, the desire to live with the other parent can be overwhelming. I usually encourage parents to support the children in these decisions if it is something the teenager feels he or she needs to do.

> **The desire to live with the other parent can be overwhelming.**

For a child to bounce back and forth between parents is dangerous. Some teenagers encourage competition for custody, and the parent who cuts the best deal wins. When teenagers succeed at this strategy, they learn a destructive lesson. They believe the world caters to their needs. Responsible parents and stepparents teach their children that a happy life includes both giving and taking.

Helping Teenagers Cope

A support group for teens provides a forum to vent anger. Teenagers discover that their individual situation is not unique. Other teens experience the same feelings and struggles.

When I first proposed the idea of a teen support group to our blending family couples, they resisted, believing their children would never attend. Having anticipated their reaction, I suggested: "Ask them to attend two sessions. After that, the decision is theirs." I felt if they attended, they would find it helpful and rewarding.

One teenager had not spoken with his stepmother in several months. His father made him attend a group. He entered the room wearing a scowl on his face. His father called me the next day and said, "I don't know what happened at last night's meeting, but he talked with his stepmother."

If you do not have such a support group for your teens, consider initiating one. Talk with your pastor and other blended family couples. Pray for God's guidance.

Healing the Wounds: Teenagers Learning to Cope with Divorce is an invaluable resource for a divorce-recovery group for teens. *Healing the Wounds* is a self-paced interactive study, like *New Faces in the Frame*, and is designed as a resource for weekly support-group sessions.

❧ **Repeat this week's Scripture memory verse to a family member. Take the opportunity to compliment a quality you have observed in him or her.**

DAY 5

ADULT CHILDREN

Couples often assume grown children will have little or no impact upon their marriage, or vice-versa. After all, none of the children will live with them. While it is true that grown children have less impact on a second marriage, they do have an effect. Adult children have a bond with only one half of the couple. They have a history with only one person, not two. They will not know or feel comfortable with this new person. They may still be stuck in the fantasy stage of hoping mom and dad will get back together.

Dealing with Change

Alice's mother was getting married again. Alice's father had been dead for 10 years; it was time. But as Alice drove with her family to the wedding 200 miles away, she felt more like she was going to a funeral than to a wedding.

Alice was 30 years old, yet she felt she was acting like a child. *What's wrong with me?* Alice wondered. *Henry seems like a nice enough guy.*

Part of Alice's grief came from knowing her mother was selling the family homestead and moving in with Henry. Alice would miss her house—the house in which she grew up. Another part of Alice's grief came from knowing instinctively that her mother's remarriage would change their mother/daughter relationship.

When her mother was single, Alice could call her and say, "Evan has a business trip. Could you come and watch the kids so I can travel with him?" Now Alice doubted her mother would babysit as often. She was helping Henry with his hardware store. Her mother had another life now.

Also, Alice's mother frequently visited for no particular reason. Alice and her mother stayed up late and talked, reminiscing about old times and the people they knew. Now when her mother visited, Henry would come with her. It would not be the same. Alice realized she was selfish. She was only thinking of herself. This marriage was good for her mother; Alice was sure of that. But it changed everything.

Remarriage changes relationships. While the couple marrying view these changes positively, children often view them with mixed feelings, instinctively knowing that some changes will affect them negatively.

If you have adult children, circle the response when you told them you were getting married?

     sad   confused   angry   pleased   neutral   ecstatic   quiet

You can help your adult children adjust to your remarriage by:
1. Letting them know you understand their sense of loss.
2. Sharing your own losses and changes.
3. Being open to their negative feelings without defensiveness.
4. Reminding them of your commitment to them as parent and friend.

When Moses led the Israelites out of Egyptian bondage, God fed them with manna from heaven. God instructed them to gather only one day's requirement of food. Some disobeyed and gathered manna for the next day. Part of our spiritual journey is learning to take one day at a time.

Why do we have difficulty trusting God to care for us in times of change? Affirm God's ability to give you and your children peace during this time of transition. Thank Him for His daily provision.

Time and distance are major factors in blending families with adult children. Today, families live all over the world. For parents to maintain a relationship with children living away is difficult. To expect that stepsiblings, who possibly met for the first time at their parent's wedding, will develop a relationship with one another is unrealistic. Family bonding needs consistent opportunity which seldom exists in stepfamilies with adult children.

The Boomerang Adult Child

When adult children return to the nest, they often are referred to as boomerang children. This idea always illicits groans in our blending family support group. Nevertheless, in blending families at least one or more adult children at some point will return home to live. To assume that once children leave for college or the service, embark on a career, or marry that they will never return is unrealistic. It happens all the time. In a blending family, whether the child has lived with them before or only visited occasionally, such a move may prove disruptive. Biological parents often feel guilty saying "No." Stepparents may either dread, tolerate, or forbid such a move. Avoid the stress and decide in advance how you will handle the situation. There is really no "right" decision.

The most successful return home situations are governed by specific contracts. Establish a certain time period for living at home, after which he or she seeks other accommodations. Decide how finances will be handled. When the time has elapsed and the adult child wants to remain in the home, the biological parent must either remain firm or with the blessing of the spouse renegotiate a new contract. Children sense and take advantage of an unwillingness to follow-through.

When an adult child goes through a divorce, economic need may dictate a return home for a time. Once again, the biological parent and stepparent should agree upon a plan. There is no question that such a return will disrupt the family. It may be especially disruptive if the child returns with grandchildren. Maintain your own marriage as the primary concern.

> Avoid the stress and decide in advance how you will handle the situation.

How would you feel about one of your adult children returning home to live? Use CoupleTalk as an opportunity to begin this dialogue.

Dividing Assets

One consideration blending family couples with adult children face is inheritance. In situations of a large estate, this factor will affect how adult children perceive the marriage. Even in cases of a minimal estate, inheritance remains an issue. Couples with adult children need to discuss decisions that affect them prior to the marriage. Update any insurance policies and wills through an attorney to assure fair disbursement in the event of your death.

More often than not, adult children are concerned about tangible assets such as pieces of furniture or other household items. Talk with the children and establish a plan. If you plan to move, allow adult children to indicate items they want. Remember, their personal heritage is attached not only to you but also to some physical items.

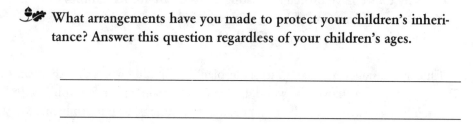 What arrangements have you made to protect your children's inheritance? Answer this question regardless of your children's ages.

_____

_____

Trade-offs for Adult Children

Adult children may regret some aspects of their parents' remarriage. However, a significant benefit is the assurance mom or dad has someone else to care for them and meet their companionship needs. It allows them to stop worrying about that parent. It may also encourage healthy separation. Some adult children hesitate to leave home and establish a separate identity due to inappropriate guilt over leaving a parent alone.

Lester's mother did not remarry after her husband died. She was in her early 50's and in good health, but Lester wondered if his mother's care was his responsibility for the rest of her life. When Lester's mother announced her intention to marry Nigel, Lester was delighted. He could relax; Mom had someone to take care of her. As a bonus, Lester and Nigel both loved to play golf.

Many adult children respond as Lester did. Others become convinced as time passes and they experience positive feelings. Time and patience are necessary virtues in all aspects of blended family living. Blending a family is certain to teach you patience, and patience is a virtue worth cultivating. So relax! Growth cannot be forced; it always takes time.

Time and patience are necessary virtues

Write this week's Scripture memory verse below.

_____

_____

1. Adapted from Beth Joselow and Thea Joselow, *When Divorce Hits Home*. (New York: Avon Books, 1996), p.3.

COUPLETALK

For you to complete

1. From the activities in days 1-3, how have you seen your children's grief, fantasy, manipulation and anger acted out? Compile a list.

_____

_____

2. If either of you have teenagers, how has their desire for independence affected your blending family? If you do not yet have teenagers, what can you do to prepare for the challenges of adolescence?

_____

_____

3. What are your feelings if an adult child should boomerang? If this has happened, evaluate your experience.

_____

_____

4. What are two ideas from this week's lessons that have helped you understand your children better? Beside each idea, write one suggestion for how to implement it.

_____

_____

For you to share with your spouse

1. Sit down facing each other and take turns sharing how each of you completed the above section.
2. Decide which ideas you plan to implement and make specific assignments for follow-up.
3. Tell one thing you really love about each other..
4. Say together this week's Scripture memory verse.
5. Pray for each other, either silently or aloud.

AVOID TYPECASTING

*D*arcy's new husband Chester was the custodial parent of two children. Although the children were a bit unruly, Darcy knew Chester was a devoted father. *We'll make a great team*, thought Darcy. From the moment Chester proposed, she determined not to become the "wicked stepmother." The children were going to love her as a mother. Although they visited their biological mother regularly, the kids would simply have two mothers.

Darcy entered her marriage in much the same way that many stepparents enter marriage—with wonderful intentions. Good intentions do not insure smooth sailing. Three months into the marriage, the children treated Darcy with distrust and disdain. She felt like a failure. What went wrong?

Darcy ultimately became a wonderful stepmother. You'll read more of her story in day 1. What she failed to comprehend in those early months was that she could not control what the children thought of her, nor could she control the timetable for blending her family. Even as she did her part to succeed as a stepmother, other family members helped or hindered the process.

The role of stepparent may look like a mine field to someone contemplating marriage to a partner with children. However, those of us who have experienced the privilege—and the frustrations—of being a stepparent, know it is a rewarding journey with many opportunities to stretch and grow as Christians and as individuals. Think of it as a blessing just waiting to happen, instead of a cross to bear.

If you are a stepparent, read this week's study looking for ways to avoid typecasting as the "wicked stepparent." If you are not a stepparent, try to put yourself in your spouse's place. Look through his or her lens at your family dynamics. You can help your spouse become a more effective stepparent.

What You'll Study

DAY 1
- **The Wonderful Stepparent**

DAY 2
- **The Wicked Stepparent**

DAY 3
- **Set-Ups for Failure**

DAY 4
- **Dealing with Jealousy and Anger**

DAY 5
- **Your Unique Family**

This Week You Will:
- examine the parts played by the stepparent, the biological parents, and the children in the way the stepparent is perceived;
- identify ways to avoid set-ups that lead to failure as a stepparent;
- determine how you will handle jealousy and anger responsibly;
- accept the challenges of your unique family situation.

This Week's Scripture Memory Verse
"Wait for the Lord; be strong and take heart and wait for the Lord" (Psalm 27:14).

THE WONDERFUL STEPPARENT

Stepparents enter marriage with great expectations. We expect to be liked–even loved–by our stepchildren. We love them, after all. Or do we? Sometimes we love the illusion of a happy family with children and how those children will respond to us. Just as love can be blind in regard to our spouse, it can also be blind in regard to his or her children.

Remember Darcy from the introduction? She knew Chester's children were unruly by her standards, but she overlooked this fact when she dreamed of married life. In her dreams, Darcy believed the children would appreciate her sincere efforts to discipline them because she loved them so deeply. Many people embrace the role of stepparent with highly unrealistic views.

Love is not enough. Love is always the best and correct way to respond, but it is not enough to make the inherent problems disappear. A stepparent may give and give love to stepchildren, only to be rejected. At least initially, the children will say either audibly or by their actions: "Who needs you? We didn't ask you to be here. Why don't you go away?" It doesn't take long before the stepparent tires of failure and considers giving up.

Which of the following best describes the situation when you became a stepparent?
- ❑ I had a very good relationship with my mate's children.
- ❑ I had problems with relating to my mate's children.
- ❑ I had illusions about who they were and how we would relate.

The Stepparent's Part

Repeatedly stepparents begin their marriages with the intention of overcoming the wicked stepparent syndrome. I am sure if the stepparents efforts were all that contributed to this scenario, they would successfully avoid the label. However, other significant players act in the family drama–the children, the biological parent, and if there was a divorce, the other biological parent. Stepparents often fail to recognize when entering a blending family that what they do is only one part of the big picture. They cannot control how the children perceive their actions. Today's study identifies parts played by the stepparent and the biological parent.

Darcy is a good example. The first time Darcy was upset over the children's behavior, she was surprised to hear Chester defend them. "They're just kids."

"And not very well behaved ones at that," Darcy replied.

"Well, they've not had much stability in their lives. They were young when their mother and I divorced; I could only do so much."

Now that we're together, we can do better, Darcy thought. She would be the mother the children needed. Darcy tried; she truly did. She ignored the remarks

What stepparents do is only one part of the big picture.

Chester's daughter Molly made about how much better her biological mother did everything. Darcy reminded herself that Molly made those comments to provoke a reaction. Therefore, Darcy smiled and said, "I'm glad you like the way your mother does it."

On the other hand, Chester's son seldom said anything bad about Darcy. Rick simply ignored her. When Darcy tried to join Rick in playing with his cars and trucks, he moved to play with something else. Darcy tried again and again to make friends with both Rick and Molly, but to no avail.

To Darcy's credit, for three months she tried her best to be a loving, supporting stepmother. However, after she was rebuffed at every attempt, Darcy gave up. *Let Chester deal with them,* she thought. Darcy began using the time Chester was home to go shopping, visit with friends and family, or retreat to her room to read. *The kids don't care if I'm around,* Darcy thought, *so I'll stop caring about them.* Unfortunately, she felt more and more isolated from the family.

Which of Darcy's experiences can you identify with in your blending family? Check all the boxes that apply.
❑ I wanted to make friends with the children.
❑ I felt rejected by them.
❑ I felt put down when compared to the biological parent(s).
❑ I became isolated from the family.

What Darcy experienced happens many times in blending families. Darcy did not consider that she was only one part of the blending family. The children, with all their past history; her new husband; and his former wife all played major roles. Darcy's part was only one factor in whether this family would blend. Remember from week 1 that on an average the blending process requires four to seven years. The three months Darcy invested was a mere fraction of the time needed.

Stepparents can give love, time, and energy to the blending process, but they are not solely responsible for the outcome. If you are a stepparent, give yourself a literal pat on the back for your efforts so far. Remember, your stepchildren are reacting to an initial situation which you did not create, and alone you cannot solve it. As this week's study progresses, look for additional ways to help the blending process.

Your stepchildren are reacting to an initial situation which you did not create, and alone you cannot solve it.

The Biological Parent's Part

As a stepparent, you may feel your mate has done a magnificent job of supporting you in your stepparenting role. Perhaps your partner has reinforced your authority with the children. You feel you are a parenting team. Most importantly, you feel your marriage takes priority when there are the inevitable choices to be made between pleasing the children and pleasing you.

Most blended couples have to work hard to achieve these goals. Think for a moment about how being the biological parent feels. Most biological parents feel they live in a war zone and are being shot at from both sides. The children aren't happy with the stepparent and the stepparent isn't happy with the children. Efforts to bring the warring sides to the bargaining table often fall on deaf ears. Many times the biological parent is asked to choose sides when, in reality, he or she wants the war to end.

Children question love and loyalty, and biological parents may hear, "You love him (her) more than me." You may shout, "You're not supporting my authority," while the children scream, "Why have we been replaced by a total stranger?" The key role played by the biological parent in the blending process is so crucial we will spend all of week 9 discussing it.

If you are the biological parent, recognize the important role you play in how the stepparent is perceived. Learn to react from a given set of principles and guidelines which you and your spouse have worked out in advance. Week 10 gives instruction on how to reach such decisions. When you and your present spouse are in agreement about actions, you are less likely to respond to emotional pressure from the children.

 What are some ways the biological parent has been helpful to the stepparent in your blending family? Be prepared to compliment him or her during CoupleTalk.

One of the wonderful qualities stepparents bring to a blending family is the ability to see clearly truths to which the biological parent has become blind. Stepparents enter the family with greater objectivity than biological parents. The difficulty is in communicating those truths. The advantage of perspective has little positive effect unless the stepparent shares the information in an acceptable way.

Share information in an acceptable way.

Patrick tried many times to explain to his wife Susan that her son behaved like a bully. Kip was bigger than other boys his age and took advantage of his size. Susan's bond with Kip prevented her from seeing his actions clearly. Whenever Patrick pointed out one of Kip's negative characteristics, Susan rushed to Kip's defense. Finally, Patrick caught on.

Rather than telling Susan to open her eyes and see the real picture (a mistake many stepparents make), Patrick affirmed Susan's close relationship with her son. And he praised Kip more often. Only when Susan was less guarded concerning Kip, did Patrick say: "I wish Kip understood how much stronger he is than some of the other boys. How can we help him use that strength and energy better?"

When offered a chance to help her son excel, rather than being faced with an attack upon Kip's character, Susan listened to Patrick. The two of them calmly discussed positive ways to channel Kip's strength. They encouraged Kip to try out for the school wrestling team, a sport he took to eagerly. If Patrick had not been sensitive to Susan's protective attitude toward her son, it is doubtful that his influence would have resulted in this win-win situation.

Re-read this week's Scripture memory verse. How can being sensitive to the Lord's timing help you deal with the stepparenting dilemma?

Wait for the Lord; be strong and take heart and wait for the Lord.
—Psalm 27:14

_____

_____

THE WICKED STEPPARENT

The wonderful stepparent (as seen through the adults' eyes) looks like a wicked stepparent to the children in the blending family. In day 1 we looked at the roles played by the stepparent and the biological parent. Today let's examine the parts played by the children and the other biological parent (the ex-spouse).

The Children's Part

Ultimately families blend when the children are ready.

Ultimately families blend when the children are ready. It does not matter that the biological parent and stepparent are ready. The children must have progressed adequately in their grief process—working through anger and their fantasies—so that blending is possible. Prior to that, the stepparent's efforts appear to be limited.

Remember Darcy? Avoiding the children was not very satisfying to her. After realizing the family would never blend without her, she continued her efforts with renewed determination.

Although Darcy knew the children resented her, she decided to like them anyway. Every time they shot her down for an effort to get close to them, Darcy regrouped and tried again. She kept a journal of her tactics. Not only did she record her plan, Darcy noted how each of the children responded. Whenever she detected the tiniest crack in an armor, Darcy focused on that toehold.

Chester was impressed with her tenacity. One night he told her: "I don't know how you do it. You truly are a wonder. I want you to know I really admire you for all your effort. I don't deserve you, but I thank God for you." Chester's comment made the effort worthwhile. He demonstrated the power to bless.

🌿 **Mark the following statements with an A for agree or a D for disagree.**

____ I've been withdrawing from my stepchildren because of their indifference or hostility toward me.

____ I've held the stepchildren's attitudes against them, feeling that I deserved better treatment.

____ I often treat my stepchildren like they treat me, instead of treating them like I want to be treated.

____ I am the adult in this relationship, and I must model the behavior I would like to see in my stepchildren.

____ I keep thinking I can make my stepchildren like me.

Stepchildren are almost certain to distrust, and probably dislike, the stepparent, for all the reasons we discussed last week. While none of these has anything to do with the stepparent personally, they receive most of the negative criticism simply because of their presence. Children can be very cruel, especially when they are hurt. A wise stepparent recognizes the hurt that exists in all stepchildren. Develop the ability to recognize what is true and what is false. When children lash out at you, look behind the words and actions to the pain that produced those words and actions; the need to respond with punishment will be less important.

I do not mean that you should ignore all negative behavior. Ignoring trouble does not make it disappear. But understanding the cause helps you to concentrate on solutions rather than further pain. Have you ever thought, *These children don't like me, and therefore I'm not going to do anything for them*? That type of thinking only makes a bad situation worse. Only as you understand that you personally are not solely the problem will progress occur in your blending family.

When Lindell began to understand this principal, his whole attitude changed. Every time the children said something negative like, "You're not my father. You can't tell me what to do," Lindell pictured them saying to their parents, "Why did you ever get divorced? I wish we could be a family again." Once Lindell had transferred what they had actually said to what was behind the words, he could deal with the children positively rather than negatively.

Now he replies, "Divorce is tough on you, isn't it. I'm sorry you have had to go through it. But I'm the one who is here right now, not your father. When you are with him, you follow his rules. When you are with me, you follow mine." By not taking their words personally, Lindell was able to respond out of love rather than anger, a much better way to relate.

 How thick or thin has your own stepparent skin been? In other words, how personally have you taken your stepchildren's remarks and behaviors? Mark an X on the continuum below.

very thin   thin   medium   thick   very thick

Think of a time when you were able to hear a negative comment from a stepchild and not take it personally. Congratulate yourself!

The Other Biological Parent's Part

Children's feelings about the stepparent may differ according to whether the stepparent is in the family due to death or divorce. In both cases, children need time to grieve and time to adjust to mom or dad's new spouse. Also, in both cases children resist someone they consider as a replacement for the other biological parent. They feel disloyal if they like the new adult. In the case of death, children at least can understand why the nuclear family is no longer intact and are less likely to blame the stepparent for their loss.

In the case of divorce, children may view the stepparent as the reason mom and dad broke up, even if that is not true. They also believe the stepparent is the chief obstacle to mom and dad getting back together again. Children who see their noncustodial parent regularly have problems adjusting to the stepparent's authority because they honestly can say, "I already have a Dad (or Mom)."

When the noncustodial parent feeds the child with doubts, worries, fears, and anxieties about the intentions or capabilities of the stepparent, the situation becomes even more problematic. They may ask the children many questions every time they visit: How does she dress? What does he watch on television? Are you being treated well? Children are perceptive about their parent's feelings. If their biological father or mother is non-accepting of the new spouse, children are more likely to be non-accepting as well. Noncustodial parents may fear being replaced in the eyes of the child. Perhaps they are threatened by the appearance, abilities, or status of the stepparent. Perhaps they, too, preferred to have the nuclear family remain intact.

Unfortunately, some noncustodial parents are just spoilers! The divorce left hard feelings and the noncustodial parents simply do not want their ex's to be happy, even if it means a difficult adjustment for their children. This position is selfish, but it does occur.

Some stepparents discover that getting to know the mate's former spouse is helpful. While most stepparents are hesitant to even meet this person, others find they can communicate better with the former spouse than their mate can. Consider your mate's former spouse as a co-worker when dealing with the children. Try to get to know their preferences and opinions. Do not rule out the possibility of coming to some mutually beneficial solutions to problems.

Ask yourself, *Am I the one with the attitude problem? Am I jealous of the children's affection for the ex? Do I give him(her) the benefit of the doubt?*

Some former spouses pose enormous difficulties for the blending family, but others are tremendous allies. Which role they choose is not within your control. As stepparents, play the hand you are dealt and live with integrity in the way you relate to them.

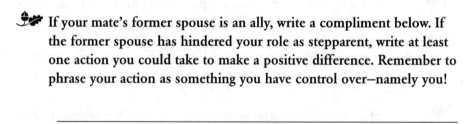 **If your mate's former spouse is an ally, write a compliment below. If the former spouse has hindered your role as stepparent, write at least one action you could take to make a positive difference. Remember to phrase your action as something you have control over—namely you!**

_____

_____

Write this week's Scripture memory verse in the margin.

SET-UPS FOR FAILURE

*I*n some ways the stepparent is set-up for failure. To foil the set-up they must overcome several obstacles. Some of these obstacles are obvious; others are not. But none of them can be ignored.

Resistance to Change

One set-up for failure is simply the fact that everything the stepparent does is different. People differ in what they eat, how they keep house, what styles they prefer, and the personal routines they follow. Since the stepparent lives in a setting where the biological parent and his or her children are already accustomed to one another, the stepparent's differences are glaringly apparent. When the stepparent tries to initiate change, the children automatically perceive it as interference. Children do not like and are resistant to change.

When Freda married Raymond and moved in with him and his eight-year-old daughter Shiela, she was appalled at their housekeeping. Clothes were piled in the floor. Dishes were stacked on the kitchen counters and the living room coffee table. *Does anyone dust or vacuum? How could people live this way?* Freda wondered.

Freda went straight to work putting the house in order–her order. Soon the house looked great, but not for long. Raymond and Shiela immediately cluttered it. Obviously, confrontation loomed imminent. The three of them had a long talk and established a list of family rules. For example, place dirty clothes in a hamper. Rinse dishes and store in the dishwasher. Keep a regular schedule for dusting and cleaning.

While none of these rules were drastic, following them consistently and all at once proved too difficult for Shiela. She resisted the change. "Why can't Freda change?" she asked her dad. When Raymond punished Shiela for failure to obey the new rules, she was really angry–not at her dad, but at Freda. "Who needs her," she said to her friends. "I wish she would leave."

Children in a blending family never embrace change graciously. They resist and resent. After all, they've experienced significant and painful change already.

Children in a blending family have experienced significant and painful change already.

Understand that your stepchildren probably will blame and resent you for all family changes. Choose your battles carefully and do not attempt to change everything at once. Decide what you can live with and what you cannot. Initiate only one change at a time, and allow everyone to observe how it benefits the family before suggesting another change.

🍂 Describe how you and your spouse effectively initiated one change suggested by the stepparent.

_____

_____

Resentment Toward the Marriage

Another set-up stepparents inherit is resentment for how their very presence interferes with the fantasy of mom and dad getting back together. Although we looked at this last week, let's focus today on how this fantasy impacts the stepparent.

When children perceive the stepparent as being an obstacle to their fantasy, some children will intentionally sabotage the marriage. It is their goal to rid the home of this invader.

Always remember that children listen to every word said about their other biological parent. Some children even listen in on an extension phone when mom and dad are talking. They want to know every detail of the interaction between their parents, good or bad. They may purposely get into trouble at school or with the law so their parents will have to talk.

Again, the stepparent should not take any of this behavior personally. It does not matter *who* the stepparent is. He or she might be the most loving, wonderful person in the world, but the children would still resent him or her.

Children under the age of 10 usually respond more readily to stepparenting; older children often do not. Depending on the children's ages, some stepparents try a different approach. When they are coming into a marriage without children of their own, they may choose to avoid the whole concept of stepparenting. Rather than accepting the role of parent, they explain to the children that they plan to simply be a wife or husband. Since they all live together, some adjustments are necessary, but parenting is left to the biological parent. Endorsing such a concept is not the purpose of this illustration. It works for some. The point is that trying to become a parent to stepchildren immediately often creates an adversarial relationship that is hard to overcome. This role can be assumed more gradually with less resistance when older children are involved.

🌿 Some stepparents are unaware the stepchildren resent them for marrying their mother or father until long after the wedding. If this was your situation, what did you do to encourage more positive feelings? If this is your present situation, what has helped/hindered acceptance by your stepchildren?

Replacement of the Single Parent/Child Relationship

The nature of a single-parent family may also be a set-up for the stepparent's failure. After a divorce or death, many children are extremely close to the parent they live with. In turn, the parents act differently toward the children. They treat them as if they are little grown-ups. Parents and children function more as a team.

This closeness not only nurtures the children through a difficult time but also helps the single parent. Being a single parent is difficult. Single parents know they cannot be both father and mother to these children. Therefore, they stop parenting in the traditional sense and begin interacting with the children as a friend. The single parent and his or her children emotionally support one another.

Eventually when the single parent meets someone and attempts to include that person in the family setting, the children consider it an intrusion. Reverting to a more traditional parenting arrangement is often like trying to put toothpaste back in the tube. Once children are privy to the freedom of single parenting days, very few welcome attempts at greater restraint. Therefore, the stepparent is set-up to be the heavy in a situation they did not anticipate nor create. Only as the stepparent begins to comprehend the social dynamics of the previous single-parent family setting is there hope for blending this new family.

One way to help the stepparent encounter less hostility among the children is to schedule sufficient alone time for the biological parent and the children. Cathy and Harry both said the worst part about their dad's marriage to Barbara was missing their time alone with him. They liked some family activities, but those times with their dad were special. Losing them left an emptiness in their lives.

The stepparent is set-up to be the heavy in a situation they did not anticipate nor create.

Fortunately for this blending family, Barbara overheard Cathy talking with friends about her new family. "Our home is not that bad. Dad could have done worse, I suppose. I just wish Barbara didn't have to go everywhere with us. Harry and I never get to spend time with Dad by ourselves. We used to have some great times together before she came along."

That night, without ever revealing her motivation, Barbara suggested to her husband that he begin spending more time with the kids without her. She said she "thought it would be good for them." And it was.

🍂 **Does the biological parent in your blending family still have quality alone time with his or her children? How can you help the transition from single parenting to blending family parenting? List some ideas in the margin.**

Grace to Remove Obstacles

Stepparents may feel they have entered a dark cave. You might well wonder if anyone finds his or her way out. Surprisingly—and thankfully—most do. This victory is not simply a result of the tenacity of the human spirit, but a tribute to the grace of God. God walks beside us as we struggle to bring order out of the chaos in the early days of a blending family. Remember the promise God made in Jeremiah 29:11: " 'I know the plans I have for you,' declares the Lord, 'plans to prosper you and not to harm you, plans to give you hope and a future.' " God wants only the best for your new family.

🌺 **Have you had difficulty feeling the presence of God in the blending process of your family? Right now stop and pray, thanking Him for His care thus far. Invite Him to continue to guide your family in this process. Remember, God cares more for your family than you do!**

Cast all your anxiety on him because he cares for you.
–1 Peter 5:7

Sometimes, we have difficulty believing and accepting that God sends others into our lives to help. Just as God sent Jethro, Moses' father-in-law, to help him organize the tribes of Israel (Exodus 18), I believe He sends many stepparents into single-parent families as an act of grace. Just because it does not happen easily, and just because the stepparent is frequently considered unwelcome, does not mean that God did not send the stepparent. With time and patience we are able to recognize His helpers in our lives.

🍂 **Write this week's memory verse from memory. How does the advice to "be strong and take heart" help you to deal with obstacles in the blending process?**

_____

_____

_____

DEALING WITH JEALOUSY AND ANGER

*P*eter's wife suffered a two-year battle with cancer and died only 18 months before he married Joan. This brief period between spouses was not adequate time for Peter's three children to grieve the loss of their mother. They were unable to accept the idea of their dad's remarriage.

Joan was totally unprepared for the difficulties she would face as the newcomer in this family. Her biggest adversary was Wanda. Wanda was "the woman of the household," not only for the year and a half since her mother died, but also for at least a year before that when her mother was sick. Although only 12 years of age, Wanda was hardly a child. She was forced to grow up quickly.

Wanda and Joan's biggest area of contention was the kitchen. Wanda had prepared most of the food (mostly microwave meals and sandwiches), but naturally Joan wanted to assume that responsibility. "You don't need to do that anymore, Wanda," Joan said. "I'll cook. You have your homework and your friends. Run along."

One day Joan rearranged the whole kitchen. When Peter arrived home that night, Wanda met him at the car. "Do you know what she did?" asked Wanda. "She moved everything in the kitchen. I can't find anything. Tell her to put it back."

After soothing Wanda, Peter walked into the kitchen where Joan was preparing dinner. "I hear you changed things around a little," said Peter.

"I arranged things where they made sense to me," replied Joan. "No big deal."

"It's a big deal to Wanda," said Peter.

"Well, Wanda isn't the mother here," said Joan. "She will have to adjust."

"Ok," said Peter, "but go slowly, will you? The kids have been through a lot. Before you change anything else, will you talk to me about it?"

Joan was furious. *Who is in charge here?* she thought. *Weren't she and Peter the parents? Didn't that mean they set the rules? Wasn't the person who does the cooking even permitted to organize the kitchen?*

The kitchen incident was the first of a long series of struggles between Joan and Wanda. Wanda felt replaced and unneeded; Joan felt unloved and unsupported. Both of them wanted to be the priority in Peter's life. Joan was certain Peter loved Wanda more than he loved her. Wanda felt to some degree she had lost both parents. Jealousy, the green-eyed monster, disrupted this family's blending process.

Roots of Jealousy

Some of us struggle more with jealousy than others. Jealousy often is rooted in low self-esteem, dating back to family-of-origin issues. When I feel insecure in a relationship, I am more likely to feel jealousy. Discovering the roots of jealousy helps us to deal more appropriately with jealous feelings.

In Joan's case, she was jealous of Peter's affection for his children. She didn't like how jealousy was affecting her actions and attitudes—particularly her relationship with Wanda. She spoke with her pastor about her feelings. He suggested that her jealousy might be related to her own personal security issues. Joan recalled a childhood incident. "When I was small, my mother took a job on the west coast and was absent for six months at a time. My grandmother took care of me while she was gone. Did that affect my feelings of security?" asked Joan.

"Imagine yourself again as that little girl," said the minister, "unable to understand where your mother had gone or why. As a little girl, you didn't know if your mother was coming back. Time is not an easy concept for children. Six months seems like forever. Fear of abandonment is one of a child's deepest fears. Is it possible that incident drives your jealousy?"

"Perhaps," offered Joan. "I never really knew my dad. I've always wanted a secure relationship. I'm sure that Peter loves me. But I want all of his love so that I can be sure he will never leave me."

Joan's pastor suggested: "The next time you feel that jealousy is controlling you, remind yourself that Peter is not going to abandon you. Remember, it's OK for him to love his kids. He loves you, too."

🍂 To what extent have jealous feelings interfered with your blending process? Put the first initial of each family member on the continuum to represent how jealousy of each has affected your blending process.

Not jealous	Somewhat jealous	Very jealous

Often it is difficult for stepparents to admit they are jealous of their spouse's affection for the children. However, jealous feelings are common. If you experience these feelings, talk to your spouse. Be specific as to particular actions which prompt your jealous feelings. Suggest to your mate ways he or she can help you feel more secure.

Anger

A major complaint among stepparents is that their spouse fails to support their discipline decisions. Sometimes, biological parents are unable to believe their child has misbehaved. Stepparents frequently are angry when the biological parent takes the children's side against them.

Angry feelings are a thermostat indicating a problem which needs addressing. This was the situation between Mary and Ron when Mary complained about the table manners of Ron's 11- and 12-year-old children. "Steve uses his fingers to put the food on his fork. And Mandy holds her fork like a spear."

Angry feelings are a thermostat indicating a problem which needs addressing.

Ron agreed Mary should teach the children etiquette. The next day when Steve and Mandy came home from school, Mary informed them they were going to have a 30-minute lesson on table manners. Although they groused at first, Steve and Mandy did pay attention. But in exactly 30 minutes, Steve bolted for the door. Mary caught his arm, "Where do you think you're going? We're not finished yet."

"You said 30 minutes," Steve answered. "Time's up. I'm out of here," and with that he ran out the door. Mandy was right behind him.

Mary was furious. These children needed to learn who was in charge. When Ron came home and Mary explained what happened, he defended the children.

"You said 30 minutes. Surely you can't blame them for holding you to your word. I would have done the same thing when I was a kid. And you said they did sit and listen."

"That's not the point." Mary was angrier by the minute. "I instructed them to stay here, and they openly defied me."

"But you also told them that they would only have the lesson for 30 minutes. Kids consider statements like that as promises. Hold the lessons to half an hour until they learn." This sounded like a reasonable compromise to Ron.

It did not sound reasonable to Mary. They argued over the issue most of the night.

 What do you believe Ron and Mary were *really* fighting about? How would you have resolved the situation?

If this scenario sounds silly, in many ways it is. Nevertheless, this battle is typical of the ones that rage in the early months of blending family life. Ron was trying to protect his children from what he believed were unreasonable demands. Mary wanted Ron to support her parental authority.

Resolving Anger

Remember, anger is a thermostat. Ron and Mary were not really fighting over who should have done what but over the larger issue of how to make parenting decisions as a team. They were learning each other's styles and temperament. Blending couples can avoid arguments similar to Ron and Mary's. Let's revisit our story and see how the scenario might have changed if Mary and Ron had followed a different plan.

When they first married, if Ron, Mary, and the children had established rules for behavior, and Ron had affirmed Mary's authority to carry out those rules, the children would have been forewarned that Mary did, indeed, have the right to discipline them for disobedience.

Mary was wise to talk with Ron about teaching his children table manners before she said anything to the children. And Ron gave her the go ahead. That was certainly better than Mary's forging ahead on her own. However, had Mary shared with Ron that she planned to give them a 30 minute lesson after school, that would have been better still. Then Ron could have responded: "OK, but stick to 30 minutes. I think that's enough time to start."

Nevertheless, when Mary came to Ron and explained the children had deliberately defied her, Ron (under these rules) would have had no choice but to tell the children their behavior was unacceptable. Any other response would undermine Mary's authority. Ron might want to discuss with Mary in private his disagreement, but he would openly support her. Only then would the children listen to Mary and obey her rules.

If children sense division, they immediately move to divide and conquer.

Parental unity is much easier to live with than division. If children sense division, they immediately move to divide and conquer. We will deal with this issue again in week 10.

Are you holding on to a source of anger toward your stepchildren? Toward your mate? Identify it below.

_____

What do you feel would be necessary to dissolve this anger? Consider sharing your reply during CoupleTalk.

Repeat this week's Scripture memory verse. How does the advice to "be strong and take heart" encourage you as you think about resolving jealousy and anger?

YOUR UNIQUE FAMILY

*B*lending families come in many sizes and shapes. Some have a stepparent who is a first-time parent. Others consist of two adults, both of whom function as a stepparent to the other spouse's children. Some blending families have stepsiblings who live together in the same household. Others have stepsiblings who are present only on holidays or occasional weekends. In today's study we will consider some implications of the various stepparenting situations.

When One Is a First-Time Parent

Which type of family would you think is the most difficult to blend—one with a first-time parent or one with children from each side of the marriage? From my experience in dealing with blending families, the first is more difficult.

This conclusion is based on my observation that stepparents who have never had children have not yet learned that many time-honored parenting techniques do not work, although they sound good in theory. Most parents approach the parenting role with great ideas. Everyone of us has said somewhere along the way, "When I have children, this is the way it is going to be." Biological parents try out their ideas on the children when they are very young. They modify their theories as they move along, discarding many and keeping a few. They learn what works with their particular children, considering temperament and personality. By the time the children are school-aged, biological parents' ideas about raising children are much different than when they began.

I noticed this distinctly as I observed my stepson and his wife rear our grandchildren. When the first child was born, they were very strict. For example, this son had to eat all his food before leaving the table. By the time our granddaughter was born, many of their childrearing ideas had changed. Our granddaughter controlled what and how much she ate. When their last child was born, these parents who began with strict ideas about childrearing were much more relaxed.

Stepparents who have never had children have not yet learned that many time-honored parenting techniques do not work.

Stepparents who have never had children do not have the advantage of time and perspective. They enter the blending family with new ideas about parenting and are ready to try them out. The children, however, are older. These children talk back. These children know which buttons to push to manipulate the biological parent. These children are not the same now as they were when the biological parents first experimented.

Childhood development is important information for stepparents. If you are a first-time parent, take a few local college courses, read books on the subject, and talk with school teachers and Sunday School teachers. If you feel your stepchildren behave inappropriately, ask persons who work with that age group to give their opinions. Recognize that parenting is an area of life in which you have no first-hand knowledge—and learn. And the faster you learn, the better stepparent you will be.

Childhood development is important information for stepparents.

 If you are a first-time parent, devise a plan to increase your knowledge of your stepchildren's developmental stage. Write that plan below.

_____

_____

If you came into the marriage with children, recall an example of a parenting technique that didn't work for you. How can you be more understanding of your mate's frustrations if he or she is a first-time parent?

_____

_____

When Both Mates Are Stepparents

When both partners are stepparents, empathize with each other regarding the obstacles discussed this week. Putting yourself in the other person's shoes helps us have compassion for what the other one is experiencing. Avoid attitudes of superiority or judgmentalism. Determining the better stepparent or complaining will not improve your relationship with each other or with the children.

Talking about feelings helps both parents understand the situation. If your mate proposes a way to ease tensions, give it a try. Be open to new ideas. Remember—our spouses are "grace gifts" from God to provide perspective.

Be prepared to discuss stepparenting issues during CoupleTalk. Use this time as an opportunity to gain perspective from each other. Prayerfully consider suggestions from your spouse for resolving tensions surrounding these issues.

Stepsiblings

When both of you bring children into the marriage, the blend of the children will affect how you feel about your stepparenting. Depending on the ages and gender of the children, the blend may be considered the greatest or the worst thing that ever happened. Some children welcome a "new" brother or sister while others resent the "intruders." Also some children are naturally more flexible and low-key while others make a fuss about everything.

Often stepsiblings disturb the birth order for a child. Overnight, the situation may force Emily from an only child position to a middle child position. These adjustments are extremely difficult for children. Emily needs time to adjust to having siblings at all, much less the fact that one is older and one is younger.

An adopted child (or children) in the family offers yet another scenario, and it is an unfortunate fact that other siblings may taunt them. Children enhance themselves by criticizing others. And friendly or unfriendly competition is complicated by blood lines, or lack of them.

When stepsiblings live together on a regular basis, expect cries of "That's not fair. You treat them differently." Children rarely view a situation from your vantage point. Pleasing them with decisions happens occasionally, but don't count on it. When children who were not reared together must share space, time, and attention, you do not have the luxury of making everyone happy. At the same time, obvious favoritism breeds resentment. Be fair and be consistent.

Remember that we discussed earlier the stepparent's lack of control over how stepchildren relate to a stepparent. In the same way, parents cannot control the manner in which stepsiblings relate to one another. The sooner children learn to settle their own differences without your involvement, the better. Intervene only when a child is in emotional or physical danger.

At least stepsiblings are on a level playing field. When a new baby arrives, the other children will question mom or dad's love for them. They may feel they have lost their special place in the family. Don't wait for the problem to rear itself. If a baby is on the way or already a part of your family, assure the other children of your love. Affirm their place in your heart.

When you look at your children and wonder if the hassle is worth it, remember that kids grow and change. Brothers and sisters do fight—yet grow up to be adult friends. Family portraits continue to change, and time is a great healer.

Being Unique Is Not All Bad

There is no other blending family exactly like yours. You are forging new trails. Perhaps a familiar landscape looks appealing to you right now, but Paul warns us not to grow weary in well-doing. (See Galatians 6:9 in the margin.)

The next time your blending family gathers together, affirm your uniqueness. Point out advantages you have as a blending family. (Look back at day 1 of week 1 if you need reminders!) Use problem-solving situations as individual and family growth opportunities. A positive attitude toward your unique family goes a long way toward creating the harmony you desire.

Let us not become weary in doing good, for at the proper time we will reap a harvest if we do not give up.
—Galatians 6:9

Say this week's Scripture memory verse. What do you feel you are "waiting for" from the Lord for your blending family? List at least one possibility.

_____

_____

COUPLETALK

For you to complete

1. If you are the stepparent, what issues from this study most closely parallel your situation?

_____

_____

2. List two new ways of being a more effective stepparent that you learned this week.

_____

_____

3. Does something need changing in your blended family? Describe how you might effectively initiate a change.

_____

_____

4. If you are the biological parent, what insight did you gain that will help you be more supportive to your mate?

_____

For you to share with your spouse

1. Sit facing each other.
2. Have each stepparent share his or her feelings about being a stepparent. (Biological parents will have a chance to share next week.) Complete this sharing before reviewing your responses above.
3. Discuss your responses to the activity above.
4. Discuss issues related to jealousy or anger that need to be resolved.
5. Tell one thing you really love about each other.
6. Say together the unit Scripture memory verse.
7. Pray for each other, either silently or aloud.

REDUCE REFEREEING

Arthur was caught totally off guard when he realized his family was not blending. Before they married, he was confident that Crystal and their three children would fit together perfectly. Crystal's older son was away at college. Arthur's children lived with their mom as custodial parent. Except for every other weekend visits from his children, he and Crystal lived alone.

With such an easy arrangement, Arthur was convinced this blending stuff would be a snap. After all, the children were with them such a small amount of time. Within just a few months, however, Arthur wondered if he had made the biggest mistake of his life. Weekend visits were a nightmare! Crystal seemed to dislike his kids. The children resented Crystal. Arthur was constantly in a war against both sides. What he believed would be easy now seemed impossible.

Arthur was very naive, but probably no more so than most biological parents who try to blend families. In fact, Arthur's situation was typical.

Although we touched on this subject earlier, this week's material concentrates on who I believe to be the most neglected member of a blending family: the biological parent. Stepparents and their struggles receive far more attention than those of biological parents. Biological parents experience an equally difficult adjustment in blending families. They, too, are overwhelmed.

This week we will explore their family position, make suggestions and seek solutions. As you study, think about God as a biological Father, sharing His Son with Mary and Joseph, who were the custodial parents. This human analogy does not fully compare, but it does remind us that God understands and cares about our family situation.

What You'll Study
DAY 1
• **Caught in the Middle**
DAY 2
• **Blaming Your Mate**
DAY 3
• **Being Defensive**
DAY 4
• **Trying to Juggle**
DAY 5
• **Redefining the Role**

This Week You Will:
• determine reasons why you may feel caught in the middle between your children and your spouse;
• replace tendencies to blame or be defensive with more effective parenting techniques;
• re-define your role in the family drama to blend more easily.

This Week's Scripture Memory Verse
"Those who hope in the Lord will renew their strength. They will soar on wings like eagles; they will run and not grow weary, they will walk and not be faint" (Isaiah 40:31).

CAUGHT IN THE MIDDLE

Many biological parents feel "pulled apart."

Many biological parents describe themselves as feeling "pulled apart." On the one hand, their mates expect their support as authority figures with the children. On the other hand, the children complain that the stepparent is unfair. Both want the biological parent to take their "side." The biological parent knows that either choice will alienate the other "side."

If you are a biological parent, have you felt caught in the middle?
❑ Yes ❑ No
What have you tried to do to get out of the middle?

How the Dilemma Develops

Arthur, whom you met in the introductory story, felt caught in the middle. He loved Crystal, and he loved his two children. He simply did not understand why they could not get along. Since the children visited only two weekends each month, Arthur tried to make these weekends special. He usually planned special trips and fun activities.

Crystal, however, implied that Arthur was a Disneyland dad. "The children need more of a home environment," she said, suggesting they spend most weekends at home. "We can work together on projects around the house and rent a movie. Trips and amusement parks should be for special occasions."

Arthur was unsure about the children's reaction, but he said he would try it. *Perhaps I have been carried away on planning every weekend as a major event*, he thought. When the children arrived for the weekend they asked, "Where are we going today?"

Arthur explained: "We're not going anywhere this weekend. Crystal and I decided that we will spend this weekend painting and decorating your rooms. Won't that be fun?" Arthur could see disappointment on the children's faces. "Come on guys, give it a chance. We're going to have a good time with this," he promised.

While the weekend progressed reasonably well, Arthur felt a little like he was walking on eggs, certain that one would break any minute. Before the children left, Brian said, "Dad, can we go to Six Flags next time?"

"Why?" asked Arthur. "Didn't you have fun this weekend? Don't you like your rooms?"

"Oh, it was OK. I just want to go to Six Flags. Mom never takes us there."

"Yeah," agreed Jill. "Let's go to Six Flags next time."

"I'll think about it," Arthur offered. *After all, they spent this weekend around the house*, he thought. *We can alternate weekends for outings*. Since Arthur assumed Crystal would not agree with his plans, he waited until the Thursday before the next visitation weekend to tell her.

"You want to do what?" asked Crystal.

"They asked if we could go to Six Flags, and I think we should. We stayed home last time, so this weekend we can go out," explained Arthur. "You can't expect us to stay home every weekend they visit. I'll take them by myself if you don't want to go," Arthur added defensively.

"That's not the point," Crystal argued. "I thought we agreed that outings were reserved for special occasions, not an every weekend thing."

"Let's just see how it goes this time." Privately Arthur hoped they would have so much fun as a family that Crystal would change her mind. Surely, he could negotiate a win/win in this situation.

From your position as a biological parent or a stepparent, how do you identify with the story of Arthur and Crystal?

Arthur: _____

Crystal: _____

Why the Dilemma Develops

Arthur was trapped in a syndrome that is typical for many biological parents. Arthur felt guilty that his children had suffered from the divorce. He saw the pain in their eyes. Therefore, he worked hard to make them laugh and have fun. Before Arthur remarried, it broke his heart when Brian would sometimes ask, "Can Mom come along next time?" Arthur could not take away their pain; it was difficult for him to say no to them about anything.

Any parent can appreciate Arthur's dilemma. Because he was separated from his children, he tried to turn every visit into a major event. Many of Arthur's actions toward his children were motivated by the fear that his children would stop loving him. Arthur's guilt over the divorce made him feel unlovable. Therefore, he believed he had to win his children's love again and again.

Arthur did not want to rock the boat. He tried to please everyone all the time—an impossible task. When Arthur tried to please only the children, he was fairly successful. But now Crystal was in the picture. Suddenly, Arthur felt trapped in the middle between the people he loved.

What motivates us to play middleman?

Identify the factors that led to Arthur's role as middleman between his wife and children.

_____

_____

What mistakes did Arthur make? Crystal?

_____

_____

Getting Out of the Middle

By putting himself in the middle, Arthur contributed to the battle raging between Crystal and the children. Let's step back and take a look at the big picture.

How do we get out of the middle?

Although the battle appeared on the surface to be about weekend visits, that issue was simply the indicator for the real problem. The basic tension came from how each family member was adjusting to and acting out his or her new role.

Crystal needed Arthur to respect her opinion and to support her as an authority figure for the children. She wanted her vote to count in family planning.

The children needed continuity in their relationship with their father. Obviously, taking trips was more fun than working around the house. They were self-centered and wanted their Disneyland dad back! They also resented Crystal's influence and were determined to resist any motherly efforts on her part.

Arthur's only way out of this dilemma was to stop trying to please both sides. Without realizing it and while trying to be fair, Arthur actually had encouraged the battle. Rather than attempting to make remarkably wise decisions on his own, Arthur needed to work with the family to determine workable solutions.

Crystal and the children needed time to develop their relationship. They needed to work out their differences without Arthur's interference. The more Arthur got in the middle, the more he got in the way. Often, the most we can do when family members are at odds is to pray for them and wait.

What about Crystal? Pressing for an immediate change in the children's relationship with their father was a battle she could not win. The weekend paint party was a beginning, but by imposing her all or nothing mentality, she set up the family conflict.

What other advice would you give Arthur? Crystal?

_____

_____

Is there a similar situation in your blending family? How can you apply your own advice?

_____

_____

As human beings, discouragement is inevitable. Isaiah 40 speaks to such discouragement. Our memory verse for this week is the closing verse of the 40th chapter. Take the time to read for yourself this magnificent chapter in your Bible.

What does it mean to you to "run and not grow weary"?

_____

_____

Pray, asking God for the energy to keep at the task of blending your family.

Those who hope in the Lord will renew their strength. They will soar on wings like eagles; they will run and not grow weary, they will walk and not be faint.
—Isaiah 40:31

BLAMING YOUR MATE

The blame game often accompanies the "middleman" game. When biological parents feel discouraged because the family is not blending as they imagined it would, they often blame the stepparent for the problem. They may say (or sometimes only think): "This chaos is all your fault. If only you were more understanding, we wouldn't have these problems. They're just kids; you're an adult. You knew what you getting into when you married me." Or, perhaps they ask, "What do you expect me to do, get rid of my children?" Of course, none of these accusations is helpful. They are just outward expressions from a biological parent in pain and feeling trapped.

Accusations are outward expressions from a biological parent in pain and feeling trapped.

🌿 **As a biological parent, how many of the above sentences have you said or thought concerning your mate? (You won't have to report on this during Couple Talk. Be honest!) Underline them.**

As a stepparent, underline those sentences above which your mate has said, or at least you felt he or she would like to have said.

Unstated Expectations

Priscilla was a biological parent. One of the things that nurtured her relationship with Charles was that he loved her children. Priscilla had three boys, and they needed a father. Their own father had all but disappeared from their lives.

Priscilla failed to realize that providing a father for her boys was actually her fantasy. Although it had been two years since their father left, the boys still imagined mom and dad would get back together. While Priscilla's sons enjoyed most of their time with Charles, they certainly did not want him to take their father's place.

After Priscilla and Charles married, Charles moved into Priscilla's house. When Charles visited the house before their marriage, Priscilla closed the doors to the boys' rooms. Now, Charles saw inside—a mess. Having spent time in the Navy, Charles knew the value of order and discipline. He decided to "whip the boys into shape." Those were the words he used in describing his task to a friend at work. Since Charles' friend also lived in a blending family, he simply smiled and said, "Good luck."

One Saturday morning, Charles woke the boys at 8:00 a.m. "OK, you guys. Roll out. We've got work to do. Breakfast is almost ready; then we're going to put these rooms in order."

The boys reluctantly followed Charles' orders and by lunchtime their rooms were spotless. After a few days, however, the boys reverted back to their routines and their rooms were messy again. Charles barked more orders at them. Not surprisingly, the boys rebelled against Charles' attempts to change them. This time, they dragged their feet on cleaning up and made the whole process as difficult as possible. Their fantasy of their real father returning was stronger than ever.

One day, when Charles ordered Sandy to make his bed and put his pajamas in his drawer, Sandy shouted, "When my dad comes back, you're outta here, man."

Barely containing his anger, Charles sent Sandy to his room. "You can stay in your room until you are ready to apologize."

When the stalemate continued into the second hour, Priscilla did not know what to do. She loved Charles. But she wished that he could show a little more compassion with her kids. *Why did he have to be so military about it?* she thought. *Couldn't he see that the children resented his presence? What was she to do?*

🍂 **What was Priscilla's unstated expectation in marrying Charles?**

_____

_____

What was Charles' unstated expectation?

_____

_____

Like many blended couples, Priscilla and Charles did not discuss their unstated expectations before the wedding. Certainly Priscilla had imagined Charles as a loving father to her sons. She never intended that he act like a drill sergeant. Although Priscilla might have overreacted to Charles' direct style, her intention was to protect her children.

Charles assumed that Priscilla would appreciate a firm stand with her boys. He had no idea they viewed him as an obstacle in their fantasy of mom and dad together again. Also, He didn't understand that his authoritarian style–after their mother's laxness and their father's absence–would produce such an uproar.

Now Charles blamed Priscilla for ineffective discipline and poor housekeeping. Priscilla accused Charles of behaving like a bull in a china closet. Neither felt warm toward the other.

Priscilla was right in resisting Charles' authoritarian rule. However, Priscilla and Charles needed to discuss the issue of discipline and establish a plan they could implement and enforce together. Without a mutual plan, Charles went ahead with what he thought was right. When Priscilla did not support him, Charles was hurt and confused.

Even when parents disagree in private about parenting methods, children need to see them as a united team. Being a parenting team was the farthest thing from either of their minds. Charles and Priscilla were more like boxers in a ring.

Moving Beyond Blame

Blame is never productive. Because it directs attention at someone or something else, blame prevents an individual from looking inward for a solution to a problem. Blame is a wish that the other person would change. I discovered that when I focus my prayers on what I believe the other person needs to do, rather than asking God what I need to be doing, I actually am blaming that other person for the dilemma. Such prayers keep us from experiencing God's work in us to change our character to reflect His likeness.

Many couples in blending families make the same mistakes as Charles and Priscilla. Blending a family is a skill, and like any other skill, it is learned and practiced one day at a time. With patience and without blame, blending families have the potential to be supportive family units.

🍃 **In the Sermon on the Mount, Jesus cautioned us against looking for the fault in another person rather than seeing our own faults. Check the response(s) below that characterize you.**
- ❏ I am a blamer. I generally look for someone else to blame for a conflict.
- ❏ I try not to blame someone else until I have examined my part in the situation.
- ❏ I go back and forth. I'd like to be more consistent in looking to my own faults rather than blaming others.

🍃 **If you have been critical of your spouse, write a prayer below asking God to help you focus on your own responsibilities.**

_____

_____

_____

🍃 **Read this week's Scripture memory verse in the margin. Allow these thoughts to encourage you about your ability to grow and change when you depend upon the Lord's strength.**

"Why do you look at the speck of sawdust in your brother's eye and pay no attention to the plank in your own eye? How can you say to your brother, "Let me take the speck out of your eye," when all the time there is a plank in your own eye? You hypocrite, first take the plank out of your own eye, and then you will see clearly to remove the speck from your brother's eye."
—Matthew 7:3-5

Those who hope in the Lord will renew their strength. They will soar on wings like eagles; they will run and not grow weary, they will walk and not be faint. —Isaiah 40:31

DAY 3

BEING DEFENSIVE

*B*iological parents are defensive about their children, and naturally so. They describe their children in glowing terms. They may see their children through rose-colored glasses. They may find it hard to believe their children would deliberately misbehave.

When I hear, "My children would never lie to me,"—or a similar statement—I almost want to laugh. Do these parents really believe their children are not affected by the same human condition as everyone else? Children are born with a sin nature. They will employ a variety of methods to get their way and avoid punishment. Lying is one of those methods, and I seriously doubt that any of us survived childhood without lying to our parents at some point.

When stepparents point out character flaws they see in their mate's biological children, they are likely to encounter a defensive wall that translates: "That simply cannot be. My children wouldn't do that." At that point, stepparents often react with disbelief and step up the accusations. "Look for yourself. Don't you see the negative behavior?" Actually, in many cases the answer is no. What may appear to be obvious flaws to you may not be obvious to a biological parent.

If you are a biological parent trying to gain objectivity about your children, avoid the trap of defensiveness. Defensiveness is a reaction to feeling threatened. We may feel like we are trapped, cornered, have our backs up against a wall. When we have not learned the skills to respond appropriately to conflict, we may react in self-defeating ways. We may think our only options are running away or fighting back. This "fight or flight" mentality may lead to several ways of defending ourselves.

What would be your general approach when you feel threatened?
- ❏ anger
- ❏ divert attention to something or someone else
- ❏ withdraw
- ❏ lash out verbally
- ❏ get depressed, moody
- ❏ give in to your attacker

We tend to be defensive about our children when we have not been able to see them as separate entities from ourselves. Therefore, to criticize my child is to criticize me. When I am able to see my children as distinct individuals, I do not have to regard their behavior as a reflection upon me. Here are some ways to develop a focused lens as you look at your children.

Recognize Your Limitations

Many times biological parents bring to the blending family an unwillingness to face their own inadequacies as parents. It is a defense mechanism. However, everyone is inadequate when it comes to parenting. We all make mistakes because we all are human. We have all thought, *When I have children, I certainly will parent differently than my parents.* We recognize the mistakes our parents made, and we probably understand why they made them. We may even excuse our parents for those mistakes. However, as adults we accept that some issues should have been handled differently.

But what happens once we have children? We revert to the old models of parenting we observed from our significant relationships when we were children. What makes us believe we can be perfect parents? There are no perfect parents. We learn by trial and error. We make mistakes. We mess up, and certainly our children pay for those mistakes. Someday our children will undoubtedly say, "When I have children, I am not going to make the mistakes my parents did." Nevertheless, they will make mistakes, and their children will say the same thing about them. That is life.

Develop a focused lens as you look at your children

Only as biological parents admit their humanness and vulnerability will they be able to acknowledge that their children are not perfect. Then, biological parents can accept the criticism stepparents offer and evaluate it as useful information. Stepparents are of tremendous value to blending families, but only when the biological parent is able to avoid being overly defensive about the children.

This defensiveness is even more pronounced when the biological parent feels guilty for having caused the children pain. Many divorced parents realize that they have hurt their children. Out of their guilt, they will try all the harder to protect their children from further pain. Thus, when a stepparent criticizes the children or suggests punishment, the biological parent jumps to their defense. "They've been hurt enough. What they did is not all that bad. I've done things a lot worse than that. They're just kids."

As we discussed in week 8, the parent/child relationship during single parenting days was quite different than now. Previously the children were treated as little adults and companions. That particular role confusion often leads to relaxed standards of behavior. Some single parents have too much on their plates to worry about every single infraction. They save their limited strength for major battles. Thus, when the stepparent seems to be nit-picking, they react defensively.

🌿 **If you are the biological parent, circle the word(s) below that indicate how open you are to hearing criticism concerning your children.**

not at all   a little   some   most of the time   always

As a stepparent, how open do you think your mate is to hearing criticism about his or her children? Circle the word(s) above.

Model the Role

Is it possible that we as parents are defensive about our children's behavior because their behavior reflects on our own? Perhaps we have failed to live up to our own expectations. Maybe claiming our responsibility in the failed marriage or coming to terms with our grief remains difficult. Being able to honestly evaluate our own behavior is a prerequisite to objectively viewing someone else's.

🌿 **Defensiveness is as old as the garden of Eden. When God confronted Adam about his sin, how did he respond? Read Genesis 3:11-12 in the margin and underline Adam's explanation for his behavior.**

Adam and Eve were punished for their sin. We do not know exactly how their relationship was affected by their defensive, blaming behavior. We do know it has affected every relationship since then! When we own our own sin, confess it, repent, and receive God's forgiveness, we are better able to parent sinful children who also need forgiveness.

Kenneth put his six-year-old son to bed and led in prayer. Feeling guilty about losing his temper earlier in the evening, Kenneth asked God to forgive him. Little Ryan's turn came to say his prayers. He obediently asked God to forgive him for picking one of Mrs. Mitchell's roses. Like father, like son. A parent who can say, "I'm sorry," is more likely to produce a child who can admit wrongdoing.

And he [God] said, … "Have you eaten from the tree that I commanded you not to eat from?"

The man [Adam] said, "The woman you put here with me— she gave me some fruit from the tree, and I ate it."
—Genesis 3:11-12

He who heeds discipline shows the way to life, but whoever ignores correction leads others astray.
—Proverbs 10:17

He who ignores discipline despises himself, but whoever heeds correction gains understanding.
—Proverbs 15:32

He who spares the rod hates his son, but he who loves him is careful to discipline him.
—Proverbs 13:24

Learn to Say "No"

Good parenting often requires saying no to children as well as enforcing restrictions. God the Father is our example of a loving parent who disciplines us for our own good and sometimes says "no" as a way of demonstrating His love.

🌱 Read the verses from Proverbs in the margin. Using these verses, summarize the purpose of discipline.

_____

_____

Children need guidelines. Discipline shows them how to live life. It increases their understanding of what behaviors will bring them the greatest happiness. Most stepparents can readily identify for biological parents their weaknesses in discipline. When both husband and wife bring biological children to the marriage, finger pointing can become a way of life. When biological parents refuse to listen to the observations of the stepparent, they block understanding. Discipline is a mark of love—God's love for parents, and a parent's love for their children.

Discipline is not synonymous with punishment. Discipline involves rigorous training. The emphasis of discipline is on building character. When a child learns that positive things happen when he behaves a certain way, that child will repeat the behavior. As simple as that statement may seem, it will profoundly affect the dynamics of your family life.

🌱 Check the ways you positively reward your children for good behavior.
- ❑ hugs, kisses
- ❑ words of approval
- ❑ a pat on the back
- ❑ treats
- ❑ privileges
- ❑ attention
- ❑ other? _____

🌱 Repeat this week's Scripture memory verse. God promises that we will "walk and not be faint." How does that promise relate to training a child?

_____

_____

_____

TRYING TO JUGGLE

During the early months—and sometimes early years—biological parents often describe their role in a blended family as similar to that of a referee. The biological parent tries desperately to keep the children and stepparent from being over the line with one another. They encourage fair treatment, and if one family member attempts to take unfair advantage of another, the biological parent calls "foul." Of course, no one assigned this role to biological parents; they just assume the responsibility and the remaining family members go along with the plan.

Some biological parents abandon their referee position and take on the role of juggler. Instead of the seemingly futile effort to get both sides to play fair, they relate to one side at a time. When biological parents play juggler, they live emotionally between the children and the stepparent, relating to each separately. This happens more often when the biological parent is not the custodial parent; however, it also can occur when the children and stepparent live in the same home.

When biological parents play juggler, they live emotionally between the children and the stepparent, relating to each separately.

The Juggling Act on the Road

Joe found the referee role so difficult that he decided he would juggle relationships and see his children apart from his wife. Joe's son Buck was away attending college. His daughter Leslie was a teenager living with her mother.

Rather than Leslie visiting his house on her regular weekends, Joe planned time with her a couple of days each week. His work schedule was flexible, so he picked up Leslie at school and they would take a picnic snack to the park or grab a milkshake and take a drive. The visits were relaxed and pleasant.

Joe also visited the college a couple of times each month and spent the day with Buck. Karen, Joe's wife, realized what Joe was doing; however, she enjoyed their life without the hassle of the kids. Joe thought, *Maybe once the children are grown, we'll be a family.*

Once Joe decided to juggle his relationships, the tension in his life abated considerably. There were no more petty squabbles, and he didn't have to hear the kids complaining that Karen was unreasonable. On the other hand, Karen had no reason to criticize Leslie or Buck. For the first time in a long while, Joe experienced some peace.

However, Joe did not realize the tremendous amount of time and energy this juggling act would require. As a single parent, Joe could hardly find time to juggle two balls—his job and his children. Now he was married and juggling a third ball—his marriage. Joe's juggling act could not go on forever. Eventually, he would drop one or more balls. Karen's ball was the first to go.

One night Karen said to him, "How long are you going to go on like this? I hardly see you anymore."

"I'm tired of it, too," Joe replied. "But I have to spend some time with the kids."

"I might as well have remained single if we are going to live like this. In fact, I think I saw you more when I was single."

Joe and Karen talked far into the night. Joe's juggling act was not a workable solution. Not only was he keeping Karen and the children from ever blending, but also he was tearing himself apart.

🌿 **If you were Joe, what would you do at this point? Check one.**
❏ Let Karen and the kids work out their squabbles over time.
❏ Stop seeing the children.
❏ Continue to juggle the relationships.
❏ Return to being referee.
❏ other? _____

Instead of becoming an expert juggler, turn that energy into blending a family.

Juggling is a skill that must be practiced continually over a long period of time in order to achieve perfection. Instead of learning to become an expert juggler, biological parents must turn that energy into blending a family. The resulting family unit will be worth the effort and the pain.

The Juggling Act at Home

Barry's situation was a little different, yet produced the same results. His wife Cali was constantly arguing with his children, Debbie and Donald. Barry felt like he was in an emotional tug-of-war. He blamed Cali for being picky concerning his kids; yet he was defensive and hard to reason with. Often, he took the children's side when Cali complained. In other words, Barry was a typical biological parent.

Many of Cali's arguments with Debbie and Donald concerned their refusal at times to speak to her. Both children came to the kitchen in the morning while Cali was sitting at the breakfast table, took a soda from the refrigerator (another thing Cali argued with them about), put a pastry in the toaster, and then ate their breakfast in the living room while watching TV. Neither of them acknowledged Cali's presence.

The first few times Cali felt ignored, she tried to initiate a conversation, but received only brief responses. Cali then decided to see what would happen if she said nothing. Nothing is what she received. Cali was not even sure they knew she was in the room.

The three of them became so good at ignoring each other that Barry felt like he lived in two worlds. If he carried on a conversation with Cali, his children tuned out. If he talked to his children, Cali went to the bedroom.

One day Cali finally exploded. "I think it's about time you kids learned some manners," she said. "Could you at least say 'Good morning' when you walk into the kitchen?"

"You don't say anything to us, either," Debbie shot back.

"I used to, but I got tired of your silence," said Cali.

"I spoke to you if you spoke to me," argued Donald.

"Yes, but reluctantly," countered Cali.

At this point Barry joined in: "Now Cali, be fair. If they spoke, you can't really know that they spoke reluctantly."

"You didn't hear them," Cali replied. "All I'm saying is it's about time they displayed some manners. I'll speak, but I expect more than a grunt in return."

Barry turned to the children and asked: "Well, kids what do you say? Does that sound fair?"

Over the next few weeks, neither Cali nor the children would make the first move. They were stalemated over who would speak first to whom. Sound silly? Perhaps so. But this issue represented the tip of the iceberg of distance between the children and Cali.

The silence became more and more a way of life. Barry conversed with his children and then with Cali. He grew more despondent as time passed.

Trying to juggle relationships between children and stepparents at home is as difficult as juggling relationships across the miles.

🍃 **What needs to happen in this family to get Barry out of the middle and bring peace to this home?**

_____

_____

The Show Must Go On

Blending requires interaction on the part of the participants. By playing the referee, Joe and Barry were stopping the interaction. They were preventing the struggle. Struggle is part of the blending process. By interfering with the struggle, biological parents halt the process. The birth of something good is seldom easy.

Let me share a story to illustrate. One day, a man walking in the woods happened upon a chrysalis that was shaking. The man could see that a butterfly was trying to get out. The butterfly struggled and struggled in its effort to break free. Feeling compassion for the insect, the man reached into his pocket and took out his pen knife. Ever so gently, the man gradually enlarged the opening to the chrysalis so that the butterfly could easily emerge, which it did. However, the butterfly was unable to fly because it had not strengthened its wings in the struggle.

None of us enjoys struggle. However, struggle often produces growth. I grew and matured more in the years following my divorce than in all the years preceding it. The growth was extremely painful, but as I look back, I am grateful for the maturing process. My blending family experience has also been painful at times. Nevertheless, the pain has proven to be worthwhile.

> **Struggle is part of the blending process. By interfering with the struggle, biological parents halt the process.**

🍃 **How have the struggles in your own life paid dividends? Tell about one experience.**

_____

_____

🍃 **How have the difficulties of blending a family strengthened you as an individual?**

_____

_____

If you are the biological parent, perhaps you are asking, "What should I do, then? Just let my spouse and children duke it out?" In week 10 you will have the opportunity to set guidelines, along with your mate, that will address issues of the children's behavior and appropriate discipline. When behavior problems are addressed on the front end, so that all parties know what to expect, you will not be drawn into a tug-of-war over each happening.

In week 11 I will give additional information on the best problem-solving tool I have yet discovered for blending families: the family meeting. For today, resolve that you will willingly give up the referee or juggler role in favor of one that is going to eventually lead to the blending of your family. If you enjoy the role in the middle, have fun. You will be there a long time!

🌱 **Repeat this week's Scripture memory verse. What would soaring on eagles' wings be compared to in your blending family? Circle the words that apply:**

> peace   contentment   joy   achievement   harmony
> relaxation   satisfaction   exhilaration

🌹 **Commit this vision to God. Ask Him to bring it about.**

DAY 5

REDEFINING THE ROLE

*T*his week we have observed the struggles and pain of a biological parent in a blending family. How can the biological parent stay out of the middle and avoid being pulled apart? How can the biological parent (and stepparent for that matter) avoid blaming the mate for the turmoil? How can biological parents stop being defensive about their children? How can biological parents avoid being referees and jugglers? Those are the questions we will consider today.

Putting Your Partner First

The couple relationship must be a priority.

In any marriage the couple relationship must be a priority. Marriage is a commitment to spouse above all others, including children. While there are exceptions to that statement (we will look at them later), the marriage vows place the commitment to husband and wife as most important.

For many biological parents, the decision to place their spouse before the children will be very difficult. But divided loyalties only invite chaos. As Jesus said, "Every … household divided against itself will not stand" (Matthew 12:25). If a biological parent exhibits greater loyalty toward his or her children, those children may use that loyalty to destroy the blending family. The marriage relationship is the basis for your new blending family.

 In your blending family, where is your primary loyalty? Put your initials on the line.

the children	both	my spouse

Where do you see your spouse's primary loyalty? Put his or her initials on the line.

The previous exercise may have been very difficult for you. Do not judge yourself or your spouse too harshly. Total commitment takes time. While I firmly believe that such a commitment is necessary before a family can blend, it still is a difficult commitment for many biological parents.

Keeping the couple relationship primary in the marriage helps the children understand the concept of marriage. They learn from the marriage model they see lived out at home. If they see a torn relationship, characterized by anger and accusations, they may struggle in their own relationships later in life. Remember—many of these children have already watched one marriage and home disintegrate. Now, more than anything, they need to see a couple totally committed to the marriage first, and then the family.

There is one exception to that standard, and that is when there is evidence of physical or sexual abuse. None of us likes to think this could happen. However, sin is still prevalent in our world. Abuse occurs more often in blending families than in nuclear families because there is not the blood relationship between children and stepparents. In nuclear families, this biological bond offers some protection for children.

Since children are more vulnerable to physical and sexual abuse, biological parents must be protective, not in a negative way to create a feeling of distrust, but in a positive way that recognizes all people sin and fall short of God's glory. When abuse is suspected, the children are the priority.

Working Together

When children believe they can exploit the biological parent's efforts to protect them, even against the stepparent, the children usually will take advantage of it. Repeatedly, children in blending families instigate a variety of episodes to increase conflict, especially if the couple is at odds concerning parenting issues. Although many blending family children fantasize about life as it used to be, another divorce would only be tragic and detrimental to their lives.

Here are some suggestions for preventing the kinds of power plays seen thus far in this week's case studies:

1. If you are the biological parent, support the stepparent, even when you disagree with what has been said or done. Do not allow the children to play one parent against the other. This approach is extremely difficult when you feel the stepparent has crossed the line. Nevertheless, by supporting the stepparent's authority, children are more likely to accept that person's role. Whenever a biological parent argues with a stepparent, the children quickly surmise that the

"Come, all you who are thirsty,
come to the waters;
and you who have no money,
come, buy and eat!
Come, buy wine and milk
without money and without
cost.
Why spend money on what is
not bread,
and your labor on what does
not satisfy?
Listen, listen to me, and eat
what is good,
and your soul will delight in
the richest of fare.
You will go out in joy
and be led forth in peace;
the mountains and hills
will burst into song before you,
and all the trees of the field
will clap their hands."
—Isaiah 55:1-2,12

stepparent has no authority in the home. Work together as a team to eliminate the need to referee.

2. If you are the stepparent, talk privately with the biological parent before announcing rules to the children. Do not disagree with your mate about the children when they are present; a united force is a winning combination.

If children observe early in the blending process that the biological parent supports the stepparent in all circumstances—and vice versa—their resistance will lessen.

 Read Isaiah 55:1-2,12 in the margin. This passage offers great hope for blending families who struggle in the early years to create a positive and nurturing family environment.

This passage is packed with hope! The first two verses invite us to eat and drink freely of that which only God can offer. If we try to blend our families on our own, we will fail. If we allow God to guide us in the process, we will succeed.

I especially love verse 12. It is a promise I have seen fulfilled for many blending families. They go out with joy and are led forth in peace. Most traveled over some rough terrain, but they arrived. Peace *is* possible for both biological parents and stepparents. Trust in the Lord!

Love Never Fails

There may be a time when you and your spouse believe that love has failed. Remember—Paul wrote in 1 Corinthians 13:8, "Love never fails." Frequently, love simply has to wait for God's timing. Our Scripture memory verse this week says, "those who hope in the Lord" will have their strength renewed. Biblical hope is not a heavenly wish but a heavenly promise. Faith carries us when all hope seems to be gone. Remind yourself of God's promises to you. He is a faithful, covenant-keeping God!

 Say this week's Scripture memory verse. Since it is longer than most, use these word prompters if you wish: hope, renew, soar, run, walk.

COUPLETALK

For you to complete

1. Look back over the notes you made each day. What are some ideas or thoughts that you would like to share with your mate?

_____

_____

2. In day 3 you each placed an X on the line concerning the ability of the biological parent to accept criticism. Share the reasons why you placed the X where you did.

3. What do you find to be the most difficult aspects of being a biological parent?

_____

_____

4. If you are the biological parent, list some ways the stepparent could help you do a better job of parenting. Or, if you are the stepparent, list some ways the biological parent could do a better job. Be constructive rather than critical.

_____

_____

For you to share with your spouse

1. Sit facing each other.
2. Allow the biological parent (both of you if you each brought children into the marriage) to share his or her feelings about being a biological parent in the blending family.
3. Allow the biological parent(s) to share some ways the stepparent can help him or her do a better job. Be constructive rather than critical.
4. Share your responses to the questions above that have not already been dealt with.
5. Tell your spouse one thing you really love about each other.
6. Say together the Scripture memory verse.
7. Pray for each other, either silently or aloud.

SET GUIDELINES FOR BEHAVIOR

*L*isa had problems with her husband's two sons, especially when they picked on her son Hank. Hank was smaller than Bobby and Gary; they called him names like "microbe" and "beetle." Hank usually wound up in a fight with them, which he always lost. When Lisa complained to her husband Terry, he replied: "They're just being boys. They don't mean anything by it."

One particular day Lisa happened to look out the window as the boys got into a scuffling match. Lisa's anger exploded. She ran out of the house, grabbed Bobby and Gary by the arms, and marched them to their father.

"What have you two done now?" Terry asked.

"She probably wants to gripe about what we did to her precious baby!" Bobby replied.

Again, Lisa's anger was out of control. Although Terry tried to calm her, she continued raging for half an hour. Terry felt caught in the middle. He agreed that his sons needed to stop teasing Hank, but Hank sometimes provoked their ridicule by acting like a baby. *He is his mother's pet,* Terry thought.

Biological parents are instinctively protective of their children. This protective instinct does not necessarily extend to stepchildren. If Lisa had seen two neighborhood bullies taunt Hank, she might have been upset, but not as intensely as she was over her stepchildren's behavior. She probably would have warned Hank to keep his distance and ignore their taunts.

Blended family couples must establish enforceable guidelines for their combined children that both parents agree to and that the children clearly understand. In order to operate as a unified front and provide stability to the family unit, couples must determine the purpose of discipline, acceptable and unacceptable behaviors, and appropriate consequences. As much as possible, older children should participate in determining consequences of misbehavior. Children feel secure when rules are established and enforced consistently by parents.

What You'll Study
DAY 1
- The Goal of Discipline

DAY 2
- Setting Guidelines Together

DAY 3
- Working as a Team

DAY 4
- Choosing the Battles

DAY 5
- Emphasizing Grace

This Week You Will:
- focus on the goal of discipline as you set guidelines;
- work together as a couple and as a family to determine acceptable behavior and consequences of misbehavior;
- carefully choose the behaviors you want to correct;
- emphasize grace over law as you enforce guidelines.

This Week's Scripture Memory Verse
"If it is possible, as far as it depends on you, live at peace with everyone" (Romans 12:18).

THE GOAL OF DISCIPLINE

*Y*ou've heard the familiar expression, "Can't see the forest for the trees." In the case of blending families, "trees" are individual needs and problems of family members. The "forest" is the goal of becoming a family unit that moves harmoniously in the same direction. In a blended family, reacting to an immediate situation is often easier than stepping back and taking the long look. However, stepping back ultimately may do more good than stepping in.

What are some of the individual needs and problems unique to a blending family?

- First, a blended family brings together children in varying stages of grief who have not shared life together and come from different backgrounds. Blending them into a cohesive family unit—especially when one or more may be hostile to the process—requires love, time, and patience.

- Second, two adults—at least one of whom has been accustomed to single parenting—are attempting to blend parenting styles. Perhaps as a single parent, you were more relaxed about rules and gave more individual attention to each child. Now you must share time with your spouse and possibly with stepchildren.

- A third issue relates to damaged egos, both on the part of parents and children. A former spouse or parent can do or say hurtful things that leave us with low self-esteem. Accepting our limitations and imperfections is difficult. "You're not my real father" is hard to hear when a parent feels personally inadequate. Children do not want to hear critical comments from a stepparent. They may interpret discipline as punishment and react negatively.

- Finally, biological parents must deal with the preferences each feels for his or her children. We desperately want our mates to love our children as much as we do. We struggle to love his or her children in the same way. Placing this unlikely expectation upon each other adds to the difficulty when discipline becomes an issue. "She's too soft on her kids," or "He's stricter with my children than he is with his own " are often-heard comments.

Like an orchestra trying to harmonize with varying degrees of musical training and ability, a blended family must practice together for a long time to accomplish a unified sound. At first, we hear only the screeching violins or the blue notes of the trumpet. Some day, we hope to project for those listening and observing a melodious, blending composition that prompts them to say, "My, don't they work well together!"

A blended family must practice together for a long time to accomplish a unified sound.

What Is Our Parenting Goal?

Don't try to be a perfect parent. This expectation may be the biggest trap for stepparents in a blended family. We easily succumb to discouragement when things

For this reason a man will leave his father and mother and be united to his wife, and they will become one flesh.
—Genesis 2:24

do not work out as we had hoped or planned. Ultimately, the goal of parenting is to work our way out of a job—the children leave home and make a life for themselves. Read Genesis 2:24 in the margin. In order for children to grow up and take care of themselves, they must learn self-control.

On the road to becoming self-controlled, a child must have parental restraints, called *discipline,* until such time as those restraints are no longer needed. Think of discipline as similar to training wheels on a bicycle. The training wheels keep the bicycle from turning abruptly to the left or right so that it maintains balance. Parents and children look forward to the day when the training wheels come off and the child balances the bicycle on his own. In the same way, parents look forward to the day when vigilant supervision is no longer necessary.

A mother noticed her three-year-old sitting in the "time out" corner. "Sarah, why are you sitting in time out?" her mother asked.

Sarah replied, "I got lipstick on your bedspread." Sarah knew she was wrong to play with her mother's make-up. She knew the consequences of such behavior. Therefore, she just eliminated the middle-man and carried out the punishment! Children cannot consistently monitor their own behavior. They need guidance from a moral authority with more life experience and wisdom than their own.

Discipline is a process by which external control becomes internal control. The test of discipline is this: Does he or she act the same way when parents/authority figures are not around? If so, the child has internalized controls.

Train a child in the way he should go, and when he is old he will not turn from it.
—Proverbs 22:6

🐾 **Read Proverbs 22:6 in the margin. There is a difference between telling and training. List some necessary elements of training.**

_____

_____

Good coaching requires practicing the drills, constant feedback, and more drills. What if the coach spent each practice lecturing or drawing plays on the chalkboard? Athletes must practice. The next time you are tempted to verbally reprimand your child, ask yourself, *Does he or she know the play (my expectations)?* If so, offer correction and decide how you can best provide positive reinforcement. Practicing good behavior is more effective than rehearsing bad behavior.

Modeling correct behavior on your part goes a long way toward producing well-trained children. When we model peace and harmony, our children are less likely to squabble and fight. If we convey stress, our children often show signs of anxiety. They may withdraw, act out, say hurtful things, develop poor sleeping patterns, or overeat. Parents who find fault with their children's behavior should be willing to ask themselves, *What am I modeling?*

The Goal Is Not a Robot

If you want to produce someone who obeys every command without mistakes, then work on plans for a robot. For years I've been waiting on one that will mow my yard. The goal of parenting is not to produce perfect children.

An obedient child does not have to be mechanical or robotic. Children display a natural curiosity about the world and a willingness to explore it. In doing so, they may place themselves in danger. Parents cannot stand idly by while a toddler heads for an open fireplace. Training children is a balancing act between encouraging risk-taking while teaching obedience. We may err on the side of authoritarianism by rigid rule-setting. We may err on the side of permissiveness when children are allowed to be in control. Finding the balance for you and your children is tricky. You and your mate have a personal comfort level with what is permissive and what is stifling. The material in day 3 will help you work as a team to determine a training plan for your children.

🍂 **What parenting style is most comfortable to you? Put your initials on the line below. Put your mate's initials where you think he or she is most comfortable.**

```
▌                                                                    ▐
```
lenient   strict

I've been asked the question, "Don't you want a child to think for himself?" I respond, "I want to inform that child's thinking!" Parents' have the responsibility of instilling values. God ordained that they demand respect for those values until the child is mature enough to make his or her own decisions. If children do not learn obedience at home, they will have difficulty obeying authority figures in society. They will also find it difficult to obey God.

🍂 **Obedience is a theme that runs throughout the Bible. Read the verses in the margin. Determine to model an obedient life to your children.**

What Do Our Children Need?

Children have three basic needs:

1. *Structure*–Children thrive in a stable, predictable environment with consistent boundaries. This statement is not meant to imply rigid structure. Children of circus performers move around a lot and keep erratic hours, yet they lead very disciplined lives. Structure offers flexibility within it. Structure implies defined limits of acceptable behavior.

2. *Consistency*–Parenting rules should remain consistent regardless of mood or circumstances. If children are not allowed to run in the hallway on Monday, then they should not run in the hallway on Tuesday. Inconsistency confuses children. They respond to parents' moods rather than developing internal monitors for control.

3. *Affection*–It is impossible to spoil a child with praise! Children need reassurance that they are OK. They also need physical touch. How often are your children corrected at school? Home should be a safe place where nurturing is the predominant mood.

🍂 **Place a star by each of the quality(ies) listed above you feel you model. Place a check by any you want to model more consistently. In the margin list one way you can model a quality you checked.**

These three childhood needs provide ample opportunity to practice and adjust your parenting style to your children's personalities.

[Jesus said] "If you love me you will obey what I command. If you obey my commands, you will remain in my love, just as I have obeyed my Father's commands and remain in his love. I have told you this so that my joy may be in you and that your joy may be complete. My command is this: Love each other as I have loved you. Greater love has no one than this, that he lay down his life for his friends. You are my friends if you do what I command."
—John 14:15, 15:10-14

If it is possible, as far as it depends on you, live at peace with everyone.
—Romans 12:18

Read this week's Scripture memory verse in the margin. Check the statement that best you or your viewpoint.
- ❑ peace-loving: Peace at any price. I can't stand conflict.
- ❑ peacemaker: Peace is not necessarily the absence of conflict. I am willing to confront if necessary.
- ❑ other? _____

DAY 2

SETTING GUIDELINES TOGETHER

Results determine the effectiveness of discipline. Continuous misbehavior points to a need to examine methods. Have you overheard the following conversation? "Johnny, don't do that. Johnny, I said don't do that. Johnny, stop doing that. Johnny, if you ever do that again, you'll be in big trouble!"

That reprimand represents ineffective discipline. We may repeatedly use a certain approach with our children that we know does not work. Why is that? Generally, we model the discipline tactics we have seen others use--whether or not the method is positive or successful. Perhaps we copy our parents' style of discipline. If they didn't allow back talk, neither do we. We may model the method used by a high school principal or coach. Perhaps we are trying an avant garde technique we learned from a television talk show!

Sometimes we react to our upbringing by using discipline methods completely opposite to our parent's. I have a friend who was reared by strict, authoritarian parents. She decided to be permissive with her daughter. The child was a terror. One day my friend confessed: "When I was growing up, my parents were in charge. Now my daughter is in charge. When do I get to be in charge?"

Discipline decisions are too important to be "spur of the moment." Just as we intentionally set business goals, we must deliberately set discipline goals. The process demands that we outline consequences for behavior on the front end. Advance guidelines in a given situation keep a parent's response from being spontaneous. Once I grounded my child for two weeks, completely forgetting the family reunion planned for the upcoming weekend!

 Recall a disastrous--or at least ineffective--example of disciplining a child. Think about how would it benefit parents and children for parents to have determined consequences prior to the incident.

Presuppositions

Lest you think there is only one way to rear children—stop and think again. Recall the different cultures and lifestyles of children around the world. Some live in igloos, others in grass huts, and still others are raised as royalty. Most grow up to become law-abiding citizens. Certainly, some God-ordained principles for living are not negotiable. But the Bible does not speak to issues such as whether children should ever be allowed to sleep with their parents or sixteen is the appropriate age to begin dating.

🌿 **Were you and your mate reared differently? List some of the differences in the margin.**

My first presupposition is that as parents we must give up our right to be right about our preferences and values. My spouse's preferences are equally valid.

Second, no one *best* way to discipline children exists. For example, in some homes, family members cannot put their feet on the coffee table; in other homes, it's OK. In some homes only one hour a day is set aside to watch television; in others the television set plays continuously. Some parents spank for discipline; others restrict privileges. Remember the test of discipline—Is internal control replacing external control? If not, change the methods.

Third, even children in the same family are different; consider this fact in parenting. I know two grown brothers, reared in a home with a father who loved sports. One son is an accomplished artist, who is still not sure whether football has quarters or innings. The other brother can't draw a straight line, but he referees Little League baseball. Consider this interpretation of Proverbs 22:6: "Train up a child in the way the child is bent." In other words, assess each child and discipline accordingly. This advice is especially pertinent in a blended family where the children do not all originate from the same gene pool! Treat them as unique human beings. Be willing to say: "You are not the same as (name of sibling or step-sibling). I reserve the right to parent you as an individual."

A Couple/Family Project

If parents are to respond deliberately to discipline incidents, they must plan and agree on methods and consequences. This process requires time discussing those decisions on the front end. The time spent is well worth it. To discuss what you will do if a child won't eat is less threatening than to be unprepared when Susie dumps her plate of food on the floor.

Parents must agree on methods and consequences.

🌿 **Would you be willing to sit down with your mate and agree to discipline decisions that you both can enforce?** ❏ Yes ❏ No
In the following paragraph, underline the advantages of advance planning.

Older children can participate in the process; include them once you and your mate have worked out the preliminaries. Often children choose a more stringent punishment for certain behaviors than parents. When children "buy in" to the consequences before an infraction, they are less likely to protest when discipline is determined. Knowing consequences before they make an immature decision may prevent some foolish choices. In week 11 we will discuss more fully the concept of family meetings. For now, contemplate ways a "meeting of the minds" might help your family cooperate in the disciplining process.

🍃 **How does being a blended family complicate decisions regarding how and when to discipline? List several ideas in the margin.**

Variables

Prior to the meeting with your spouse and/or children, consider your options. Here are some variables to keep in mind:

1. *Discipline must be age-appropriate.* Don't lecture a two-year-old or send a teenager to "time out" in a corner. If you have children of differing ages, one discipline size won't fit all.
2. *The same discipline tool won't work indefinitely.* You may need to "up the ante" if a behavior is repeated. Losing the privilege of watching a favorite television show may need to be followed by not watching television for an entire evening.
3. *Build up to the big deals.* In other words, don't drop an atom bomb on a village. What will be the "big gun" in your arsenal? Save it for a major infraction.
4. *Keep restrictions short term.* A child's memory is short. Two weeks is a lifetime to a 10-year-old. Long restrictions lose their force. Better to ground a preteen for three days than three weeks. Short-term restriction gives a child good reason to improve rapidly. Otherwise, he might as well take two weeks to reform. If you realize you restrict your children often, perhaps your expectations are too high. Or, you may need professional help.
5. *Every childish mistake does not require punishment.* Children learn from their mistakes just as adults do. A "gotcha" after every overturned glass of milk teaches a child to fear making errors and can lead to a failure syndrome.
6. *Help your child find constructive alternatives to troublesome behavior.* Instead of saying "stop running around the room," suggest playing an active game. Also, eliminate the need to discipline where possible. "Don't touch that" becomes unnecessary when the object is removed from a child's reach.
7. *Help children learn which rules are negotiable and which are not.* If a rule is non-negotiable, then don't argue. If it is negotiable, negotiate! Once you've made a decision, let the child know the discussion is over. Curfews are an example of a negotiable rule. If a movie is over at 9 p.m., a midnight curfew makes little sense. On the other hand, if a chaperoned church event is scheduled to last all night, the curfew is adaptable.

Develop a discipline philosophy that fits you, your mate, and your children. Incorporate the best options and discard the ineffective ones.

🍃 **Write this week's Scripture memory verse below.**

_____

_____

Consider making this verse a family motto. How would repeating it at family gatherings improve the climate in your home?

_____

_____

WORKING AS A TEAM

hether you establish consequences of misbehavior as a couple or as a family, parents must function as a unit to implement an effective plan. Otherwise, children play one parent against the other to determine who offers the best deal.

Must you and your mate agree on everything? Of course not. That's an unreasonable expectation. Each parents according to individual personality style. Dad may not mind if the kids scream in the backseat of the car, but Mom may insist on "inside voices" while driving. Children learn what is acceptable to each parent. This process is good training for the adult world where they will experience a variety of managerial personalities throughout their careers. Exercising individual rights as parents does not mean working against each other. Consensus about acceptable behavior stabilizes the child's world and provides him or her a safe predictability.

In a blended family, arriving at consensus on rules is complicated by the issues discussed in day 1 of this unit. Unity requires give and take.

> **Consensus about acceptable behavior stabilizes the child's world and provides him or her a safe predictability.**

Place an *X* on the continuum below to indicate the degree to which you and your spouse presently work as a team on discipline decisions.

not a team	becoming a team	a team

Standing Together

Our children were almost grown before Betty and I truly felt we were a team. We profited from our mistakes and want to pass on the resulting wisdom to you.

1. *Don't criticize your spouse's decisions in front of the children.* Our children got used to frequently hearing one of us say to the other, "Can I see you in the bedroom for a moment?" That meant Mom and Dad were talking it over out of earshot. Allowing a decision to stand—even if it is a bad decision—is better than disagreeing about the decision in front of the children. Of course, the exception is if anyone would be in danger as a result of the decision.

2. *Don't change a decision your spouse made and announced to the children.* If you disagree, share your idea with your mate and implement your plan the next time. Who's right is a matter of opinion. Your spouse just might have a better idea.

3. *Don't practice "one-upmanship."* Be careful about creating a win/lose atmosphere, where if she concedes to my views I am in control, or if he does it my way, I've scored a point. Both of you are winners when you agree. Don't model a competitive relationship where winning is more important than parental unity.

4. *Don't pass the buck.* Do you feel you are left to make the unpopular decisions or to be the "bad guy" on a regular basis? The good-parent/bad-parent syndrome

may hinder a close relationship between the parent who enforces the tough decisions and the children. Discipline follow-through is a shared responsibility.

🍂 **Look over the previous team suggestions. Place a check by those you feel would help you function better as a couple. What other ways of functioning as a team would you add?**

Team Rules

Together, Betty and I developed several team rules. These rules helped us to avoid arguing about each other's parenting styles. Consider them suggestions. You'll have an opportunity during CoupleTalk to establish your own team rules.

"Simply, let your 'Yes' be 'Yes,' and your 'No' 'No'; anything beyond this comes from the evil one."
—Matthew 5:37

1. *Don't say no until you mean it.* Read Matthew 5:37 in the margin. No does not mean maybe. No is not a word used to allow more time to think. Be honest with your children. "I need more time to think about this before I make a decision." An even better solution is, "I need to talk to your Dad (Mom) before I say yes." I've said no prematurely, only to realize later that I had jumped to a conclusion. Saying yes after some thought is much better than changing a no to a yes.

2. *Reserve the right to change your mind.* Even good choices frequently need altering. Allow yourself the option of reversing an undesirable decision. Children can handle, "I've been thinking about the ballgame, and although it is a school night, I've decided to let you go." This kind of flexibility validates for your children the right to rethink some of their positions.

3. *Don't give warnings.* Warnings imply that parents don't mean what they say. "Please stop" may be interpreted, "wait and see what happens if I don't stop." If you count to three before taking action, you teach children it is not necessary to obey until the number 3 is called.

4. *Don't use physical punishment unless you have agreed in advance that it is appropriate.* Betty and I decided hitting or slapping a child out of anger was unacceptable to us as parents. We held each other accountable in order to avoid this common parenting reaction.

🍂 **What rules would you like to propose during the CoupleTalk session? Write them here for later reference:**

What Discipline May Cost You

Children are notorious for making their parents feel they are the meanest parents in town. Part of our sin nature is the desire to be self-ruled. We all experience the drive to be in control of our world and our homes in particular. Children need you to be in control of the home. But it may cost you.

It may cost your popularity. The children may say they hate you or wish you were not their parents. If a parent accepts this statement at face value, the comment is a painful, offensive message. Then the parent responds defensively and threatens action. The child learns he or she can really upset Mom or Dad. "If I can't have what I want, I will make Mom (Dad) pay for this injustice."

Avoid being hooked by anger. Send a message that you understand the feelings, but encourage children to express the feelings in a more appropriate way. A "time out" may provide emotional space to think of a better response. Our need for love and affection is a trap if we allow children to control our emotions.

Discipline may cost your desire to be understood. Have you ever tried to convince a child that your position is the right one? Obviously, we want to be fair. We allow our children to express their feelings and to present a reasonable case for their proposal. But fairness does not promise that once all is said and done, the child will agree and say: "Thanks, Mom (Dad) for pointing this out to me. You're a genius!"

Finally, discipline may cost relying on your mood of the moment. The time-worn excuse, "I'm just in a bad mood," does not excuse poor decision-making. Mental or emotional well-being is not an appropriate gauge for dispensing discipline. Generally, most parents react rather than act. Spontaneity is an easy way out, but it is an ineffective means to establish parental authority. Learn to put your emotional state on hold when making a decision, and your children will learn to control their emotions as well.

🍂 Repeat this week's Scripture memory verse to a family member. Tell him or her you are seeking to be a peacemaker in your family. Enlist this person as an ally.

Divorced Parents Can Be a Team

If your ex cooperates with you on setting rules and enforces them in a similar style, you are indeed fortunate. It is more likely that you and your former spouse practice different parenting styles.

Children quickly adapt to different households and are not irreparably harmed if Dad or Mom allows them to stay up later or eat junk food occasionally. When moral issues are involved, you may have to use maximum negotiating skills. If you run out of options with your ex, talk to the children and discuss your personal standards. Avoid a judgmental attitude. Explain why you think the behavior is harmful and why you are concerned for them. Assure them you have confidence in their ability to make wise choices, and pray for them. Depending on the circumstances, you may want to consult a lawyer and/or your pastor.

Some remarried persons believe their ex-spouses deliberately attempt to sabotage their discipline process. A constant battle between biological parents hurts the children and reinforces an adversarial position between the ex-mates. Refer to the material on problem solving in unit 11. State your expectations clearly. Limit your intervention to those matters that pose a moral or physical danger to the child. Then, respond appropriately if your ex refuses to cooperate.

Don't abandon the idea that you and your ex can be a parenting team. Consider sharing ideas from today's study with him or her. Enlist your mate's help to establish and reinforce guidelines. You may be surprised by a positive response!

Don't abandon the idea that you and your ex can be a parenting team.

CHOOSING THE BATTLES

*I*n the process of becoming individuals, children quite normally test our belief systems. Usually they learn Mom and Dad have good reasons for their beliefs. Allowing children some room to experiment helps them to develop confidence in their own decision-making abilities. We all learn by trial and error.

When children feel tightly reigned with little freedom of thought or action, they often feel discounted, even worthless. They may conclude the world is not a safe place and they are not capable of living in it without extreme supervision. Consequently, they may become dependent.

The net effect of such parenting is a win/lose atmosphere in the home where the child's efforts at becoming an individual result in punishment rather than affirmation. Too much control literally drives children crazy. Their acting out is a way of fighting for their right to exist. The ultimate consequence may be loss of relationship with the parents.

Winning the Battles and Losing the War

You've heard the expression, "You may win the battle but you will lose the war." I grew up during the 1960's when parents reacted strongly to long hair on boys. One couple I know kicked their son out of the house because he would not cut his hair. The son moved in with friends and later was murdered by a drug dealer. They won the battle—but they lost the war.

Another way of expressing this concept is to ask: Is it a hill to die for? Am I willing to engage in this battle as long as it takes and no matter the cost? In a blended family, there are ample chances to engage your combined children in combat without provoking unnecessary fights.

> **In a blended family, there are ample chances to engage your combined children in combat without provoking unnecessary fights.**

🌿 Put a check in the blank to analyze your parenting style.
- ❏ I let most things go.
- ❏ I pick my battles.
- ❏ I am always ready for a fight!

Ask yourself these four questions as you choose your battles:

1. *Is it a winnable fight?* I gave up the dream of a clean room when after twelve years of nagging, my son convinced me he would never meet my cleanliness standards. I've also given up on his eating broccoli or liking my music. These are not winnable fights. Before you lay down an ultimatum, determine whether or not you can win. You *can't* make a child go to sleep. You *can* enforce a 9 p.m. deadline to be in his bed.

2. *What will winning the battle cost me?* Assuming you can win, the battle may be too costly. It may cost you some peace—constant monitoring, bickering, or nagging.

There may be countless displays of temper, and your child may be on constant restriction. Do I want a sulking teenager confined to my house for three weeks? Three weeks can be an eternity! Make your battles important ones.

3. *What will losing the battle cost me?* I closed my son's door when company visited, but since I did not have to clean his room, I could live with his messiness. At times his clothing tastes were bizarre, but we survived his experimentations. If your children's physical, mental, emotional, or spiritual health is not jeopardized, surrender a few battles along the way. Being different from their peer group may be more psychologically damaging to your children than their choice in clothes.

4. *Is compromise possible?* Compromise allows children to save face and you to make your point. Perhaps you do not want your child to spend the night with a friend whose family you do not know. However, you may be willing to let the child play at his house for two hours on Saturday. Modeling the art of compromise is one of a parent's most important virtues.

🐝 **Select a typical behavior problem with one of your children (stepchildren). Ask these four questions about that particular behavior. Write your responses below.**

The child's name: _____

The behavior: _____

1. Is it a winnable fight? ❑ Yes ❑ No

2. What will winning the battle cost me? _____

3. What will losing the battle cost me? _____

4. Is compromise possible? ❑ Yes ❑ No

5. What is the possible compromise? _____

_____

Why Children Misbehave

When choosing battles with your children, look beyond the disagreeable behavior to the reasons behind the behavior. Psychologists tell us there are four reasons children misbehave:

1. *To receive attention.* Children will get negative attention if they do not get positive attention. When you feel annoyed with your child, ask yourself if the child is simply trying to get your attention.

2. *To feel powerful.* Children seek control, especially when they feel threatened. Power plays emerge from insecure feelings and the need for boundaries. Reassure your children, work through their insecurities, and provide appropriate boundaries.

Look beyond the disagreeable behavior to the reasons behind the behavior.

3. *To retaliate or get revenge.* Generally children hurt others because they have been hurt. In a blended family, children may lash out at a stepparent because that stepparent dared to take their biological parent's place. When children seem vengeful, acknowledge their hurt. Refuse to take their behavior personally.

4. *To withdraw.* Passive/aggressive behavior, such as procrastinating, may be a child's way of saying he or she feels inadequate. Help children confront their inadequacies. Encourage them to believe they can succeed.

> **Which of these reasons accounts for most of the misbehavior in your family? Put your children's initials in the appropriate blank(s).**
> ____ to get attention
> ____ to feel powerful
> ____ to retaliate
> ____ to withdraw

A Common Battle

Sibling rivalry flourishes in a blended family. A vast majority of the parents' time is spent proving they are fair and impartial, as well as intervening in daily fights and aggravations.

Distinguish between harmful rivalry and healthy give-and-take. Draw the line at hateful speech and vengeful behavior. Teach children that jealousy, pride, and selfishness are sins against God. Read Philippians 2:3-4 in the margin.

Children face conflict and competition in every area of their lives. The idea that two people can disagree without being disagreeable is a lesson that will help your children to develop appropriate social skills. What better place to learn these skills than at home?

Do not interfere in a sibling squabble unless your intervention is necessary to prevent injury to body or spirit. Children eventually settle most disagreements among themselves. Your intervention implies a parent will always be around to take care of them. In the long run, this message does not benefit the child.

> **Identify a typical sibling squabble in your home. How does such a scenario differ from the picture painted by this week's Scripture memory verse? List ways to encourage peace in your home.**

_____

_____

Building Strong Families is a national effort to support parents in training children to develop good habits and Christlike character. Home activity books offer 30-day suggestions for building character qualities and come complete with reward cards, mottoes, goal-setting sheets, scripture verses, and daily devotional thoughts. Consider using the home activity book entitled *Peace in the Family* to encourage attitudes and actions that contribute to a peaceful family.

Do nothing out of selfish ambition or vain conceit, but in humility consider others better than yourselves. Each of you should look not only to your own interests, but also to the interests of others.
—Philippians 2:3-4

You can order Peace in the Family by calling the Customer Service Center at 1-800-458-2772. Ask for item 0-7673-2584-2.

EMPHASIZING GRACE

Grace is sometimes defined as unmerited favor. An acronym is "God's Riches At Christ's Expense." In choosing to redeem us rather than banish us to eternal hell, God revealed Himself to be a God of grace. His judgment is on those who refuse His grace. He disciplines for the purpose of restoring His children to grace.

🔖 Relate this concept to a blended family. What does grace look and act like between members of a blended family? Write in the margin.

What does a judgmental atmosphere look like? Write your responses in the margin and be prepared to share them with your group.

A grace-filled home stands in stark contrast to a judgmental home. Do you remember having to chin the bar in physical education classes? Judgmental homes can be compared to always having to chin the bar around our parents' expectations. The feeling of never quite measuring up is a common one among children who grow up in homes where keeping the letter of the law is expected. In his letter to the Galatians, Paul describes a life of slavery to the law as foolish. Read Galatians 2:21 in the margin.

A grace-filled home recognizes our inability to live up to the law's demands. Such a home is made up of persons who own their sinfulness, stand ready to confess their sins to one another, and give and receive forgiveness.

🔖 Consider making a banner for your home with the words: *The Grace Space.* What do you think are the implications of such a motto?

Children need to know that regardless of the wrongs they have committed or how far they may have wandered from the truth, as a parent you offer grace. The parable of the prodigal son illustrates for us a loving parent who welcomes an erring child. Every biblical truth has a balancing truth. Often God must discipline His children before they willingly return to His loving arms. The prodigal lived with the pigs for a while before he came to his senses.

🔖 Place a mark on the line to evaluate your "grace-filled-ness."

lacking grace   full of grace

Cal, a friend of mine, has three teenagers. All three dented their first cars in minor traffic accidents. In each case, Cal remained calm. The kids had to pay for

A grace-filled home:

A judgmental home:

I do not set aside the grace of God, for if righteousness could be gained through the law, Christ died for nothing.
—*Galatians 2:21*

the damage and find rides to school and work while their cars were in the shop, but none of them got the traditional parental tirade. Cal told a friend: "I remembered doing the same thing when I was a kid. My parents yelled at me and grounded me. I already felt terrible. What I needed was mercy, not judgment. I said then that when I became a parent, I'd think about how I felt."

Creating a Grace-Filled Atmosphere

Create a grace-space by observing these principles:

1. *Positive parents encourage positive kids.* An optimistic spirit, even in the midst of trouble, teaches children a "can-do" spirit. Looking on the bright side may seem idealistic at times, but it lifts your own spirits as well as your children's.

2. *Model forgiveness.* Children know parents are fallible, even when we do not act like we know it. Acknowledging your own error gives a child permission to say he or she is wrong. Every day brings an opportunity to admit our humanity!

3. *Model respect.* Treating a child with respect builds self-confidence. Disrespect includes name-calling (lazy, stupid) and insults. Put-downs also damage tender feelings, even if we are teasing. Often children try out their ideas on us. When we offer encouragement to continue thinking through a problem—rather than belittling their ideas—they are motivated to think creatively.

4. *Avoid vengefulness on your part.* When a child disappoints us, we may consider seeking revenge. Saying hurtful things, sulking, displaying temper, or refusing to relate demonstrate a desire to retaliate. Instead, discipline with actions—not with words and attitudes.

5. *Avoid favoritism.* One of God's greatest gifts is His love for each of us. Grace is extended to all, not reserved for a select few. Emphasize each individual child's strengths. Explain how the family benefits from his or her presence.

> 🍃 **Select a family member you feel would benefit from some special time alone with you. Tell this person how much you care for him or her. Give a hug or other appropriate physical expression of your love.**

6. *Avoid comparisons.* When children are compared to other family members, they lose their sense of specialness and individuality. An exception is if the comparison is a compliment and relates to character and not appearance.

Developing Grace-filled-ness

Become a grace-filled person.

Do you feel somewhat deficient as a grace-filled person? Join the crowd! All of us could use some growth in our capacity to extend grace to others.

> 🍃 **Check the ways you want to pursue developing graciousness.**
> ❑ Make a study of the word grace in the Bible. Use your concordance to find Scriptures that relate to grace.
> ❑ Study a biblical character who demonstrated grace, such as Ruth or Lydia.
> ❑ Study the life of Jesus. Look for ways He showed grace to those considered unimportant by the world's standards.
> ❑ Ask someone whose opinion you trust to evaluate your lifestyle. Ask, Do I demonstrate grace in the way I treat others?
> ❑ If you are really brave, ask your family the same question.

Many of us grew up in homes that emphasized law over grace. None of us wants to repeat past mistakes. We want to model the best of what we've learned from our role models. We are not doomed to repeat their mistakes.

🌿 Set some parenting goals for yourself in creating a grace-filled home.

I want to:

_____

I don't want to:

_____

The theme of this week's study has been setting guidelines in advance of behavior as much as that is possible with growing children. Being intentional about behavioral guidelines enables us to identify and practice good parenting techniques and exclude less than successful ones.

🌿 List some parenting techniques you want to copy from significant role models and some techniques you wish to avoid.

I want to:

_____

I don't want to:

_____

🌹 Repeat this week's Scripture memory verse. Pray, substituting the word *me* for the word *you*. Ask God to make this verse characteristic of your life.

COUPLETALK

For you to complete

1. List some ways you and your spouse can be a more effective parenting team. Refer to p. 166.

_____

_____

2. (If applicable) Identify at least one way you and your ex-spouse can be a more effective parenting team.

_____

_____

3. Name at least one advantage of setting guidelines and consequences before an incident occurs.

_____

_____

4. How can your home become more of a "grace space"?

_____

_____

For you to share with your spouse

1. Sit down facing each other and take turns sharing how each of you completed the above section.
2. If you are in agreement, discuss how you will go about setting guidelines and consequences of behavior as a couple and as a family.
3. Review your lists of parenting goals from day 5. Choose several from your combined lists you wish to implement. Plan how you will implement them.
4. Tell one reason why you love each other.
5. Say together this week's Scripture memory verse.
6. Pray for each other, either silently or aloud.

DEVELOP PROBLEM-SOLVING SKILLS

On Saturday Ted's boss called to see if he could come to work for half-a-day. Ted asked his new wife if she would mind watching his two children while he was gone. Peggy agreed. *What a good opportunity for Peggy and the kids to get to know one another better*, Ted thought. While they were dating, Peggy and Ted had only occasional outings with the children. Now that they were married, the children visited them every other weekend.

When Ted returned home, the children were restricted to their rooms. Peggy had grounded them for playing inside her car. "Were they hurting anything?" asked Ted.

"No, but I told them to get out and they didn't. They disobeyed me."

"I don't see the harm of pretending to drive. They are just kids."

"I suppose I should have given them the keys and let them drive away," Peggy said sarcastically.

That incident ruined the entire day. By evening, Ted felt like the whole family was mad at him. *What did I do?* he wondered.

If problems truly aid spiritual growth, then blended families are blessed! They experience a multitude of problems. Why? Because of the many complicating factors we have considered during the past 10 weeks—as well as the baggage that every family member brings to the blended family.

But problems can be solved. Learning how to resolve the most difficult ones facing blended families is the purpose of this study. This week we will focus on a specific problem-solving technique: the family meeting. This tool has been as helpful as any I've used and recommended in my years of working with blended families. If you already use this method, look for ways to improve your technique. If you are not presently conducting family meetings to resolve problems, consider the reasons to begin such a practice.

This Week You Will:
- seek to identify the *real* problems that face your family and find solutions;
- use the family meeting approach to solve problems;
- look for the blessings of growth through problem-solving.

This Week's Scripture Memory Verse
"Let us not become weary in doing good, for at the proper time we will reap a harvest if we do not give up" (Galatians 6:9).

What You'll Study

DAY 1
- **The Need to Solve Problems**

DAY 2
- **Steps to Solving Problems**

DAY 3
- **Family Meetings to Solve Problems**

DAY 4
- **Guidelines for Family Meetings**

DAY 5
- **Problems as Blessings**

THE NEED TO SOLVE PROBLEMS

*M*ost of us would like to live life like an ostrich—with our heads in the sand! Let the world go by. As long as it doesn't bother me, I won't bother it! Fortunately, God gave us the unique ability to solve problems. Some people, however, fail to exercise that ability. They bury their heads in the sand by ignoring the problem, hoping it will go away. Some people choose another problem-solving option—a "winner take all" attitude—and then fight to the death. I recommend a third problem-solving option that seeks to find a win-win situation for everyone involved. It is called consensus decision-making, where family members come to an agreement about a solution.

Today we will explore the reasons why ignoring on-going problems never contributes to blending a family. We will study an example of assertiveness and ways to be assertive without being offensive to those we love.

Ignoring on-going problems never contributes to blending a family.

Problems Don't Go Away

Clint, Gail's former husband, seldom paid child support for his two sons. Nevertheless, he insisted Gail allow visitation whenever he wanted to see them. Gail was not a confrontational person. She usually complied with Clint's demands because she did not want to make waves.

Stuart, Gail's present husband, saw red whenever Gail gave in to Clint's demands. "Why don't you hire an attorney and sue him for all the back child support he owes?" Stuart asked.

"Then he will just become more unreasonable," Gail replied. "You don't know him like I do. It's just better to go along."

Of course, nothing got better. Gail's former spouse continued to disrupt their lives. Clint's refusal to pay child support, in addition to Gail's passive attitude toward Clint's demands, increased the strain on Gail and Stuart's marriage.

Do you think this situation can go on forever? Ignoring a problem seldom solves it; usually the problem gets worse.

🌿 **If you were comparing your problem-solving approach to an animal, check the animal which best describes you.**

❑ ostrich—I turn the other way and therefore problems don't exist.
❑ beaver—I just allow problems to pile up, without dealing with them.
❑ lamb—I allow others to walk all over me or make all the decisions.
❑ bull—I get defensive and attack at the slightest provocation.

Confrontation Is Difficult

Like Gail, many of us are frightened of confrontation and avoid it whenever possible. Others, like Clint, take advantage of our failure to confront. When dominant persons continually get their way, they are more likely to abuse their power in the future. Standing up to those who take advantage of us is one of life's developmental tasks. If you are not a person who feels comfortable with confrontation, take heart! It is a skill that can be learned.

One weekend Clint called on Saturday morning to say he wanted to take the boys to an afternoon ball game. Gail and Stuart had already planned a weekend camping trip with the boys. Stuart was standing nearby and could hear Gail's phone conversation with Clint. Stuart looked at Gail and silently mouthed the words, "Tell him no."

It took all Gail's courage to say: "I'm afraid that idea won't work this weekend, Clint. We're taking the boys on a camping trip."

"Let me talk to the boys," demanded Clint.

Gail almost relented, but she looked at Stuart and instead said: "I'm sorry, but not this time, Clint. We're going camping. You can call the boys Sunday night." With that, Gail hung up the phone.

Gail was trembling, not at all sure she had done the right thing. Stuart, sensing her indecision, put his arms around her and said: "I'm proud of you, honey."

Just then, the phone rang again. Gail was certain that it was Clint and he would be angry. Stuart answered the phone. Clint yelled, "Let me talk to Gail."

Very calmly Stuart said: "She can't come to the phone right now, Clint. She's packing for our camping trip."

"Then let me talk to one of the boys," replied Clint.

"They're getting ready too, Clint. Call them Sunday night." It was Stuart's turn to hang up on Clint.

This time Clint did not call back. To Gail's surprise, Clint did not call again until the following Wednesday to arrange for weekend plans. Rather than making more trouble, Clint seemed to respect Gail for standing up to him. With Stuart's support, Gail grew stronger.

Perhaps you have tried standing your ground with an aggressive personality only to reap more belligerence, not less. Assertiveness is not a quick fix; it requires consistency and a long-range strategy. An assertive person determines his or her rights, maintains a win-win focus, and observes the Golden Rule.

"Do to others as you would have them do to you."
—Luke 6:31

🌿 Label the following with an *A* for aggressive, *S* for assertive, and *P* for passive.

____ Clint demanded the right to visitation with his children every weekend, although the court awarded visitation only every other weekend.

____ Gail placed no time restraints on Clint's weekend visits with the children. When he asked to keep them longer, she always said yes.

____ Stuart encouraged Gail to return to court to receive back child support payments.

Clint's aggressive style consistently won out over Gail's passive style, until assertive Stuart helped Gail deal with her ex in a more effective manner.

Problems Have a Purpose

I suspect that the prophet Jonah was similar to those of us who read the newspapers or watch the news and say, "Someone ought to do something about that."

Jonah knew that Nineveh was a constant threat to the Israelites. He observed their sinful behavior and thought: *I might do some wicked things sometimes, but certainly nothing as bad as the people in Nineveh. God should do something about those sinners!*.

Now, I don't really know what Jonah was thinking. But I do know God told Jonah to go to Nineveh and Jonah didn't want to go. In his attempt to run away from God, Jonah was swallowed by a great fish. Even today, problems have a way of swallowing us when we try to run away from them.

When God saw what they did and how they turned from their evil ways, he had compassion and did not bring upon them the destruction he had threatened.
—Jonah 3:10

🕊️ **Read Jonah 3:10 in the margin. When Jonah obeyed God and preached to the Ninevites, God worked a miracle in their midst. Underline the blessing that resulted from Jonah's faithfulness.**

🕊️ **Are there problems within your blended family that you have been avoiding? If so, list one or more here.**

_____

_____

Check why you believe these problems haven't been solved.
❏ We don't know what to do.
❏ I've tried but other family members do not support me.
❏ So far our attempts at a solution haven't worked.
❏ One (or more) in the family sabotages our efforts.
❏ Other _____

Compare problems to the math homework you had in elementary school. Problems are only difficult until we learn the solutions. God does not intend that we struggle through life without relief from painful situations. When we look for and discover His solutions, problems can become allies, moving us closer to Him and to His purposes for our lives.

We must not give up the process of resolving problems simply because solutions do not magically appear. Unless we are familiar with the dynamics of blended families, we learn mostly by trial and error. In our introductory story, Gail learned that confrontation often works better than giving in. She also realized that Stuart was extremely supportive when dealing with Clint. Other aspects of problem solving will be presented in day 2.

Let us not become weary in doing good, for at the proper time we will reap a harvest if we do not give up.
—Galatians 6:9

🕊️ **Read this week's Scripture memory verse in the margin. Rate your "weariness index" by putting an *X* on the continuum below.**

energized   growing weary   weary

🌺 If you feel weary, claim the strength promised in this verse. Catch a vision of the harvest that awaits you as you learn to resolve difficulties.

STEPS TO SOLVING PROBLEMS

Good problem-solving skills are imperative to successful blending. In day 5 of week 4 we learned the six steps to resolving conflicts. Today we will concentrate on two of those steps. While the ones recommended here are not unique to blended families, your application will be.

Identify the Problem

When a problem arises, each family member views it differently. Some family members may not see it at all. Regardless of who surfaces a particular issue, identifying the problem is the priority. Defining a problem is not as simple as it sounds. Problems–like onions–have many layers. The apparent problem is often the presenting problem, or the problem that first appears on the outside of the onion. As the problem is "peeled," deeper layers surface. These less-obvious problems may need resolution before the top layer can be addressed.

Involve as many family members as possible in the initial stages of defining the problem. Involving the children early will encourage them to buy into the solution. Let's look at a typical example. Ethan married Kate after dating her only six months. While Ethan knew upfront that Kate's daughter Nora was not happy about the marriage, he was certain Nora eventually would come around. After the wedding, Nora remained hostile toward Ethan, going out of her way either to ignore him or to be rude to him.

Kate's appeals to Nora fell on deaf ears. After months of rejection by Nora, Ethan confronted Nora. Ethan began: "Nora, we have a problem. I know you don't want me here. You've made that clear. But I am here, and I plan to stay. I've tried to be friends with you, but you don't even treat me in a civil manner. I don't think I can live this way. What can we do to make living together more pleasant?"

🍂 **Let's stop and analyze this situation. Do you feel Ethan has identified the "real" problem? ❏ Yes ❏ No If not, what is the real problem?**

_____

Ethan wanted to change Nora's behavior before learning the reason for Nora's rejection. After Ethan asked, "What can we do to make living together more pleasant," Nora glared at him.

"That's your problem," she answered. "I told Mom she shouldn't marry you."

Ethan and Nora then began to debate whether or not the marriage should have taken place. Obviously, they were way off base in defining the problem – and thus solving it. You can't change the past.

Problems–like onions–have many layers.

The family seemed to be stalled. Finally Ethan said: "As I understand it, you are determined to just live here, hate every minute of it, and make everyone else as miserable as possible until you leave for college. Is that about right, Nora?"

Nora thought about Ethan's assessment of the situation and replied: "Well, I don't like this anymore than you do."

"Then why don't we decide how each of us can move beyond what has happened," said Kate. "Nora, I'm sorry that I didn't listen to you before Ethan and I married. I don't know that I would have waited. But I am sorry we didn't have this discussion before the wedding."

Ethan agreed: "That goes for me, too. I love your mother so much that I believed everything else would simply fall into place. I knew that you wanted us to wait. But, we should have talked."

It took some time but Ethan, Kate, and Nora finally identified the real problem: Nora felt she was left out of the decision-making process when Ethan and Kate decided to marry. The next step was to work out a solution to how they would relate as a family. A positive solution is impossible until the problem is clearly defined.

Look for Solutions

Defining the problem and everyone's contribution to the problem is the first step in problem solving. Obviously, there can be no long-lasting solution until everyone involved wants to solve the problem.

There can be no long-lasting solution until everyone involved wants to solve the problem.

"Since we didn't wait to get married, what do you think we should do now?" Ethan asked Nora.

"I don't know," replied Nora.

"Do you think I should move out?" he asked. Ethan thought Nora probably would say, "Yes," so he was pleased when she replied, "Don't be silly."

"Give me a little time," Nora said. "I don't hate you, Ethan. I'm just hurt that you didn't consider my feelings before you decided to get married."

Ethan thought to himself, *It wouldn't have changed anything*, but he did not make the statement aloud.

Nora continued: "I'll try to be more civil. I don't know about being friends yet. We'll see."

Confrontations such as Ethan, Kate, and Nora experienced are not pleasant. However, the events of that night changed things considerably. They had the courage to move past their hurts and talk to one another. Now the three of them had to agree on a description of "civil behavior".

Ethan had higher expectations than "I'll speak to you when you come into the room." Nora thought that was a great concession. Kate, however, had a better idea. She drew a line down the middle of a sheet of paper, making two columns. In one column she listed Ethan's ideas of "civil behavior." In the other, she listed Nora's ideas. Kate then suggested they each pick three items from the other's list to implement. They agreed to meet again in two weeks to evaluate how the plan was working.

This win-win approach softened Nora's resistance and gave her a voice in the decision making. Ethan's willingness to go along with Nora's minimal effort was crucial to the plan's success. Fortunately Ethan realized that Nora would later offer other concessions if given time, patience, and respect.

Once a solution is agreed upon, set a time for follow up conversation to evaluate the success of the solution. Frequently, adjustments are necessary. Be willing to try multiple solutions until you feel comfortable with the issue.

 What would have happened if Ethan had just given up and ignored Nora's behavior?

_____

_____

 Read our Scripture memory verse for the week in the margin. Underline the promise.

Let us not become weary in doing good, for at the proper time we will reap a harvest if we do not give up.
—Galatians 6:9.

DAY 3

FAMILY MEETINGS TO SOLVE PROBLEMS

*I*n the past families gathered around the table for dinner and often spent the evening together talking, singing, sewing, playing games, and listening to someone read aloud the Bible and other great books. Then came the light bulb! Now we live in a 24-hour-a-day society that never stops. In most families, finding time for meals together is a major hassle. Dinner is rushed—hardly the atmosphere for discussing family problems and struggles.

Blended families need a set-aside time to connect. Although nuclear families experience their share of problems, they do not include members who have not bonded from birth. Emotional bonding makes a tremendous difference in how well families function, and blended families need time together in order for bonding of any degree to occur.

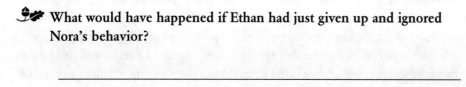 **When is your blended family most likely to be together? What is happening during that time? Does it contribute to family bonding?**

Schedule Family Meetings

I encourage blended families to conduct a family meeting at least once a month—and every week if possible. A productive meeting includes all family members (unless a child is away at college or is an infant). The purpose of such meetings is to catch up on what is going on with each other and to solve problems. If the meetings become only a time for complaints, they will lose their effect. Positive, affirming, encouraging words are necessary items for the agenda.

At first, family meetings will feel awkward for everyone. The children will probably resist attending. That reaction is normal; no one accepts change readily. Schedule the first meeting far enough in advance so that it does not conflict with previously set plans. Giving notice cuts down on excuses for missing the meeting.

Select a time that can be observed weekly, if possible, but remain flexible and adjust to changing circumstances. When a schedule conflict occurs, plan for an alternate time. In many blended families, noncustodial children will not be able to attend every week. If that is the case, change the meeting schedule so they can be present.

Hold meetings in a comfortable place for everyone. An ideal location is a table large enough for everyone to sit around. Keep the meetings brief—one hour is adequate. There may be occasions when everything on the agenda does not get considered. That's all right. It is better to accomplish less and end on time than to extend the meeting. You cannot solve all the family's problems at one time. Strive for fairness, making sure everyone has a voice.

Plan only one or two agenda items for your first family meeting. Follow-up meetings can allow a more extensive agenda. At the first meeting have a parent to preside. Later, the task may be passed around. I know of one family that bought a gavel and the person presiding used the gavel. The children loved the idea of being in control of the meeting, and the gavel was the symbol of that control. Just as everyone takes turns at presiding over the meeting, everyone old enough to write can take turns as secretary, recording the decisions made.

Close the time together with some family fun. Play a game together or go out for a movie or ice cream. Meeting closure is as important as its beginning. Sometimes families experience more productive sharing during the fun time and without agenda than during the actual meeting. Prior to each family meeting, enlist a different family member to plan the after-meeting activities.

🍃 **If you have family meetings, when do you meet?**_____

If you do not, when could you meet?_____

Benefits of a Family Meeting

🍃 **As you read the following benefits, underline those qualities you would like to build into your family.**

Family meetings offer positive rewards to blended families. They enable the family to cooperate as a single unit rather than existing as a grouping of individuals. Meetings nurture a common identity among family members. Family members understand how each person impacts the others. For example, if my being slow in the bathroom causes you to miss the school bus, I will understand why you want me to set my alarm fifteen minutes earlier. Hopefully, after a few family meetings, family members will have a better understanding of one another.

Family meetings also teach children problem solving. In some ways, the family meeting is a laboratory where everyone learns how to get along with others. It improves social skills and teaches democratic principles—skills children and adults apply throughout their lives.

Meetings nurture a common identity among family members.

Setting the Agenda

Consider the following family meeting agenda:

1. Open the meeting with prayer by the presiding family member.
2. Allow time for each person to share one good experience from that week.
3. Read the minutes from the previous meeting.
4. Discuss old business (situations not addressed at the previous meeting).
5. Discuss family finances. The family meeting provides a wonderful opportunity to demonstrate money management; however, carefully choose financial information to share. Involve children in financial planning for major purchases. They may be happier with the decision to miss summer camp if they know the family is saving for a new car. Also, if children compare the electric bill from month to month, they might be more likely to turn off the lights when they leave a room! If you provide weekly allowances, the family meeting is an appropriate time to distribute the money.
6. Present new business. Post agenda items prior to the meeting. Tape a sheet of paper on the refrigerator or some other prominent place where anyone can list items they want discussed. Here is a sample agenda:
   1. Linda comes into my room without knocking. (Joseph)
   2. Raising allowances (Linda)
   3. Holiday planning (Mom)

   An agenda helps parents stay neutral when children squabble. When children enlist your help in settling a quarrel, suggest they add it to the family meeting agenda. Serious issues will make it on the list; frivolous complaints rarely do.
7. Use the problem-solving method to resolve issues. Family meetings should not be democratic in terms of voting. Parents are in charge of the home. However, it is important to seek consensus (general agreement) where possible. If one family member feels that he or she has been treated unfairly, the whole family suffers. We will explore the dynamics of a family meeting in day 4.
8. Close with prayer by the presider.
9. Initiate family fun time. Allow the family member who planned the activity to explain the outing or game.

Write a one-sentence rebuttal to these objections to family meetings.

I could never get our family together. _____

_____

The kids would hate the idea. _____

_____

I wouldn't know what to do. _____

_____

It would never work in my family. _____

_____

Do you see the value of holding regular family meetings? Family meetings encourage everyone's involvement in developing a strong, positive family structure.

 Repeat this week's Scripture memory verse. Thank God for the good work He is doing in your family. Thank Him for the harvest you can see and the harvest yet to come in your family's future.

DAY 4

GUIDELINES FOR FAMILY MEETINGS

*F*amily meetings could easily become your worst nightmare if they are not conducted according to several time-tested guidelines. After several years of evaluating family meeting reports, I've compiled a set which contribute to harmony and positive results.

It's fun to be an innovator. In the case of family meetings, however, I don't suggest launching out on your own. Follow the pattern I'm suggesting. Opportunity to improvise will occur later. But if you attempt to alter these suggestions from the outset, please don't hold me responsible for the outcome!

Keep the Meeting Running Smoothly
Let's look at some principles for conducting a smoothly-run family meeting. Ahead of time, post this list to be discussed at your first meeting. Abide by these principles if the family agrees with them.

1. Everyone's voice is important—regardless of age. Each family member is encouraged to give his or her opinion.
2. Decisions are made by agreement rather than by vote. We will discuss problems until a solution is acceptable to everyone.
3. All decisions remain in effect until presented again and changed at another family meeting.
4. Some decisions are made, enforced, and explained by the parents. (You may want to add examples, such as where the family lives, bedtimes, and curfews.) However, children may add these items to the family meeting agenda for discussion and are encouraged to give their opinions and share their feelings.
5. All family members will preside and record on an alternating basis. Everyone should participate in discussion time. (Some children—especially teenagers—believe their silence will sabotage the meeting. Explain to them that their tactic is their way of forfeiting input in family decisions.)
6. The family meeting is a safe place to solve problems—not complain. Rephrase a complaint as a problem statement. We will seek to find a solution that is satisfactory to all.

7. Family meetings will include a time for praise, encouragement, and evaluation of results and change. (Brag on each other! Look for signs of "we-ness." Some families select an MVP each month. Avoid this idea if the recipient would be the same person. If a "problem child" is never a candidate, poor self-esteem is the result.)

🌿 **Perhaps you would want to add to this list of guidelines below and talk them over with your spouse during CoupleTalk.**

_____

_____

Build Consensus

Consensus decision-making occurs when the disagreeing parties discuss the matter until all are in agreement. It does not mean that a vote is taken and the majority rules.

The reason the majority rule approach doesn't work in family meetings is obvious. Any family with three or more children would eventually live at Disneyworld or allow the children to drop out of school! A more serious reason has to do with how persons feel when they lose. The minority generally feel resentful and may even sabotage the decision. Respecting one another's feelings is important in any family, but in a blended family, riding roughshod over feelings deters the blending process.

A consensus decision may not be anyone's first choice. But if everyone can live with it, then progress is made. If a family cannot reach agreement, then the matter may be held until the next meeting. If the issue is too important and too immediate, parents may exercise their right to make a decision.

Parents must discern which decisions are their responsibilities and which can be made by the entire family. A parent being transferred by his or her company cannot ask the children for approval. However, the children can be encouraged to share their personal thoughts, concerns, and feelings about the move. And they can be involved in planning for the move. Remember—democracy does not mean you will get your way; it means you will get your say.

Democracy does not mean you will get your way; it means you will get your say.

🌿 **Does your family already use consensus decision-making to some degree?** ❏ Yes ❏ No

What concerns, if any, do you have about using this approach? Share these with your group at your next meeting.

Build "We-ness"

The family unit is the backbone of society. We not only thrive but also survive by forming small, cooperative units. Families have been a source of support, encouragement, and sustenance for centuries, often against overwhelming odds. Our culture has been described as hostile to family togetherness. Our busy schedules and constant media bombardment often work against bonding.

A family meeting is one of many ways to build "we-ness." Family members learn to function as "one for all and all for one." Decisions are made to help the family as a unit, not to please only one individual. Problems that affect one member are taken seriously by the others. "We-ness" stands in stark contrast to "me-ness."

Other ways to build "we-ness" include activities in which the family works, plays, and worships together. Develop family traditions for your family. Pass on family stories of courage and persistence. Build an identity of pride in who you are and what you have to offer to each other and to those outside your family.

Read 1 Corinthians 12:12-26. Paul was comparing the body of believers—the church—to a human body. How can this same illustration be applied to our families? Write your thoughts below.

_____

_____

_____

In this Scripture, Paul gives an example of how individual parts of a body are interrelated. If one body part hurts, the remaining parts suffer as well. If a person breaks his toe, his head cannot say it doesn't matter. He will have a difficult time thinking clearly as long as his toe is in pain. This analogy illustrates how all Christians are tied together. We need one another just as the parts of a body need one another. One part is never more important than any other part.

The same analogy applies to families. Family members are not independent. They are interdependent. If one person hurts, they all hurt. Your family may not feel this corporate pain now because you are still in the blending process. But that is the goal. What happens to one, happens to all. Read 1 Corinthians 12:12-26 to your family and explain this concept to them.

The family meeting is living proof that the family is trying to become a single body, tied together not only by kinship and marriage, but also by common purposes and common problem solving and decision making.

Let us not become weary in doing good, for at the proper time we will reap a harvest if we do not give up.
—Galatians 6:9

How can a family meeting contribute to a "harvest" of benefits for your family?

_____

_____

Say this week's Scripture memory verse to a family member. Compliment one way he or she is "doing good" for your family.

PROBLEMS AS BLESSINGS

Seeing the potential good in a problem takes eyes of faith. None of us enjoys problems. On the other hand, almost everyone enjoys solutions. Solving a problem builds self-respect and gives us a positive sense of accomplishment. The more difficult the problem, the better we feel at having solved it.

Solving Problems Builds Self-Respect

Remember Gail and Stuart from day 1? If not, go back and re-read their story. A few weeks after the camping incident, Clint called again. Gail was not home at the time, and he spoke with one of the boys. He offered to take the boys fishing for the weekend and instructed them to be ready in an hour. Stuart learned of the trip when the boys came downstairs carrying their overnight bags. "What's up guys?" he asked.

"Dad called. We're going fishing for the weekend," answered Mark, the older boy.

"Really," said Stuart. "I think it's time your dad and I talked."

"Go ahead," Mark replied. "I don't think it will make any difference."

When Clint arrived, Stuart met him at the car. "Clint, you really need to call ahead of time to set up plans with the boys."

"Yeah, yeah, I know," Clint admitted. "But I don't know my own schedule very often."

"I'm serious Clint," said Stuart. "The next time you don't give us at least two days notice, the boys will not be allowed to go with you."

"You can't deny me visitation," said Clint, getting a little huffy.

"No," said Stuart, "and I don't want to. However, you either will plan time with the boys according to our regular schedule, or you will call two days in advance. That's it. Otherwise, you are going to need a court order. I will not allow you to disrupt our lives like this."

Clint sat there for a minute, almost as though he had never thought about how his calling at the last minute impacted their lives. "OK Stuart," he relented. "I guess you're right. I'll give you more notice. By the way, I think you're doing a good job with the boys. They seem to like you. Now, will you tell them to hurry along?"

The two men shook hands. When Gail returned home, she was surprised at the turn of events. "He really told you he thought you were doing a good job with the boys?" she asked.

Clint tested the waters a few more times, but when he realized that Gail and Stuart were serious about their rules, visitation became a regular happening. Gail and Stuart felt better about themselves for having stood up to Clint. The boys were happier because Dad was not the subject of family squabbles.

Develop Problem-Solving Skills **187**

🍂 **Think back to a problem you have solved. How did solving it build your self-respect?**

_____

_____

What life lessons do you continue to use today that you learned through the process?

_____

_____

Solving Problems Produces Growth

I often say if I could go back in my life and remove some of my worst moments, I would not dare. Why? Because I grew and matured as a result of each one. That declaration includes my divorce and my struggles throughout the early years of our blended family. Don't misunderstand. I would not want to live through those times again. They were painful. But they produced good growth.

God allows problems in order for us to grow. I like to imagine life as a classroom with God as our teacher. As a wise teacher, God promises that we will never be presented with a situation He has not prepared us to face victoriously. See 1 Corinthians 10:13 in the margin. Until we learn the easier lessons of life, we are unable to resolve the more difficult.

I was amazed when I graduated from high school and went to college. In college, the work was considerably more difficult than it had been in high school. My freshman year was an enormous struggle. After that, having developed much better study skills and having learned what was expected, the remainder of my college years were easier. When I went to seminary for graduate work, once again I discovered the work to be more intense and difficult. And again, I struggled. However, I graduated. But had I tried to enter seminary without having first gone to college, I suspect I never would have completed either. The more difficult lessons could not be learned until I had mastered the less difficult ones.

Such is life. God trains us with lessons geared to where we are at the moment. Once we have mastered those, we are able to move on. Until then, we are doomed to repeat the same mistakes.

Groundhog Day has always been one of my favorite movies. The main character, a television weatherman, goes each year to Punxsutawney, Pennsylvania, to cover the story of the groundhog looking for his shadow. His character is very negative and makes fun of all the local people. Due to a freak snowstorm that he failed to predict, he is stranded in the town and forced to spend the night. When he awakens the next morning, he discovers it is Groundhog Day all over again.

Each day is the same—one Groundhog Day after another. At first, he is frustrated and angry. Later, he realizes he can use his knowledge of the immediate future to manipulate and take advantage of people. When that begins to bore him, he tries to make the best of the situation. Finally, when he seems to have gotten it right, the day moves on and so does he.

No temptation has seized you except what is common to man. And God is faithful; he will not let you be tempted beyond what you can bear. But when you are tempted, he will also provide a way out so that you can stand up under it.
—1 Corinthians 10:13

Life is a little like that movie. We receive the same lesson to learn (in one way or another) until we learn it. Then, we move on because there are still lessons waiting. The new lessons are simply different and usually require skills we did not possess before. God is a good teacher.

Peter studied under the Greatest Teacher ever. Peter learned many lessons from his brief time with Jesus. He learned that he couldn't walk on water without Jesus' help. He learned that he could not control his temper without divine intervention. In the courtyard when Peter denied that he knew Jesus, he found that he was as susceptible to peer pressure and fear as the rest of us.

🌿 **In your Bible read John 21:15-17. This is a story of Jesus and Peter following the resurrection. Do you think that Peter would have been ready to "feed my sheep," as Jesus instructed him, without having walked through these other experiences? ❏ Yes ❏ No**

Is there a particular lesson you feel Jesus wants to teach you through your blended family experience? Write it in the margin.

Problems are indeed an important ingredient in the growth process. While they usually are appreciated only in retrospect, problems are intended to result in a blessing, not in a curse.

Problems Produce Strength

Our approach to problems often determines how quickly we are able to solve them and move on to others. Occasionally I encounter people who consider problems as punishment. In the midst of a struggle they say, "Why is God doing this to me? I've tried to live a moral life. Why would God let something like this happen to me?"

Such reasoning baffles me. Where did we ever get the mistaken notion that if we lead good and moral lives, we will not encounter struggles or problems? I wonder if people who think like this read the Bible. The apostle Paul certainly was one of the greatest Christians ever to live. Yet, he suffered considerably.

🌿 **Take a moment to read 2 Corinthians 11:22-33. List five ways in which Paul suffered for what he was doing.**

_____

_____

_____

_____

If someone to whom Christ himself appeared could then struggle and suffer so, how can we ever imagine that the Christian life was meant to be one of ease and comfort? It is not. Struggle and problems are means by which God blesses us and helps us to become a blessing to others.

Although I did not enjoy the early struggles of our blended family, without those struggles and the growth that resulted, I would never have been able to develop our church's existing stepfamily ministry. I may not have even observed the need. Today I can claim the blending process as a blessing. God has enabled me to watch hundreds of blended families move through their struggles successfully. He has permitted me to help them. He continually allows me be a part of His creative work. I can't imagine a greater blessing!

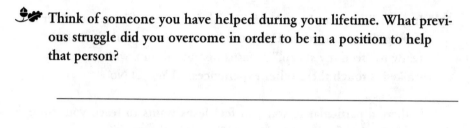 Think of someone you have helped during your lifetime. What previous struggle did you overcome in order to be in a position to help that person?

_____

_____

Do you now consider what was a problem as a blessing? Do you think that perhaps the problems you are experiencing even now are blessings? Your problems may ultimately benefit others as well. We never know, but one thing I have learned about God is that He never wastes anything. God was into recycling long before us.

Think of a problem you want to allow God to turn into a blessing. Ask Him to do so right now.

Say this week's Scripture memory verse to a family member.

COUPLETALK

For you to complete

1. Did you list problems in day 1 that you have been avoiding but now might want to face? ❑ Yes ❑ No

2. Would you like to try to resolve any of those problems?
   ❑ Yes ❑ No

4. What do you think needs to happen in order for this (these) problems to be resolved?

_____

_____

5. Check your attitude at present toward a family meeting:
   ❑ wouldn't work in our family
   ❑ a possibility I'm willing to consider
   ❑ definitely a good idea
   ❑ already applying the principle

For you to share with your spouse

1. Sit down facing each other and share your responses to the above questions.
2. Discuss the possibility of holding regular family meetings.
3. Share how a problem from your past has been used to produce a blessing.
4. Tell one thing you really love about each other.
5. Say together the week's Scripture memory verse.
6. Pray for each other, either silently or aloud.

SEE GOD AT WORK

I remember the day Nancy and Al first attended our blending family support group. They were obviously nervous. Al had not wanted to come, but Nancy had said, "We either go to this group and get some help, or I'm out of here." So Al came–reluctantly.

Al had determined that he would simply sit and listen. *I will not parade my family's problems before strangers,* he thought. Is it possible that God in His wisdom intervened and only 5 of our usual fifteen group members attended that night? Absolutely. In a large group, one can hide. In a small group, it's next to impossible.

Can you guess what happened? Al talked. We zeroed in on Al and Nancy's situation, almost as though it was a private counseling session. And it helped. Nancy and Al attended nearly every meeting during the next five years, growing and learning. Eventually they were leaders in the group, sharing insights with others.

I celebrate all the Al's and Nancy's I have encountered through the years. I was an Al once, with a wife demanding change. I will share more of my journey during this week. Hopefully you believe you are on a similar journey. Have you enjoyed the positive feeling of encouraging someone in your group? Would you consider leading a group to study *New Faces in the Frame?*

Although it is our final week of study, think of it as a beginning for you and your blended family. Day 1 is the first day of the rest of your blended family life. Seize the day, practice what you've learned, and as you move on from your group, be sensitive to opportunities to encourage other blending families. Share the good news that with Christ, all things are possible! (Philippians 4:13).

What You'll Study
DAY 1
- **Redeem Your Mistakes**
DAY 2
- **Develop Patience**
DAY 3
- **Move Through the Pain**
DAY 4
- **Revisit the Stages**
DAY 5
- **Live God's Plan**

This Week You Will:
- allow God to use your mistakes for personal growth and ministry to others;
- implement actions that lead to developing patience;
- deal constructively with personal and family pain;
- revisit the stages of blended family living to determine progress;
- affirm God's plan for your blended family.

This Week's Scripture Memory Verse
"Trust in the Lord with all your heart and lean not on your own understanding; in all your ways acknowledge him, and he will make your paths straight" (Proverbs 3:5-6).

REDEEM YOUR MISTAKES

*B*lending families resemble a chess game in progress. If you don't play chess, you may not know that chess is an extremely intricate game. Even the greatest chess masters are able to see only about three moves ahead. Beyond that the variables are too great. Thirty-two pieces, each with different moves, make it impossible to predict how your opponent will play.

The variables are also great in a blending family. Because of varying backgrounds, every blending family is different, and each family member is unique. As family members work at blending, the way they interact with each other changes and grows. What works well in one blending family may not work at all in another. While there are similarities, the variables make your blending family one-of-a-kind.

Although the ideas in this workbook have been successful in other blending families, you must apply them to your own situation. God understands that. He knows you are trying to build a foundation based on solid principles, and He will be with you in the effort. This week we are focusing on practical helps during times of stress, and my purpose is to give hope to those of you who are struggling. Hope does not necessarily spring eternal during stormy times. My advice to you is to stay with the process and look for God's footprints in your life. I have found Him to be a faithful guide and teacher.

Growing Through My Divorce

Blended family couples often enter a subsequent marriage feeling like failures. Divorce and single parenting take their toll on self-esteem and self-confidence. Then the fear sets in. Perhaps you have asked yourself, *Will I manage this new family better than I did my former one?*

God knows that we will make mistakes. All of us sin and fall far short of bringing glory to God. While that is not an excuse for wrongdoing, we only fool ourselves if we pretend otherwise. Much of the blending family process is trial-and-error. Hopefully, we learn from our mistakes, but mistakes cause consequences—hurt feelings, conflicts, distrust, and misunderstanding. The flip side is that mistakes also provide built-in opportunities for growth.

I think of my own divorce that way. Looking back, certainly I regret the mistakes in my first marriage and I'm ashamed of the many failures. Everyone of us in that family, including my children, bears scars as a result of those failures. I struggled more and felt more depressed after my divorce than at any other time in my life. I was lost and in deep trouble. There were times when I even doubted that God was with me.

Now I realize God never left me. He was at my side every step of the way, waiting to take my failures and use them as only He could to build something new

We know that in all things God works for the good of those who love him, who have been called according to his purpose.
—Romans 8:28

and worthwhile. Even now, this fact truly amazes me. At the time, I believed the only way I could ever be happy again was to find someone else (this time the right one) and get married. I had bought into the "they lived happily ever after" fairy tale all the way. I was a half-soul, searching for my other half in order to be whole.

Over a four year period and through a very painful journey, God led me to a singles ministry that changed my entire life. At the time, I was in the process of leaving the ministry and studying journalism at Ohio State University. I actually thought God was leading me out of the pastorate to do something different. In a way He was. I have not pastored in the traditional sense of the word since that time. However, I have continued to pastor in a specialized way.

It seems to me that from the very first time I attended a "Positive Christian Singles" group, I knew God was calling me to work with single adults. *Every church needs something like this,* I thought. Soon I began working with a pastor to develop a singles ministry in another church. That particular program was so successful that I began consulting with other churches to develop similar ministries. God used my pain to help others, and that in turn brought healing to my own life.

Today, through my consulting efforts and the use of my book, *Launching and Sustaining Successful Singles Ministry,* I have been involved in over two thousand singles ministries around the world. In my wildest dreams, I would never have imagined such a thing. And still, God is not finished. God will use some of you in successful ministry to other blending families. Your mistakes, like mine, will become another of God's building blocks for new and challenging ministries.

God will use some of you in successful ministry to other blending families.

🐾 **Have you sensed God's leadership to use your blended family experience as a ministry to others?** ❑ Yes ❑ No

If yes, check possible ministry options to which you are open.
❑ pray for other blended families
❑ lead a group through *New Faces in the Frame.*
❑ promote and publicize *New Faces in the Frame* in your church/community
❑ take an ongoing responsibility in singles ministry
❑ other? _____

Growing Through My Remarriage

In 1982 I married again. As I said earlier in the workbook, I was totally naive about blending a family. I assumed this marriage would incorporate the best of my first marriage and the best of all I had learned since then. I knew I had grown in the intervening years, and Betty and I anticipated a wonderful life together.

Well, today, we have that wonderful marriage. But it did not come easily nor quickly. I continued to make mistakes as a husband. I still remember the pain and struggle. You may recall from week 1 that Betty considered leaving our marriage at one point. When the Stepfamily Association of America states that it takes four to seven years to achieve a good working blended family relationship, I agree and share that expectation with other families because it was very much our family experience.

When Betty and I started our blending family support group at the church where I presently serve, we did so because we needed it—desperately. At the time,

I did not understand that God could use our family struggles to help others. Today, once again, I see how God has used my mistakes and sculpted them into something useful. God does that. Christ took our sins and redeemed them for eternal life. In the same way, God takes our mistakes and redeems them for personal growth and help for others we influence along the way.

❧ Identify at least one area in which you have noticeably grown as a result of your remarriage.

_____

_____

Growing Through Parenting and Stepparenting

Betty and I discovered that our growth as parents and stepparents was exceedingly slow. We caught glimpses of what our family could be like only to watch them slip away. One of the most difficult times in my own blending family occurred when my grown daughter pulled totally away from my wife and me. For almost five years we had no communication with her. I did not know where she was living or how she was doing. For a parent, it was a terrifying feeling.

During this time, I prayed for her daily. Many times I wept and asked God to restore her to my life. Time dragged on. I knew God loved me; however, I could not imagine anything good coming from this separation. I was wrong.

In the fullness of God's time (which was certainly not my time), our relationship was restored. During our separation, my daughter matured into a fine young woman. She needed this time away from us to grow into the person God intended. Betty and I needed that time to cement our relationship. With my daughter gone, eliminating the reason for many of our arguments, we were able to concentrate on our marriage. God redeemed the experience.

When the relationship with my daughter was restored, my son stopped writing, answering letters, and calling. Again, I experienced a great deal of pain, and again, God was faithful to sustain our family.

God gave Betty and me the ability to endure the set-backs and disappointments with our children. Instead of concentrating on our mistakes as parents and stepparents, we put our trust in the One who makes paths straight.

❧ Identify at least one area in which you have noticeably grown as a result of parenting and stepparenting:

_____

_____

❧ Read this week's Scripture memory verse in the margin. Underline the phrases you want to express to God as prayer thoughts today.

Trust in the Lord with all your heart and lean not on your own understanding; in all your ways acknowledge him, and he will make your paths straight.
—Proverbs 3:5-6

DEVELOP PATIENCE

Cathy was depressed. This marriage was not at all what she hoped it would be. While she had anticipated some problems in blending their two families, she had never imagined it would be this tough. Surely, after six months they should be further along in the process. *How long will it take for these two families to feel comfortable together?* Cathy wondered.

Cathy failed to understand that her timetable for blending was unrealistic. Many who enter blending families anticipate that their problems will last only a year at the most. One day a concerned woman called me about her brother and his blending family. Her brother had been married three months and was experiencing typical difficulties with the blending process. She said to me, "After three months, I would think they would have worked out all of these problems."

I said to her: "If they had been married six years and were no further along in the blending process than they are, I might be concerned. At this point, what you have described sounds perfectly normal." Her expectations were impractical. I urged her to have patience.

Patience Is a Virtue

No matter where you are in the blending process, patience is indeed a virtue. The way we learn patience is by living through situations that call for patience. Blending families are a good place to develop this spiritual discipline.

Many of us have mistaken ideas about patience. Some think patience means never getting upset or angry, and never questioning circumstances or situations. I would not describe such behavior as patience. Rather, I would define it as denial—refusing to face trouble.

The Bible personality, Job, has often been referred to as a prime example of patience. However, Job certainly is not an example of someone who never got upset, expressed anger, or questioned life. Job did all of these things. He became very upset with his three friends (Job 6:14-15,21). And He expressed his anger at what they told him (Job 13:1-4). Job even expressed his anger with God (Job 16:1-8) and then questioned why God was allowing him to suffer (Job 19:7). If Job was patient, then patience definitely is not as many people define it.

Patience, real patience, has to do with trust. It involves trusting and believing that regardless of the situation, God is still there. He cares for us, and He will provide. Job's story, while probably more dramatic than anything most of us will experience, is our story at times. Haven't we all known times when the world seemed to fall apart? when God's will was unclear? when we prayed and then wondered if God even heard us?

Such times call for trust that reaches far beyond understanding. We have no real difficulty in trusting God's goodness and love when everything is going our way. Who needs to be patient when only good things are happening? When we are overwhelmed by life, then we reach down deep for patience. If we trust God to make it happen according to His perfect timing—that is patience.

> **Patience involves trusting and believing that regardless of the situation, God is still there. He cares for us, and He will provide.**

✎ Recall a time in your life when you exercised patience. Looking back, how was God working in the situation?

_____

_____

In what ways did your faith and trust grow?

_____

_____

Near the end of Job's story, Job says, "My ears had heard of you but now my eyes have seen you" (Job 42:5). Job's story described a man going through great agony. Nevertheless, Job held to his trust that God was in control. Finally, his faith was vindicated.

✎ Read Job 42:10 in the margin. Draw a line to connect the following words that illustrate Job's journey through life in the order they occurred.

restoration   disasters   doubt

prosperity   forgiveness   faith

After Job had prayed for his friends, the Lord made him prosperous again and gave him twice as much as he had before. —Job 42:10

Note that Job's faith and forgiveness came before his restoration. God honors our sincere attempts to trust Him and be obedient. Faith is stepping out into the darkness. If Job had seen restoration before exercising faith, his faith would have been "by sight" and thus not faith at all.

Why Blending Families Need Patience

Let's get back to Cathy and her husband Rob. When they married, Cathy had a 7-year-old son and a 4-year-old daughter. Rob had a 15-year-old daughter and a 9-year-old son. All of the children lived with them most of the time but frequently saw their other biological parents.

✎ From what you know about blending families, which child is likely to give Cathy and Rob the most heartbreak? Why?

_____

_____

If you answered Rob and Cathy were likely to experience the most difficulties with Rob's 15-year-old, you were absolutely right. Teenagers are trying to pull away from their families and become independent. Additionally, teenagers are generally more vocal than younger children. Each of the children, as well as Rob and Cathy themselves, faced massive readjustments. We will read more of their story in day 3. Blending families need patience while growing and changing. Patience provides the ability to trust in God's goodness in the midst of turmoil. Patience allows us to progress according to God's timetable instead of our own.

How to Develop Patience

Some persons are more patient by nature than others. A more laid-back personality style is more inclined to be patient than a Type-A personality who is always on the go. Some use their personalities as an excuse for being impatient. Others grew up with impatient people and never saw patience modeled. Still others believe, like Benjamin Franklin, that "God helps those who help themselves." If God seems slow in providing a solution, they think they are helping Him out by pitching in and doing it themselves!

🌿 **How does a person learn to be patient? What advice would you give to an impatient person?**

_____

_____

A friend once told me to be careful about praying for patience. He said whenever we pray for a character quality, God gives us the opportunities we need to develop it. Praying for patience invites God to place us in situations that demand patience. Since that conversation, I have hesitated to ask God for patience!

However, I believe my friend is right. God does teach us through life experiences. We learn patience through situations that call for us to be patient. In trying times I pray: "Lord, I will wait for Your perfect time. I trust in Your love. I know Your goodness. I leave this in Your capable hands."

Humans want everything immediately, according to our expectations. However, God really does know what is best for us. He sees the big picture, while we see only a small piece of the puzzle. Therefore, we plunge ahead blindly, not knowing where we are going. We need His guidance because only God can see the completed puzzle.

Waiting for God's time requires believing that God truly loves us in a personal way. Believing and claiming the truth of John 3:16 for everyone else is much easier than accepting God's love for me as an individual. Something within me refuses to accept this act of grace. Perhaps knowing my personal sins causes me to think that God can love everyone else but me. However, the truth of the gospel is that God actually loves you and me that much. He loves each of us far more than we love ourselves, and He wants good things for us—His children.

🌿 **Our Scripture memory verse for this week gives us a clue to developing patience. In the margin underline the word that leads to patience.**

🌿 **Patience is the ability to trust in God and wait on His timing. Waiting is not passive. Our memory verse also indicates what we are to do while waiting. Circle the words that describe our actions while waiting.**

"For God so loved the world that he gave his one and only Son, that whoever believes in him shall not perish but have eternal life."
—John 3:16

Trust in the Lord with all your heart and lean not on your own understanding; in all your ways acknowledge him, and he will make your paths straight.
—Proverbs 3:5-6

MOVE THROUGH THE PAIN

Have you noticed that most of the case studies thus far in this workbook have had happy endings? Families have worked out their problems and come to terms with all the variables that were hindering the blending process. I hope you have identified with these real-life stories and have a similar family story to tell.

A more realistic assumption is that many of you do not have happy endings to share. You have tried the approaches suggested in this workbook but have not yet seen visible results. You may want to say to me: "I'm trying to wait patiently on the Lord. But isn't there anything else I can do?"

Real life is not a movie—complete with a happy ending. I don't want to rush past your pain of today with a syrupy statement about what may yet lie ahead for you and your family. Today is today. And today you may feel terrible!

A corrolary truth is that you must move through the pain. We easily get stuck in ruts of self-pity and recriminations. How is it possible to look ahead with bright expectations, while at the same time dealing honestly with today's heartbreaks? We will explore the tension of living in the present and believing there is hope for the future.

Pain's Origins

Life would be so simple if we could just ascribe pain to the devil and his legions. The fact is that some pain results from doing good! Read Hebrews 11:35-38 in the margin. The persons mentioned in this section from the heroes of faith chapter were persecuted for being obedient to God! Some of your pain as a blended family member is the result of trying to do the right thing, yet being criticized for it. Perhaps a family member has misunderstood or disagreed with your decisions. They may be reacting out of their own pain and are oblivious to the pain they cause you.

Cathy and Rob faced a situation of this kind with his daughter Mary Ann, who did everything possible to disrupt their home life. She led them on a roller-coaster ride over four years of skipping school, occasional drug use, breaking curfews, and petty shoplifting. Discipline tools that worked well with the other children—loss of phone privileges, car, dates, television, to name a few—seemed to make little impression. In fact, Mary Ann became more belligerent.

Cathy and Rob began family therapy. Mary Ann remained uncooperative and unresponsive. At one point, she ran away from home. After three days, they located her at the home of a friend who lived in a nearby town.

One day in the counselor's office Rob asked, "What have we done wrong?"

The counselor responded: "If you were totally responsible for Mary Ann's behavior, you would have four unruly children! As it is, you only have one. Mary Ann makes her own life choices; now she must live with the consequences."

Others were tortured and refused to be released, so that they might gain a better resurrection. Some faced jeers and flogging, while still others were chained and put in prison. They were stoned; they were sawed in two; they were put to death by the sword. They went about in sheepskins and goatskins, destitute, persecuted and mistreated—the world was not worthy of them. They wandered in deserts and mountains, and in caves and holes in the ground.
—Hebrews 11:35-38

🌿 **Do you relate to Cathy and Rob's story? If so, what are your feelings as you assess the problems in your family? Circle them.**

depression   discouragement   low energy   sadness
shame   self-pity   despair

God made us different from all His other creations. He gave us a free will, and He allows us to choose His way or our own way. As parents we must remember that our children reach an age of accountability when we can no longer dictate their choices. Blaming ourselves for their choices is unproductive. Instead, become responsible for your own emotions, actions, and reactions to their choices.

Pain's Responses

Our reactions to pain vary with our individual differences. Some people have a high tolerance for pain; others, a low tolerance. Some personalities roll with life's tides, and others of us are agitated when the smallest change comes our way.

It would be presumptuous for me to tell you how to respond to pain, but I can share some responses that produce better results than others. Nonproductive responses include displays of temper, blaming, holding grudges, bitterness, self-pity, judgmental attitudes, and self-condemnation. When we turn on ourselves or others with a critical spirit, we lose our ability to influence the situation positively.

I am not recommending that we stuff our feelings. I am talking about getting stuck in our pain. Pain can become a time-warp with no visible end in sight. What if you cut your finger on a piece of paper and two years later you still felt that sharp jab of pain? A healthy body regenerates itself; the wound heals. God intends for our emotional wounds to heal also. He wants to work with us through the process to promote healing. The Holy Spirit was sent to comfort us, so that we in turn can comfort others (2 Corinthians 1:3-5).

Productive responses move us forward so that resolution is possible. Acknowledging our pain is a necessary step toward healing our wounds. We may need to ask forgiveness from God, from one or more persons, and from ourselves. Living as a forgiven person allows us to take appropriate actions of restitution and act responsibly in the situation. Remember—you are only accountable for your attitudes and actions. You cannot control the attitudes and actions of others.

Cathy and Rob determined that they would not allow the use of drugs or alcohol in their home. When they discovered drug paraphernalia in Mary Ann's bedroom, they admitted her to a drug treatment facility. Rob said it was the hardest decision he ever made. After high-school graduation, Mary Ann lived with friends in an apartment. She worked on and off, losing as many jobs as she kept. But Cathy and Rob together decided not to bail her out by paying her rent.

I wish I could tell you that today Mary Ann is doing well. As this workbook is being written, she remains estranged from her family. Cathy and Rob continue the blending family process with the other children. Their marriage has grown stronger through the struggles.

Pain's Effects

You may have heard the expression, "life's experiences make us better or bitter." Where do you find yourself at this point in life?

Acknowledging our pain is a necessary step toward healing our wounds.

🦋 On the following continuum, put an X to mark your response:

better   bitter

Peter said that although we must suffer grief due to life's trials, these trials prove the genuineness of our faith. Read 1 Peter 1:7 in the margin.

James, in his boldness, suggested that we rejoice in our trials. Times of testing build perseverance, which results in maturity (James 1:3). Pain is not the source of our joy; God gives the joy as we trust Him to bring us through the pain.

I have a friend with cerebral palsy. He is married and the father of two children. A deacon in his church, he is often called on to give his personal testimony. Recently he was honored as handicapped person of the year in his community. Life's pain has made him better, not bitter.

🦋 Read this week's Scripture memory verse in the margin. Identify a problem you want to trust the Lord to bring you though. Pause to thank Him for His commitment to you as His child.

These have come so that your faith—of greater worth than gold, which perishes even though refined by fire—may be proved genuine and may result in praise, glory and honor when Jesus Christ is revealed.
—1 Peter 1:7

Trust in the Lord with all your heart and lean not on your own understanding; in all your ways acknowledge him, and he will make your paths straight.
—Proverbs 3:5-6

DAY 4

REVISIT THE STAGES

*D*o you remember when you began this study nearly twelve weeks ago? It seems like forever, doesn't it? During week 1 you looked at the various stages blending families usually experience as they grow. Today we will revisit those stages and evaluate where you have been and where you are going. You may have entered a new stage during this study. If so, looking back and looking ahead will provide some perspective.

Remember that stages are not something you pass through and never see again. We revisit various stages throughout our lives. Therefore, we may repeatedly experience times of crisis and times of growth. As we review the stages this time around, we will consider the children's experiences. Often, parents may be in one stage, while the children are in another. Realizing this fact can help us better understand one another.

The Infatuation Stage
The first stage we studied is the Infatuation Stage. For the couple, it is the time period during which you fell in love. Take a moment to recall those exciting days. Return to this stage periodically and remember those wonderful feelings.

Betty and I became quickly infatuated with each other. I can still picture Betty as she stood by that door at the church where we met. I probably will always look back on those days as some of the happiest of my life. Infatuation is like that.

Our children experience a period of infatuation also—at least some do. While some children oppose a mother or father's remarriage, most wish for a home with two parents. Some of our children remember happy times when mom and dad lived together. During the infatuation stage, children imagine that when mom or dad marries again, life will return to what they perceive as normal. The infatuation stage for children can end abruptly when they realize how different their new family is from what they wanted and expected.

🌿 **Did your children or stepchildren have unrealistic expectations about your remarriage? What were they?**

_____

_____

The Questioning Stage

The second stage for blending families is the Questioning Stage. The couple doubts their earlier certainty concerning the family's future. Children enter this stage when the reality of blending family living overcomes their fantasy expectations. The Questioning Stage is not pleasant. It's a time when we ask ourselves, _What have I done? Did I make a mistake?_

The Questioning Stage moves us past infatuation and begins to teach us about real love. Infatuation is based upon fantasy. Real love is based on reality. Infatuation requires nothing and costs nothing; it just happens and overwhelms us. Real love requires hard work and commitment; it forces us to grow.

No one moves straight from total infatuation to constant questioning. The questioning stage begins with little nagging doubts that creep in when you begin to discover that this other person is not entirely as you pictured him or her. Perhaps that person has little annoying habits. The habits may have always been there, but now they are more irritating. Little by little, questions form in your mind.

It is possible to enter the Questioning Stage even before the wedding. Many couples (perhaps even most) do. This stage is not enjoyable, but, thankfully, it is part of a progression of stages.

🌿 **If your children had positive feelings before your marriage, but then changed afterward, what led you to believe they were questioning the benefits of their new family? Circle your responses.**

anger   withdrawal   sadness   misbehavior   grief

other?   _____

The Crisis Stage

Not every family experiences a distinct crisis stage during which someone threatens to leave. However, most blending families move through a stage when they are aware that family life needs considerable improvement. One or more family members is calling for change.

Infatuation requires nothing and costs nothing; it just happens and overwhelms us. Real love requires hard work and commitment; it forces us to grow.

I call this the Crisis Stage because for a large number of blending families they reach a distinct turning point. Consider this stage as a positive event because it is the pathway to the latter stages. When a couple (or more often one part of the couple) reaches the point where they will no longer accept an inferior marriage and family life, positive things happen.

Some couples remain in the Questioning Stage for years, afraid to enter the Crisis Stage. They sense that this stage is a fork in the road that could lead to another broken marriage. Some couples fear this relationship stage so much that they sit on their pain, hoping that ultimately the family will be happy.

🌿 **If you have lived through the Crisis Stage, what was that experience (those experiences) like for your children? How were they affected?**

_____

_____

Betty and I experienced crisis every time my daughter came home from college. Without thinking, my daughter and I would make plans and then invite Betty to come along. Looking back, I can hardly believe I was so insensitive to her feelings; she felt like an outsider. Her resentment grew until it became a crisis. The positive outcome of this crisis was that Betty and I sought help. We were forced to look at and talk about our relationship. We saw the need for a support group and began our blended family ministry.

Crises faced honestly and boldly–along with a conviction that those involved will not walk away without doing everything possible to hold the family together–almost always reap positive results.

The Possibility Stage

By now, some of you may be in the Possibility Stage of your blending family. Others may have at least caught glimpses of this stage. For many, the Possibility Stage is a great relief following the Crisis Stage.

🌿 **If you have been through the Crisis Stage, when did you first realize that your family was going to make it?**

_____ months(years) into the marriage

What led the children to come to that conclusion?

_____

_____

For Betty and me, the Possibility Stage began when we attended a stepfamily seminar at Georgia State University. Attending that seminar was an act of desperation. We knew we needed help. Several wonderful things happened at that seminar. First, we met other blending family couples who were also experiencing

When a couple (or more often one part of the couple) reaches the point where they will no longer accept an inferior marriage and family life, positive things happen.

problems. Second, we were given some tools to work on our problems. We learned about books that addressed blending family needs. We heard experts speak in specific terms about particular struggles concerning our children.

Third, Betty and I were able to meet real people who were successful in their blended family journey. We began to feel normal again and were able to say, "If they could make it, so can we." While we certainly had not solved all of our problems, we left the seminar with something we didn't have before—hope! Possibilities loomed ahead!

The Growth Stage

The longest stage in the blending families process is the Growth Stage. Growth is a slow process. When Betty and I bought our house in a new subdivision, there were two maple trees planted in front of the house. When we moved in, those trees were about twelve feet high. That was nine years ago. Now, those trees are taller than our house. There has been a lot of growth in nine years.

During the Growth Stage, blending families begin to develop family closeness. Stepparents begin to feel accepted by the children. Biological parents stop juggling relationships and begin to relax. They no longer feel pulled apart. The children accept the new family situation and may even like it. The blending process is now visible, whereas before it was less visible.

Although you may not have moved into the Growth Stage yet, what signs of growth have you observed in your children?

_____

_____

For several years, Betty and I seemed to move repeatedly from the Possibility Stage into the Growth Stage, then back to the Crisis Stage, into the Possibility Stage, then into the Growth Stage. Some lessons are extremely difficult to learn. Also, keep in mind that it is not just the couple learning; the children (no matter their ages) are learning too. You cannot learn their lessons for them. You can help them, but in the end, the children must work to overcome their own struggles.

The Reward Stage

The Reward Stage is the goal for blending families.

The final stage is the Reward Stage—the goal for blending families. Finally, family members can talk together comfortably. There is less of the "walking on eggs" feeling because family members are more relaxed. What a joy!

When you reach the Reward Stage, you have to wonder, _What took us so long?_ Betty and I only recently entered the Reward Stage, and we have been married almost fifteen years. There were many times during the Growth Stage that we experienced the rewards of blending family living. But there still were missing pieces. It was a little like an incomplete puzzle. The picture was obvious—but a few details were missing.

Don't settle for less than the Reward Stage. Keep it as your goal. Ask God to give you hope and patience as you work to attain a successful blended family.

🕊️ **If you have been through one or more stages during this New Faces study, identify it.**

from _____ Stage to _____ Stage

🕊️ **Which stage would you say your children (stepchildren) are in? Use the margins for more than one child.**

_____ Stage

💗 **Think of ways to encourage movement toward the next stage.**

DAY 5

LIVE GOD'S PLAN

*D*o you believe that God has a plan for you and your blending family? He does! We may think our lives are moving along in random fashion, without order or design. We make choices, and based on those choices, our lives become better or worse. While there is some truth in that concept, never forget that God is ever present, working to mold our lives into something beautiful. Even when we do not choose His way, God does not give up on us. He is constantly calling us back to Him and away from danger and foolish choices.

The Faith Walk

We may find that even when we want to follow God's plan, that plan seems unclear. We may pray, "Dear Lord, show me what to do," and still hear nothing. Only silence! Most of us have felt God was not listening or answering.

Although our knowledge of God's plan may be vague at times, realize that God is guiding even when it is not clearly evident to us. One of the great advantages of growing older is the opportunity to look back over my life and recognize how often God's grace was at work even when it was unseen by me. Today I recognize God's constant watch care during many times I felt I was stumbling along.

While I do not believe that God intended my first marriage to end in divorce, I can see how God redeemed that tragedy. Also, I can see His love and grace during those painful years when I was estranged from my daughter and then my son. Although I can accept that now, at the time it only hurt. God nurtured spiritual growth and maturity in all our lives.

In 1 Corinthians 13 the apostle Paul wrote: "Now we see but a poor reflection as in a mirror; then we shall see face to face. Now I know in part; then I shall know fully, even as I am fully known" (v. 12). Such is life. As earthly mortals, none of us are capable of seeing the complete picture. That's why we need faith! God sees everything. We must keep our eyes on Him and be obedient.

Take a moment and read Numbers 9:15-23. How did the Israelites know God's will for their lives?

_____

Has God's will ever been this obvious in your own life? List some times when you knew of God's will at a given moment.

_____

_____

I have had three such times in my life: when I knew my task was to help develop single adult ministries; when I met my wife Betty; and when Betty and I attended the stepfamily seminar at Georgia State University.

Most times we don't get to see the fire and the cloud as the Israelites did. That's where faith comes in. If everything in our lives were always perfectly clear, we would not need faith. As Hebrews 11:1 says, "Now faith is being sure of what we hope for and certain of what we do not see." We learn and practice faith during times when we are unsure of the path ahead.

Faith is trusting in God's love enough to know that He is always working for our good—even when it is taking much longer than we want and we are not seeing the results we desire. I had to rely on faith after my call to singles ministry. An avenue for following that call did not materialize very quickly. Churches were not standing in line to invite my help. Economically, my decision to consult with churches developing such ministries was a disaster. At one point, my income was only $300 a month, and my rent was $350.

Anyone could see that my plan was not working. A minister asked me: "Why are you so stubborn? Why don't you just take a church like the rest of us?" But I knew I had heard God's call to singles ministry. How could I do less than wait on God? Nevertheless, I did question whether I had heard His call correctly.

There is a humorous story about a farmer who looked up into the sky and saw that the clouds formed the letters *PC*. The farmer believed it to be a clear call from God to "preach Christ." Therefore, he left farming and went into the ministry. However, he was not equipped for preaching, visitation, or other important aspects of ministry.

One day a friend questioned his decision to be a minister. The farmer/minister explained about his call. The friend thought for a minute, then said, "Did you ever stop to think that maybe God meant for you to plant corn?"

Had I heard God correctly? Surely, if I had, I would not be starving, I thought. I grew very close to God during this time, and my call was confirmed. My faith had to grow up. Perhaps your faith needs to grow, too. Understand that God is not punishing you when He gives you faith lessons. He is training you so that you can live a more productive life for Him.

Understand that God is not punishing you when He gives you faith lessons.

 Is God teaching you a faith lesson through experiences in your life right now? Think about what He may be saying to you. Ask Him how you can cooperate with His plan.

Can We Lose the Way?

One of the Bible's greatest mysteries is why God chose to work through fallible human beings to make Himself known to the world. He could have announced Himself through angels exclusively. Today, He could use any means known to us and many more we know nothing about. Yet, God still depends on you and me to spread the word about His saving grace.

While scars from our sins may last a lifetime, God still uses those experiences in a positive way. No one is as helpful to an alcoholic as someone who has overcome alcohol addiction. No one can offer comfort and encouragement to a person experiencing divorce as well as someone who has been there and moved on. No one is as helpful to blending families as someone who has traveled the same journey. God can take all of these circumstances and use them to His glory.

Throughout the Gospels, Jesus expressed His anger with those who pretended they had no failures. Jesus said they were like "whitewashed tombs, which look beautiful on the outside but on the inside are full of dead men's bones and everything unclean" (Matthew 23:27). Failures are only failures if we quit. God is always working with us to transform those failures into successes.

Have you ever watched a tree grow over the years? Five years ago I planted a sweet gum seedling. It was only a twig with a few roots. Today, that tree stands about four feet tall. While it is still small, other sweet gum trees that stand nearby rise to over thirty feet. It will take years for this tree to reach its full height, and it will need a larger and stronger root system to sustain such height. But given time and nurture, that is its destiny. The same is true for us. While we might desire instant results, God in His wisdom designed us to grow slowly. In His hands and according to His time schedule, we *will* grow.

You Are Not Alone

God leads us in so many unseen ways that often we may regard them as coincidences. I heard a good definition of a coincidence. A coincidence is a little miracle where God chooses to remain anonymous. God has a plan. He will help you discover that plan. Using this workbook as a couple and participating in the weekly group meetings has already helped you discover part of that plan.

God wants your blending family to be a supportive family unit that nourishes and encourages every individual member. He is willing to lead you in making that become a reality. Even the journey toward that end is exciting when we acknowledge that God is in control. Relax in that confidence. God is with you. You are not alone.

🌿 There is a wonderful promise in Paul's second letter to the church at Corinth. Read it in the margin and underline the promise.

Heed Paul's admonition to "not lose heart." Keep in mind "what is seen is temporary." Momentary troubles are "achieving for us an eternal glory that far outweighs them all." From the perspective of eternity, the struggles to blend your family will pale in comparison to the blessings of relationship you have yet to see.

Therefore we do not lose heart. Though outwardly we are wasting away, yet inwardly we are being renewed day by day. For our light and momentary troubles are achieving for us an eternal glory that far outweighs them all. So we fix our eyes not on what is seen, but on what is unseen. For what is seen is temporary, but what is unseen is eternal.
—2 Corinthians 4:16-18

COUPLETALK

For you to complete

1. How have you allowed God to use your mistakes for personal growth and as a ministry to others?

_____

_____

2. What actions are you willing to take to become a more patient person? _____

_____

_____

3. How are you attempting to deal constructively with personal and family pain? _____

_____

_____

4. Dream about your future as a blending family. Describe what the Reward Stage would look like.

_____

_____

For you to share with your spouse

1. Sit facing each other and share your responses to the questions above.
2. Compare your responses to what stage you feel your marriage and your family are in at this point in time. Refer to p. 205.
3. Share what you feel is necessary to move individuals and the family to the next stage.
4. Tell one thing you really love about each other.
5. Say together this week's Scripture memory verse .
6. Pray for each other, silently or aloud.

GROUP LEADER GUIDE FOR SMALL-GROUP SESSIONS

This section is intended for the facilitator of a group studying *New Faces in the Frame: A Guide to Marriage and Parenting in the Blended Family.*

Scheduling the Course

New Faces in the Frame is divided into two 6-week studies. The first 6 weeks focuses on the blended couple relationship, and the second 6 weeks targets parenting issues in a blended family. You may schedule the course as a 12-week commitment or you may offer it as two 6-week studies, either back-to-back or with time between each study.

Some couples will more readily commit to 6 weeks instead of 12. Be sure to include those couples in your promotion plans when the second 6 weeks is offered.

Preparing to Lead

Familiarize yourself with the Contents page and the course map, "The Blended Family Tree," located on the inside cover of this book. Read the Introduction and the first week's lesson to prepare for the introductory session. The first page of each lesson summarizes the content for that week. Read as much as possible of the remainder of the book. The more familiar you are with the content, the more helpful you will be to group members as you overview and teach the course.

Each week this leader guide will give you suggestions for processing what you and your group members studied during the week. Adapt the suggested session plan to fit your situation. Be flexible. When discussion is flowing readily, stay with the topic, even if it means omitting the next activity from the lesson plan.

Some of the activities call for small-group discussion. If your group has fewer than five couples, simply do all of the activities together. If you have five couples or more, divide into subgroups of two to three couples for small-group activities. Then, allow members to report in the large group what they have gleaned from their small-group time.

The suggested session guides are designed for a 90-minute meeting. If you have more than 90 minutes, spend more time on each activity. If you have less than 90 minutes, select those activities which best fit your group.

Look over the next week's lesson plan early in the week in order to collect needed supplies or formulate your thoughts for discussion times. Check off each Before the Session activity as you complete it.

Leading the Session

Begin and end each session on time. Groups benefit from structure and predictability. During the session, seek to maintain an atmosphere of safety and caring for group members. Monitor the discussion and move to the next topic when you feel the group is ready.

Encourage group members to talk to one another rather than focusing on you. Share the leadership by redirecting a question to the group: "That's a good question, Susan. What ideas would you be willing to share with Susan?"

Give permission for group members to disagree. Our purpose is not to promote uniformity. Each marriage and parent represented will have unique personalities and styles, as well as value systems. We are in the group to support one another, not to become carbon copies of one another. Allow differences to emerge without feeling you must resolve them.

Our purpose is not to solve group members' problems. Often the group is most helpful by offering care and concern rather than advice. Some issues are resolved only through time and effort. Sharing someone's pain may be more healing than offering a "quick fix."

Since this study is based on biblical principles, encourage members to use and read from the Bible. Use biblical examples where appropriate and focus on attitudes and behaviors that are pleasing to God. Make prayer a significant part of each group session. At the same time, don't allow religious words, the Bible, or prayer to become a club to batter struggling individuals. Encourage "grace space" where fears, doubts, and spiritual struggles are acknowledged without criticism or judgmental attitudes.

Model the behavior you desire for group members. Demonstrate encouragement through eye contact and body language. Be authentic. Share from your own personal journey. If you are open about your own struggles, chances are group members will open up as well.

Operate the group on a feeling level. Help group members to identify and express their feelings in a comfortable way. Your comfort level with emotions will model acceptance for other group members.

Plan ahead and follow your lesson plan. Spontaneous changes may prove unwise. Remember that no perfect group facilitator exists and be patient with yourself. Communicating positive regard for others is more important than a well-executed lesson plan.

Evaluating the Session

After each session, spend a few minutes evaluating the session. Here are some suggested questions you might ask yourself:

1. Was any couple not represented this week? Do I need to make a follow-up call or send a note of encouragement?
2. Did I create a feeling of safety for sharing?
3. Did I communicate acceptance and concern?
4. Did I manage the group time wisely?
5. Were group members encouraged to help and support one another?
6. Did I practice good listening skills?
7. Did one person dominate the discussion? If so, how did I respond? What can I do to encourage participation by additional group members?
8. Did anything totally unexpected occur? How did I handle it? What should I have done differently?
9. How did I point participants to God's Word?
10. Would I recommend someone from this group to lead another group through *New Faces in the Frame?*

Introductory Session

Prior to the beginning of the 12-week study, offer an introductory session to accomplish these objectives:
- explain the purpose of the study;
- overview the content and resources;
- introduce yourself as facilitator;
- distribute copies of *New Faces in the Frame;*
- review the requirements for individual study and group sessions;
- secure a commitment to the group;
- assign the first week's lesson.

You may need to adapt the introductory session guide, which is designed for 90 minutes.

During the Introductory Session present the group covenant on p. 212. Have participants read the covenant together and verbally agree to its provisions. Or, reproduce it and ask members to sign and return it to you.

Couple Leadership

If you and your spouse are leading the group together, divide the responsibilities according to your individual gifts and abilities. Some couple leaders prefer both to give input throughout the session. Others divide the session plan and alternate leading activities. Still other couples have a primary facilitator and one who takes care of housekeeping issues, such as attendance, name tags and other printed material, weekday contacts and follow up.

Couple leadership has the advantage of providing a role model for both husband and wife. Both male and female viewpoints are represented. When participants observe a couple working together harmoniously, they feel hope for their own blended couple relationship.

Target Audience

Most churches have several blended couples who would benefit from studying *New Faces in the Frame*. Check with your pastor, minister of education, singles minister, and adult department directors to identify potential group members. Announce the study in your church bulletin and newsletter.

Consider the outreach potential of *New Faces in the Frame*. Invite blended couples in your community. This group could be an entry point for unchurched and unsaved adults. Place an advertisement in your local paper. Urge church members to distribute announcements to friends, relatives, and co-workers in blended families. Child-care centers and schools may allow you to promote *New Faces in the Frame*.

Ordering Materials

Order sufficient copies of *New Faces in the Frame* in advance of your first meeting. Order your workbooks through the Customer Service Center at 1-800-458-2772; or you may purchase them at a Baptist Book Store or LifeWay Christian Book Store.

INTRODUCTORY GROUP SESSION

Before the Session

1. Have available enough copies of *New Faces in the Frame: A Guide to Marriage and Parenting in the Blended Family* for each participant to have a copy.
2. If members are paying for part or all of their workbooks, make arrangements for collecting the money.
3. Prepare a group roster or attendance sheet. Keeping attendance records allows you to follow up on absentees. Regular contact is essential to prevent dropouts. Often participants need encouragement to complete the course.
4. Prepare to overview the course and week 1.
5. Duplicate copies of the Group Covenant found on p. 212 if you choose to have members sign it.
6. Arrange chairs in a semicircle. Arrange for a chalkboard or marker board, or attach tear sheets to the wall. Place name tags and markers near the door.

During the Session (80 minutes)

1. As participants enter the room, have them prepare their name tags and take a seat in the semicircle.
2. Begin the session promptly. Welcome everyone to the group. Open with prayer.
3. Ask one person representing each blended family to tell the length of time they have been a blended family and to share names and ages of the children in their blended family. Explain that there will be time for more sharing later in the session. Begin the sharing time yourself to model the role.
4. Ask, *What is the definition of a blended family?* Write the group's consensus definition on the chalkboard or another surface. Lead the group to identify some differences between blended families and nuclear families. List these under the definition.
5. Invite participants to share why they chose to be a part of this blended family study. Share your own reasons for participating in the group. Identify with group member's expectations. "I, too, am looking forward to...."

6. Clarify your role as facilitator. Point out that you are not the official answer-giver or fact-finder. Explain that you, too, are a group member, seeking support and encouragement in your own blended family.
7. Distribute copies of *New Faces in the Frame* and, if necessary, explain procedures for payment.
8. Ask participants to turn to the Contents page in their books. Present the course overview, using information you reviewed prior to the session. Then, direct members to look at the course map on the inside cover of the book as you explain it: The two sections of the book–Marriage and Parenting–are represented as branches of a tree, with the leaves representing each week's lessons. When these branches function well, the result is a strong sense of blendedness.
9. Direct members to the Introduction, p. 4. Ask one participant to read the Introduction aloud as members follow along, or you may read it aloud.
10. Ask members to locate week 1 in their books. Invite them to look over the unit page and read the week's objectives at the bottom of the page. Call attention to the weekly Scripture memory verse. Encourage the group to memorize each week's verse.
11. Lead members to look through the week 1 daily lessons. Then review the purpose of the CoupleTalk exercise at the end of each week's study. Explain that CoupleTalk allows couples to discuss the week's lessons before the group session, so they will feel more comfortable sharing with others. It also provides a built-in opportunity for couple communication, while providing time to establish mutual goals for the family.
12. Call for questions about the book or weekly assignments. Recap the importance of completing the reading and learning activities on a daily basis. Affirm the privacy of each member's book.
13. Instruct group members to complete week 1 before the next group meeting. Announce meeting time and date if different from the introductory session.

14. In the remaining time allotted for During the Session, allow members to tell their blended family story. Divide the time as equally as possible among families. Some couples will be more open than others. It often takes two to three sessions before participants feel comfortable sharing with one another. Do not force intimacy. Begin by sharing your own story.

Closing the Session (10 minutes)

1. Distribute copies of the Group Covenant. Ask participants to read and sign the Covenant and to give it to you before leaving the room. Or, read the Covenant aloud and ask for verbal commitments.

2. For the next session, ask each couple to bring a picture of a blended family tree similar to the course map including the names and pictures of individual family members (if possible) on the husband's and wife's tree branches. Couples may substitute a recent family portrait. If pictures are not available, include ages of the children on the family tree.

3. Ask for specific prayer requests and lead in a closing prayer. Collect Covenants as members depart.

GROUP COVENANT

To encourage a high level of trust, love, and openness in my *New Faces in the Frame* group, I covenant with my group's other members to:

1. Make attendance at group sessions a priority.

2. Complete each week's assignments prior to the group session.

3. Treat information shared in the group as confidential.

4. Support other group members as they share. I will try not to give advice or pressure other persons to see things my way.

5. I will pray for myself, my spouse, my group leader, and other group members.

Signed _____ Date _____

PROGRESS THROUGH THE STAGES

Before the Session

1. If you are combining this session with the introductory session, use the appropriate portions of that session to introduce this study.
2. If the group consists of more than five couples, be prepared to divide participants into smaller groups of two to three couples each for small-group assignments. If you are not dividing the large group, give the small-group assignments to the entire group.
3. Display your family tree picture. If you have newcomers, allow time for them to complete their pictures as an arrival activity. Provide extra paper and markers for newcomers as well as others who did not complete the assignment. Or, duplicate and provide copies of a fill-in-the-blank family tree. Use masking tape to mount pictures.
4. Plan to omit some activities if you have less than 90 minutes.
5. Arrange chairs in a semicircle. Place name tags near the door. Check attendance as members arrive.

During the Session

1. (10 minutes) Ask couples to mount their blended family tree pictures on the walls around the room. Welcome everyone to the group. Introduce newcomers. Open with prayer.
2. (10 minutes) Ask each couple to present their family tree. Instruct couples to share how long they have been married as well as children's names and ages. Also ask them to share if theirs is the primary home for their children or if children visit regularly.
3. (10 minutes) Give small groups (or the one large group) the following assignment. Say, *At the end of day 1 you listed helps and hindrances to the blending process. Share these ideas with one another. Select no more than three ideas from each category, and designate a group spokesperson.*
4. (5 minutes) Call for group reports. Affirm participants' ideas. Say to the group: *You already know a great deal about how to blend a family. We will learn other ways to facilitate blending during this study.*

5. (5 minutes) Invite participants to share their top three adjustments from the learning activity on p. 11.
6. (20 minutes) Review each stage of blended family living by asking members to describe an event or circumstance from each stage. Only two or three stages may be represented in your group. Ask volunteers to summarize the main distinctions of stages not covered by the testimonies.

    To encourage participation, prepare to share a personal example for the stages. Remember–not everyone will feel comfortable sharing at an indepth level. Affirm all responses. Do not allow the group to debate the stages nor the particular stage in which an experience may fit.
7. (10 minutes) Ask members to share with their small groups the particular stage of blended family living they see themselves in at this time. As they share, encourage them to explain their reasoning:
    • Why did they place themselves at this stage?
    • What does this stage feel like?
    • At what stage would they like to be?
    • How long do they anticipate it will take to reach that stage?
8. (10 Minutes) Point out that God is faithful to us in all situations. Read Deuteronomy 7:9. Affirm God's commitment to each person. Ask for testimonies of God's provision during their blended family experience.

Closing the Session (10 minutes)

1. Invite participants to share additional insights they gained this week about blended families.
2. Answer any questions about the workbook, CoupleTalk, or the group sessions.
3. Ask couples to bring one or more of their wedding pictures to the next session. Contact participants during the week and remind them of the assignment.
4. Ask for prayer requests. Close with prayer.

GIVE YOUR MARRIAGE PRIORITY

Before the Session

1. Remind members to bring a wedding picture as you contact them during the week.
2. Display the family tree pictures from session 1 if you do not use the "Name that Parent" game. Encourage couples to look over one another's trees in an effort to get to know each other better.
3. Print the five stages of grief on the chalkboard or poster board for display during step 5.
4. Arrange chairs in a semicircle. Continue to use name tags as you feel necessary.

During the Session

1. (5 minutes) Welcome participants to session 2. Check attendance. Open with prayer.
2. (5 minutes) Play "Name that Parent." Using the family tree charts, call out the name of a child and ask for the name of the biological parent in your group. Parents cannot identify their own children.
3. (10 minutes) Ask each couple to show their wedding picture(s) and tell about the wedding. Monitor the time or establish time limits. Follow up with the question, *How were your expectations for this marriage different?* Conclude by saying, *Although we believe we have set aside former relationships when we marry again, often grief, guilt, and past experiences affect the present relationship.*
4. (15 minutes) Ask, *How does the past interfere as we attempt to make our present marriage the priority?* Allow for several responses. Lead the group to list several criteria for claiming this marriage as a priority. For example, one criteria might be considering the needs of our spouses as equal to our own needs. List these criteria on the chalkboard or tear paper.
5. (10 minutes) Display the five stages of grief first identified by Dr. Elizabeth Kubler-Ross: 1) Denial: "This isn't happening"; 2) Anger: "I am angry about . . ."; 3) Bargaining: "If I do such-and-such, this won't happen/will happen again"; 4) Depression: "I feel helpless/hopeless"; 5) Acceptance – "I have come to terms with my grief." Instruct members to respond to

the following assignment in the margin of their books on p. 23. Say, *Think of a significant loss in your life. What stage of grief are you in at the present time?* Allow for writing time; then invite testimonies from members about ways they have dealt with grief.

6. (5 minutes) If you have unsaved persons in your group, take this opportunity to review the steps to forgiveness. If not, discuss, *How can we know we have been forgiven by God for our mistakes in the past?*
7. (10 minutes) Divide members into small groups and give this assignment: *List qualities Joseph demonstrated in overcoming his past that would be helpful for blending family couples (See p. 30). Be prepared to share these qualities with the large group.* Allow 5 minutes for small-group sharing and 5 minutes for the group reports. Summarize the importance of moving beyond our past experiences.
8. (10 minutes) Lead a discussion on the importance of trust in blended family relationships. Ask, *Why is it difficult to trust? What helps/hinders you in trusting again?* Affirm the importance of trusting God as a basis for trusting others.
9. (10 minutes) Invite participants to share one or more of the marriage goals they agreed to during CoupleTalk. Compliment couples for setting goals. Emphasize the importance of reviewing these goals throughout the *New Faces in the Frame* study. Suggest couples post their goals at home as a reminder.

Closing the Session (10 minutes)

1. Allow unstructured time for individuals to ask questions, make comments, or share insights. Avoid being the "answer-giver." Model the role of a good group participant.
2. Get input as to whether members are working through the learning activities, keeping up with their reading, and participating in CoupleTalk. Do not be critical. Simply evaluate participation and offer encouragement.
3. Call for prayer requests. Close with prayer.

BUILD COMMUNICATION SKILLS

Before the Session

1. Make two signs on poster board or chart paper. Label one "Talkers" and the other "Quiet Ones." Mount these on opposite walls of your meeting room. Place chairs in a semicircle under each sign.

2. Provide tear sheets, markers, and masking tape for use in small groups.

3. Contact your pastor to learn if he offers family counseling and his procedure for scheduling appointments. Ask him to recommend Christian counselors in your area. Consider duplicating and distributing names during the session. Always provide more than one referral source. A single referral may be interpreted as a recommendation. Gather information about upcoming marriage enrichment opportunities in your church or area.

During the Session

1. (15 minutes) As members enter, ask them to sit under the sign that best describes their communication style. When most members are seated, give this assignment: *Considering your communication style, compile a list of ideas that will help you become a better communicator.* Ask groups to write their suggestions on a tear sheet and post it when they are finished.

   Suggest members review week 3 of *New Faces in the Frame* for ideas. Allow time for group reports.

   Lead a discussion of the issues involved when a talker marries a quiet person.

2. (10 minutes) Have members move their chairs to the usual room arrangement. Ask them to turn to p. 48 in their workbooks. Assign the Proverbs Scriptures to volunteers to read aloud and identify the communication tip from their verse(s). As a group, say together Colossians 3:14. Suggest members adopt this week's Scripture memory verse as a motto, tempering all communication with love.

3. (15 minutes) Say, *Communication style is only one of many potential differences between husbands and wives.* Invite participants to share ways they differ from their

mates. Ask them to tell how they have learned to live with these differences.

   Point out the potential dangers of attempting to change each other. Instead lead the group to focus on ways to adapt to differences.

4. (10 minutes) Refer participants to week 3 CoupleTalk on p. 55. Invite members to share ideas they listed for 1) what to share, 2) when to share, and 3) how to share. Be prepared to give examples from your own marriage to stimulate discussion.

5. (5 minutes) Ask, *Who kept a schedule during the week to determine possible alone time?* Invite respondents to share what they learned.

   Brainstorm obstacles that keep couples from having time with each other. List these on the chalkboard or tear sheet as members contribute.

6. (10 minutes) Ask willing couples to share their plan for a specific date night or other alone time. Commend them and offer encouragement.

   If a couple or couples have not devised a definite plan for alone time, ask if they would like the group's input. If so, allow members to brainstorm with the couple(s) ideas to resolve their dilemmas. Offer prayer support as well.

7. (15 minutes) Review the importance of establishing an action plan for troubled times. Emphasize the benefits of agreeing in advance.

   If you or someone else (whose permission has been given in advance) have personally benefited from individual, couple, or family counseling, tell about that experience. Do not ask members if they have visited a counselor. That information is private.

   Tell or distribute information about Christian counseling services and future marriage enrichment opportunities in your church and area.

Closing the Session (10 minutes)

1. Allow unstructured time for individuals to ask questions, make comments, or share insights.

2. Call for prayer requests. Close with prayer.

LEARN TO LIVE TOGETHER

Before the Session

1. Compile a list of 8 to 10 opposite characteristics, such as neat/messy, organized/disorganized, thinker/feeler, morning person/night person, spender/saver, outgoing/shy, athletic/couch potato, spontaneous/predictable. Use these in the arrival activity.

2. On a poster board, draw a simple floor plan of a house with a living room, bedroom, bathroom, and kitchen. Display it during step 3 of During the Session.

3. Write the five statements listed in step 4 of During the Session on a chalkboard, or duplicate them for use during small groups.

4. (Optional) Decorate the room using an upcoming holiday theme.

During the Session

1. (10 minutes) Play "Opposites Attract." Ask members to stand in the center of the room. Give these instructions: *I will call out a pair of opposite character traits. As I name each one, I will point to a wall in the room. If the trait describes you, go stand against that wall.* Before you go on to the next set of traits, note which couples are opposite on that characteristic. When you have finished calling the list, ask members to sit in your usual room arrangement. Lead the group to decide whether, in their cases, opposites attract.

2. (10 minutes) Display the floor plan you prepared earlier. Ask couples to identify rooms in their house that have been the location for the most conflict in regard to sharing space. Put an *X* for each response in the designated room.

   Discuss possible ways to resolve differences in sharing space. Allow volunteers to tell what they have learned from this group about adjusting to a marriage partner (see activity p. 59).

   Allow members to tell about a family member who has been flexible and creative in adjusting to living in a blended family (see activity p. 62).

3. (15 minutes) Divide members into small groups. Ask groups to discuss how their individual families could benefit from the following suggestions. Give groups a copy of the assignment or call attention to the statements on the chalkboard:

   • Develop a win-win mentality.
   • Practice the art of compromise.
   • Offer your mate a love gift.
   • Develop the virtues of patience and flexibility.

   When small groups have finished, reconvene the large group.

4. (15 minutes) Call attention to room decorations or mention the next approaching holiday. Ask volunteers to share how they will spend the holiday as a family and how they reached that decision. Depending on the response, discuss Christmas, Thanksgiving, and Easter specifically as they affect blended families. Discourage "war stories" of past conflicts. Focus on workable solutions. Emphasize the value of making holidays "holy days."

5. (15 minutes) Lead a discussion of finances in the blended family. Ask couples to share how they responded to the first activity in day 4. Be prepared to address issues such as child support, debt acquired prior to the marriage, separate financial responsibilities, and joint or separate bank accounts.

   Ask someone to recount briefly the author's beach house story on p. 68. Discuss the spiritual implications of how we handle money. Read Paul's affirmation in Philippians 4:11-13.

6. (15 minutes) If possible, illustrate the problem-solving method suggested on p. 71 from your own experience. Choose a true-to-life example and work your way through the steps. Call for responses from CoupleTalk as to how others used the problem-solving exercise .

Closing the Session (10 minutes)

1. Allow time for couples to share joys, crises, breakthroughs, or other happenings from the past week.

2. Call for prayer requests. Close with prayer.

MINIMIZE INTERFERENCES

Before the Session

1. Prepare four signs using four different colors of paper. Label the signs: *The Former Spouse, The Couple's Parents, Friends,* and *Work.* Display one sign in each corner of the room, and arrange two or more chairs around each sign. If you have fewer attendees, select the two or three topics you consider most pertinent, based on your knowledge of members. Adjust the room arrangement to that number.

2. Write the following small-group assignment on the chalkboard: *Suggest ideas to minimize the negative effects of this influence.*

3. (Optional) Provide chart paper and markers or paper and pencils for small-group work.

4. Prepare to lead a discussion based on Mark 2:13-28 (activity p. 76).

During the Session

1. (30 minutes) As members arrive, ask them to choose a small group assignment and sit in that group. Partners should feel free to choose different groups. If no one chooses a particular group assignment, prepare your own brief synopsis of that topic while groups work.

   Point to and read aloud the small-group assignment written in advance. Instruct groups to appoint a recorder/reporter. Participants may use the information from week 5 and life experience.

   After 10 to 15 minutes for discussion, call for reports. If groups have used chart paper, display the lists. If not, compile ideas from reports and list on a chalkboard. If necessary, present your report on the unassigned topic.

2. (10 minutes) Emphasize the importance of placing the needs of your blending family above other concerns. Say: *Protecting your family's best interests may require you to confront others, even members of your extended family. We often think of Jesus only as "meek and mild." Jesus was willing to defend Himself and His mission against those who sought to undermine Him.* Lead a discussion of Mark 2:13-28 based on the learning activity on p. 76. Lead the group to summarize the difference between paying back evil for evil and allowing oneself to become a doormat for another person's bad behavior.

3. (10 minutes) Invite the group to share ideas for ways to include the stepparent who feels like an outsider to the family. As a discussion prompter, use the case study in the unit introduction of week 1 (p. 5).

   Encourage couples to share from their own experiences without allowing one or two individuals to monopolize the sharing time. Remember, you cannot solve everyone's problems. But allowing participants to vent feelings is a positive expression of care.

4. (10 minutes) Discuss ways to help a child who feels like an outsider in his or her blended family. Ask: *Since children have trouble verbalizing their feelings, what behaviors might indicate they feel like outsiders? How can we help children feel important, loved, and accepted?*

5. (10 minutes) Invite volunteers to share insights that resulted from their CoupleTalk experience.

6. (10 minutes) Call attention to this week's memory verse. Lead the group to give examples of the word *kindness.* What does kindness look like in a family?

   Brainstorm ways our faith helps us relate to others in a Christ-honoring way. Ask members to find and read together 2 Thessalonians 1:11-12. Remind members that it is God's desire to fulfill every good purpose in their lives.

Closing the Session (10 minutes)

1. Allow couples to share family issues or concerns not addressed in today's study. Do not be overly concerned if the situation is covered in a later session. Instead, share that information as a source of encouragement.

2. Ask for prayer requests. Close with prayer.

RELY ON GOD

Before the Session

1. Provide art supplies, such as tear sheets and markers, for use in step 1 of During the Session.

2. Enlist a member or someone outside your group to give a five-minute testimony about the difference God has made in his or her blended family. If possible, select someone who has experienced family life from two perspectives: a family struggling without God and a family that now relies on God.

3. (Optional) Prepare a display table of resources for couple Bible study. Refer to p. 99 for suggestions.

4. Bring supplies needed to lead the worship activities mentioned in step 6 of During the Session.

5. Prepare to overview the next 6 units of *New Faces*, which deal with parenting issues. Refer to each week's first page for a summary of content and objectives.

During the Session

1. (10 minutes) Ask each couple to work together to draw a picture illustrating God as Head of their family. As couples finish, display the pictures. Give each couple opportunity to explain their drawings.

   (Optional) For couples who are not artistic, provide chart paper and markers to list characteristics of a family with God as the Head. Display lists along with the pictures.

2. (10 minutes) Call on a member or pre-enlisted person to describe how relying on God has made a difference in his or her family life. Use the testimony as a springboard for other spontaneous testimonies, or share your own experience.

3. (10 minutes) Discuss the meaning of the word *covenant* and God's covenant with Noah, Abraham, and Moses. Ask, *What is the distinction of the New Covenant through Jesus Christ?* (Based on faith and not works; required Jesus' shed blood for our sins).

   Ask members to re-read the characteristics of the covenant on p. 93. Discuss the implications of a covenant both with your spouse and with your children or stepchildren.

4. (10 minutes) Ask members to share ways they intend to encourage prayer as a couple and as a family. Discuss obstacles members identify. Encourage couples to make prayer a personal habit and a part of their family's routine.

5. (10 minutes) Ask a member to read Matthew 7:24-27 (p. 96). Invite testimonies from couples who plan to implement any of the ideas from day 3.

   Call attention to the resource materials for couple Bible study. If there is time, allow a few moments for browsing, or encourage members to browse at the end of this session.

6. (10 minutes) Review the importance of practicing our faith in our homes (day 5). Ask, *What is your response when I say that our homes should be mission stations for the Lord?* Invite suggestions on ways to evidence faith as a family.

7. (20 minutes) Spend the remainder of the time using several of the suggestions for home worship on p. 102. (Couples may be more inclined to try an activity they have experienced.) Select two or more of the activities you feel comfortable leading. As needed, provide extra Bibles, hymnals, art supplies, or nature items such as pine cones or leaves.

   After completing the worship activities, ask for feedback. Assure couples of their ability to lead out in building a family of faith.

Closing the Session (10 minutes)

1. Remind couples that the first six units of *New Faces* focused on the couple relationship. The next six units will deal specifically with parenting issues. Overview the remaining weeks to build interest and promote participation.

   If *New Faces* is being offered as a two-part series and this is your final session, provide closure by asking members to share testimonies about what the group has meant to them. Give schedule information for the remaining six units.

2. Share prayer requests. Close with prayer.

Understand the Children

Before the Session

1. Analyze your group to determine which questions you will use from During the Session. Depending on the ages of your members' children, you may choose to spend more or less time on step 5 that deals with teenagers and adult children.
2. (Optional) Display a picture of Jesus with children. Check with your preschool Sunday School departments for a picture you can borrow.
3. Interview an older child or teenager who has lost a parent to death or divorce. Ask the child to give suggestions to couples who have remarried that would help their children cope with the new marriage.

During the Session

1. (10 minutes) Call attention to the picture of Jesus and the children or read the week's Scripture memory verse from Matthew 19:14. Brainstorm, *What qualities of Jesus do you think endeared Him to children?* List responses on the chalkboard or chart paper.

   Continue, *What qualities of children are evident in persons who belong to the kingdom of Heaven?* List these alongside the first responses.

   Lead members to silently evaluate themselves according to these qualities. Instruct members to list in the margin on p. 108 in their workbooks qualities they want to develop more fully. Allow time for thoughtful evaluation; lead a prayer of commitment.
2. (20 minutes) Say, *This week we have concentrated on understanding what our children experience when we marry again.* Ask members to review silently the activities from day 1. Invite members to share answers to the following questions:
   - What evidences of grief have you seen in your children following your divorce or the death of your mate?
   - What feelings have your children shared about how the divorce or death experience has affected them?
   - How did your children react when you told them you were marrying again?
   - What have you done that helped your children move beyond their grief?
3. (20 minutes) Ask members to review the activities from day 2, dealing with children's fantasies. Ask willing members to share:
   - In what ways have any of your children demonstrated fantasies concerning an absent parent?
   - How have fantasies concerning an absent parent affected your blending family?
   - Have any of the children in your blending family seemed reluctant to become close to the stepparent?
   - Have any of the children indicated they would like mom and dad to get back together?
   - What seems to help your children get in touch with reality and live in the present?
4. (20 minutes) Review the material in day 3 on ways children express anger and attempt to manipulate the people in their lives. Invite couples to share how they answered the following:
   - In what ways have you found your children trying to manipulate you or their biological parent?
   - How have your children demonstrated their anger after the death of a parent or your divorce?
   - How have you helped your children manage anger?
   - How have you identified and resisted manipulation?
5. (10 minutes) Review days 4 and 5 which took a specific look at teenagers and adult children. Ask couples to share ways teens or older children have impacted their blending families.

   If your group has younger children, have members mention ideas that will help when they eventually confront certain issues.

Closing the Session (10 minutes)

1. As a summary and challenge, present the results of your interview with a child. Be encouraging as you share ways couples can help children adjust.
2. Debrief other group issues or concerns.
3. Share prayer requests. Close with prayer.

AVOID TYPECASTING

Before the Session

1. Prepare team assignments for step 1 on separate pieces of paper and distribute when teams are formed.
2. Write the case study in step 1 on a poster board or flipchart for display or duplicate individual copies for group members.

During the Session

1. (30 minutes) Divide members into four teams of one or more persons by counting off around the semicircle. Do not attempt to match assignments with the real-life roles of members. Distribute the following written assignments:

Team 1: The Wonderful Stepparent. Describe the hopes and dreams stepparents bring to the blended family. Are these expectations realistic? What generally happens to "burst the bubble" of the new stepparent?

Team 2: Stepchildren. Why does the wonderful stepparent look "wicked" to you? What are your issues in accepting the stepparent into your family?

Team 3: Biological Parent. Describe how it feels to be caught in the middle between the stepparent and your children. What are your issues in being the biological parent?

Team 4: Noncustodial Parent. What role do you play in how the stepparent is perceived and how the blended family functions? Why do you react the way you do?

Allow 10 minutes for discussion. Call for reports.

Present the following case study: Alex and Jennifer have one child each who live with them. The two children are only 10 months apart in age and compete for time, attention, and possessions. Jennifer's ex dislikes Alex and tells his daughter. Alex was a widower and his son adored his deceased mother. Neither child likes the stepparent. Alex and Jennifer are planning a family vacation, but both children refuse to go. What can they do between now and the vacation scheduled in three months to build relationships? (Note: Details, such as children's ages, have been purposely left out to encourage brainstorming several scenarios.)

Ask teams to interact by discussing possible ways to resolve the difficulties presented in the case study. Team 1 members should offer appropriate ideas for the stepparents; team 2, the stepchildren, etc.

2. (10 minutes) Ask, *What does it mean to be typecast?* Use the week's title to prompt discussion of ideas that have helped members overcome the set-ups for failure listed in day 2: resistance to change, resentment toward the marriage, and replacement of the parent-child relationship. Affirm responses and portray confidence that these barriers can be removed.

3. (15 minutes) Brainstorm ways children demonstrate feelings of jealousy. Write responses on a chalkboard. Then ask, *How do spouses display jealous feelings?* List responses. Discuss ways to deal with or prevent jealousy between stepparents and stepchildren.

4. (15 minutes) Erase the chalkboard and draw a line to make two columns. Label one column "sources of anger" and the other "resolving anger." Divide members into two groups. Ask group one to complete the first part of the sentence and group two to finish the sentence: *I feel angry because … and what I can do to resolve the conflict is ….* Complete as many of these statements as time permits. Consider trading group assignments after a few responses.

5. (10 minutes) Say together this week's Scripture memory verse from Psalm 27:14. Invite testimonies of how the Lord has enabled individuals to "be strong and take heart." Encourage members to patiently wait on God's timing in blending their families.

Closing the Session (10 minutes)

1. Provide unstructured time for couples to discuss issues not mentioned in today's study. Encourage others to offer support.
2. Call for prayer requests. Close with prayer.

REDUCE REFEREEING

Before the Session

(optional) Decorate using a sports theme to emphasize the refereeing imagery in today's study. Wear a whistle and a red or yellow handkerchief. Encourage a casual and fun atmosphere by throwing the handkerchief indicating a penalty each time someone makes a particularly insightful comment. Award a piece of candy for each "penalty."

During the Session

1. (10 minutes) Open with prayer. Review the roles played by the four components of a blending family: the biological parent, the stepparent, the children, the ex- or deceased spouse. Point out that just as the stepparent alone cannot solve a blending family's dilemma, neither can the biological parent. Ask and discuss, *Why does our author say the biological parent may be the most neglected member of the blended family?*

2. (10 minutes) Ask persons who have been members of an organized sports team to explain the role of the referee. Ask: *What is the referee's purpose in the game? Why is a referee often disliked by both sides? What feelings do you think a referee experiences when either side is displeased with a call?* Relate these ideas to the role of the biological parent in a blended family.

    Consider using the story of Arthur and Crystal as a springboard to discuss ways the biological parent can exit the role of middleman. Refer to the group's responses to the learning activities on pp. 143-144.

3. (20 minutes) Invite those in the group who are biological parents to share their experiences of being the biological parent in a blending family. After each response, categorize and list on the chalkboard. Then, ask the group to select two or three priority issues to discuss in detail. Divide into small groups of two or more members and assign one priority issue to each group.

    (Alternate idea) You may choose to discuss the issues as a large group. If so, refer to specific ideas and suggestions from this week's study to supplement members' contributions. If you use small groups, allow time for discussion and call for reports.

    Include the remainder of the session plan if the following ideas are not covered during discussion of priority issues.

4. (10 minutes) Review the material from day 2 which relates to blaming the mate. Ask: *Why do we blame others for our problems? Why does blaming your mate fail to solve the problems of blending? Which strategies are more productive?* Encourage members to define their unstated expectations of one another.

5. (10 minutes) Using the material in day 3, discuss reasons for defensive behavior and the ways we generally respond when we feel threatened. Ask the group to share ideas for behaving in a less defensive manner.

6. (10 minutes) Ask, *Has anyone here tried to juggle relationships?* If persons respond, ask them to share their experiences. Or, use the case studies from day 4 to review problems caused by relating to spouse and children separately. Invite group reactions to the statement on p. 153: "By interfering with the struggle, biological parents halt the process of blending."

7. (5 minutes) Review the author's two suggestions on pp. 155-156 for reducing children's power plays. Encourage couples to work together to build a united parenting team.

8. (5 minutes) Repeat this week's Scripture memory verse. Lead in a time of sharing ways this verse has encouraged members to renew their strength.

Closing the Session (10 minutes)

1. Invite members to share if this has been a good week in terms of blending family relationships. If someone has struggled with a special problem, allow time for sharing. Encourage others to offer encouragement or positive results to similar situations.

2. Ask members to read together Isaiah 55:12 as a parting meditation.

3. Call for prayer requests. Close with prayer.

SET GUIDELINES FOR BEHAVIOR

Before the Session

1. Prepare a poster indicating a target zone surrounded by 4 circles. Keep a marker handy to write on the poster as the session progresses.
2. (optional) Invite to the session or interview an experienced blended family parent who is willing to share parenting tips with the group.
3. Provide extra paper and pencils for step 6.

During the Session

1. (10 minutes) Open with prayer. Display the target poster. Review points from day 1 and day 2 using the following questions: Ask, *What is the goal of parenting?* (to work our way out of a job). Write the group's paraphrase in the center target area. Then ask, *What is the goal of discipline?* (to change external control to internal control). Write the group's paraphrase on the second circle, surrounding the target.

   Say: *Discipline methods are numerous and individual parents need to determine methods according to situations. However, the goal of discipline remains the same.* Ask, *How do we know if our discipline choice is effective?* (It produces the result we intended). Write this response on the third surrounding circle.
2. (10 minutes) Assign each of the three needs of children (p. 161) to small groups of two or more. Ask each group to list practical ways parents can meet these needs. Call for reports after 2 minutes.
3. (5 minutes) On the fourth circle, write *Our parenting style*. Discuss differences in parenting styles from day 2. Remind couples to talk in terms of styles and preferences rather than "right vs. wrong" when deciding on discipline methods.
4. (15 minutes) Say, *In order to hit the parenting target, couples must set guidelines together and work as a team.* Ask couples to share any rules they have developed as a team for their blending family. Ask those who share, *How has working as a team enhanced your parenting?*

   Then ask couples who have allowed their children to participate in setting family guidelines and conse-

quences to share the results of that experience.

   Follow up by asking those who have worked with ex-spouses as a discipline team to share their experiences. Anticipate response from those who are not yet able to work as a team with their ex's. Encourage them to continue efforts toward teamwork.
5. (10 minutes) Refer to the material in day 4 concerning choosing your battles. On the chalkboard draw a line down the middle to make two columns. Label the left hand column "Battles to Fight" and the right hand column "Battles to Ignore (for now)." Lead the group to list items in each category based on their personal family decisions. This exercise may lead to helpful discussion. Be willing to invest additional time.
6. (10 minutes) Ask members to turn to day 5. Ask couples to work together to describe what grace looks and acts like between members of a blended family. Provide paper and pencils as necessary.

   Allow time for couples to talk. Call on each couple to give their report. Affirm responses. There are no incorrect responses.

   Ask for members willing to share from page 171 how they characterized a judgmental home and a grace-filled home.
7. (20 minutes) Have members report on the goal-setting activity on p. 173. (Optional activity) Use your interview notes or introduce the guest to share parenting tips from an experienced blended family parent. Allow for question/answer as time permits.

Closing the Session (10 minutes)

1. Ask and discuss: *How are things going this week in your families? Is there a problem you would like to share with the group?* Allow time for input.
2. Repeat this week's Scripture memory verse as a meditation thought.
3. Call for prayer requests. Close with prayer.

DEVELOP PROBLEM-SOLVING SKILLS

Before the Session

1. Prepare for the role-play in step 1 of During the Session by arranging a table and chairs for the "family" and additional chairs for the "audience."
2. On the chalkboard or a piece of chart paper display the listening team questions from step 2 below. Refer to them during step 1.
3. If you are using the optional lesson plan (begins with step 3), prepare to display the questions.

During the Session

1. (30 minutes) Open with prayer. Remind members that week 11 recommended a family meeting approach to problem-solving in a blended family. Invite four volunteers to role-play a family meeting. The characters are a father, mother, and two children. Ask the remaining group members to function as a listening team and be prepared to provide feedback after the role play.

    Lead the group to determine the children's ages and the problem to be solved during the new business portion of the meeting. Encourage "characters" to act like a real family, not a perfect family.

    Suggest that the father preside and follow the suggested meeting agenda on page 183. Assign one of the children to record minutes. Allow the "family" 5 minutes away from the group to decide issues related to agenda items 3, 4, 5, and 9. While the "family" is away, refer the listening team to the questions displayed from step 2.

2. (40 minutes) Conduct the role play. Monitor the time and move the meeting along as necessary. After the role play, call for listening team reports. Ask:

    • *What benefits of a family meeting did this "family" model?*
    • *What other ways could the problem addressed as "new business" have been resolved?*
    • *How do you think family members felt about one another and the family as a whole as a result of their meeting?*

    As members discuss the role play, remind them

that they are not evaluating the actors' performances. Discourage criticism. Phrase suggestions as additional ways to handle the situations. Conclude with steps 5 and 6 below (10 minutes).

3. (20 minutes) If you feel your group would not respond well to a role play, display the questions below for discussion starters and follow the remainder of this lesson plan.

    • *Why is consensus a helpful approach to problem-solving in a blended family?*
    • *Why is assertion more productive than aggression or passivity when solving problems?*
    • *How do you peel the layers of a problem to get to the root cause?*

4. (30 minutes) Refer members to day 3 which looked at family meetings as a method for problem solving. Ask: *Who has held family meetings? Were the meetings successful? What difficulties did you encounter? What additional ideas about family meetings did you discover?*

    If no one has experienced family meetings, use answers to the rebuttal questions on page 183 as a way to encourage members to try this approach.

    Brainstorm family meeting benefits identified by members as valuable to them (p. 182).

5. (10 minutes) Ask members to turn to page 188 and share a problem their family solved. Then ask, *How has God used a problem from your life to bless someone else?*

6. (15 minutes) Invite volunteers to share problems they have solved since the beginning of this group. How has solving those problems enhanced their marriage? parenting?

7. (5 minutes) Repeat this week's Scripture memory verse. Ask for testimonies based on this verse.

Closing the Session (10 minutes)

1. Allow volunteers to share a problem which is an ongoing issue in their blended family. Pray for these during the prayer time.
2. Close with prayer.

SEE GOD AT WORK

Before the Session

1. Since this is the final week of this study, prepare to share information at the end of the session concerning additional study opportunities available through your church in the coming weeks.
2. Prepare to lead a brief review of weeks 7-11.
3. Note that the session plan calls for 15 minutes instead of the usual 10 to close the session.

During the Session (75 minutes)

1. (15 minutes) Open with prayer. Lead a review of weeks 7-11 by asking members to turn to the introductory page of each week and review the daily lesson titles and objectives. Lead the group to recall each week's highlights.

   If the group has met together for 12 weeks, consider using the course map on the inside front cover of *New Faces* as a way to review the content. Give a one sentence review of each week.
2. (5 minutes) Ask members to turn to week 12 introduction on p. 192. Say, *Think back to your first day in this group. Who identifies with Nancy? with Al?* Encourage members to share ways they have changed and grown during the past weeks.
3. (10 minutes) Ask for volunteers to share from day 1 what the expression "redeeming your mistakes" means to them. Share a mistake you feel God has redeemed from your life and encourage others to do the same.
4. (10 minutes) Day 2 related to patience. Ask the group to compose and then write a definition of patience on the chalkboard. Call for responses to the learning activity at the top of p. 197. Then ask, *How would you advise a friend to develop patience?*
5. (10 minutes) Reaffirm the concept from day 3 that all blended families do not have happy endings—at least for the foreseeable future. Read 2 Corinthians 4:16-18. Discuss the concept that our troubles are considered "light and momentary" in comparison to our future with God.

Be sensitive to your group as you deal with the issues from day 3. You may choose to spend additional time with this content.
6. (10 minutes) Ask the group to name the six stages of blending from day 4 and list them on the chalkboard. Allow members who feel comfortable doing so to identify the stage where they see their families at this time. Ask: *Have any of you moved through any stages during this study? What did you determine about your children's movement through the stages as you read and responded?*
7. (10 minutes) Review day 5 by asking the group to reflect on how they have seen God guiding them during the 6 or 12 weeks of this study. Invite them to share glimpses they have had into God's plan for their future.
8. (5 minutes) Repeat this week's Scripture memory verse together. Emphasize the difference between trusting in the Lord and trusting in our mates, or children, or circumstances.

Closing the Session (15 minutes)

1. Present information about additional studies that will be offered during the coming weeks.
2. Thank the group for their participation. Affirm their openness to God's leading in their blending families. Use encouraging words to inspire further growth. Ask couples to consider leading a *New Faces* group and to let you know of their availability.
3. Ask the group to stand in a circle and join hands. Invite members to share one-sentence testimonies affirming the group and individual members. Invite sentence prayers from volunteers, and then close with your own prayer. Leave with hugs, handshakes, or other appropriate expressions of affection.